Psychology Revivals

Psychology and Morals

Originally published in 1923, this book had enjoyed constant and wide success, being reprinted fourteen times. In this new and thoroughly revised edition, published in 1964, the author has reconsidered his conclusions in the light of modern psychology of the time, and includes many case histories from his long experience as a psychiatrist. The book was important for its insistence that there is no intrinsic conflict between analytical psychotherapy and ordinary moral behaviour.

Psychology and Morals

An analysis of character

J. A. Hadfield

Routledge
Taylor & Francis Group
LONDON AND NEW YORK

First published in 1964
by Methuen & Co Ltd

This edition first published in 2016 by Routledge
2 Park Square, Milton Park, Abingdon, Oxon OX14 4RN

and by Routledge
711 Third Avenue, New York, NY 10017

Routledge is an imprint of the Taylor & Francis Group, an informa business

Publisher's Note
The publisher has gone to great lengths to ensure the quality of this reprint but points out that some imperfections in the original copies may be apparent.

Disclaimer
The publisher has made every effort to trace copyright holders and welcomes correspondence from those they have been unable to contact.

A Library of Congress record exists under LCCN: 50003142

ISBN: 978-1-138-64801-2 (hbk)
ISBN: 978-1-315-62669-7 (ebk)

Psychology and Morals

An Analysis of Character

by

J. A. Hadfield
M.A. (Oxon.), M.B., Ch.B. (Edin.)
Late Lecturer in Psychopathology and Mental Hygiene, University of London

UNIVERSITY PAPERBACKS

METHUEN : LONDON

This book was first published June 7th, 1923
It has been reprinted fourteen times
Fifteenth edition, revised, March 1949
Reprinted 1955
First published in this series (sixteenth edition) 1964

Printed and bound in Great Britain by
Cox & Wyman Ltd., London, Fakenham and Reading

University Paperbacks are published by
METHUEN & CO LTD
11 New Fetter Lane, London EC4

Contents

Preface to the Sixteenth Edition

AT THE TIME this book was written, now over forty years ago, it was generally considered that the New Psychology, as it was then called, was opposed to both religion and morals, just as a century before the theory of evolution had raised a cry of alarm amongst theologians. My purpose in writing the book, though not stated in so many words, was to counter this popular idea, and to maintain that the findings of the New Psychology were not incompatible with morality; but that, rightly considered, they were quite consistent with moral principles.

At the same time, as in the case of Evolution, a certain revision of older concepts was called for. As the Bible story of the Creation as literal history had to be scrapped in the face of the discovery of physical science, so certain old-fashioned moral concepts such as that the instincts of man were essentially evil had to give way in the face of psychological discoveries.

In this revised version I have re-written some of the sections; and have also included some new material such as the chapters on 'The Development of Conscience', 'Individual and Social Conscience', 'What is a Neurosis?', and 'Dreams' to help to bring the subject a little more up to date.

The reception of the book at that time surprised me. I had letters from prominent Nonconformists commending the book for its emphasis on the need for morals: from High Anglicans to say that it confirmed, by its insistence on analysis, the theory of the Confessional; and finally a kind letter from Professor Margoliouth, the eminent Jewish scholar, to say that the book exactly confirmed Rabbinic teaching! The only conclusion one can draw from such a reception is how slight, when one gets down at all to the fundamentals, are the differences dividing the various creeds.

The substance of the following chapters was delivered as the Dale lectures at Mansfield College, Oxford, in 1920.

I have refrained from discussing the more debatable

theories of the 'new psychology', and have confined myself to those, such as 'conflict' and 'repression', which are most generally accepted not only by psycho-physicians but also by psychologists.

Nor have I stayed to point out where I agree or differ from the schools of Psycho-analysis (Freud) and of Analytical Psychology (Jung). Those who are not acquainted with their writings would find such a discussion tedious, and those who are so acquainted will be able to detect the differences for themselves.

In spite of the dogmatic tone I have had to assume for the sake of brevity, I fully recognize that on the theoretical side the book is only tentative and suggestive. It attempts merely to present a point of view and makes no claim to be a systematic treatise on ethical theory – that is the province of the philosopher and the divine. Its object is rather to set out facts and principles revealed by modern Psychology, especially in its application to nervous disease, some knowledge of which is of vital importance to all who, like parents, teachers, clergy, and general practitioners, are called upon to give practical direction and advice to individuals in regard to the actual problems of life and conduct. In doing this I have ventured from time to time to indicate ways in which these facts and principles may modify, at any rate, the expression, if not also in some respects the nature, of ethical theory. As a practical physician I neither claim the equipment, nor acknowledge the obligation, to produce a complete and intellectually rigid system of moral philosophy. The psychologist, however, is in a position to speak of facts which neither the moral philosopher nor the practical pastor or teacher can afford to ignore.

However inadequate, therefore, the theoretical treatment of the subject may be, the principles which I attempt to set forth have stood the test of practical experience. They are the result not of work in the study or laboratory but are the outcome of many years' experience in dealing with the practical needs and problems of men and women.

Where I have quoted cases from my patients, I have either obtained their permission to do so, or have so disguised them that they cannot possibly be identified. To them and to the various friends who have assisted me in the preparation of this book I desire to express my gratitude.

To my mother, who taught me the ways of freedom, and to my wife and boys, through whom I have realized joy and happiness, I gratefully dedicate this book.

J. A. H.

WHITHURST PARK
KIRDFORD, W. SUSSEX

CHAPTER I

Introductory

IF ONE VISITS the wards of a 'shell-shock' hospital, one sees there men paralysed, blind, deaf, dumb, and suffering from severe headaches and other pains. It seems incredible and yet such is the fact, that all these men are suffering from disorders which, though physical in their symptoms, originate not in the body, but in the mind – disorders due, in fact, to disturbances of the emotions. One may visit a ward of another hospital and find men suffering from what appear to be exactly the same symptoms – they, too, are paralysed and blind – but the disease in these cases is of an entirely different nature, being due to some bodily injury or sickness. The former are 'psychogenic' disorders, that is, disorders originating in the mind, and are variously distinguished as the 'psychoneuroses', 'functional nervous disorders', or, more popularly, 'nervous diseases'. They include neurasthenia, hysteria, anxiety neuroses, phobias, and obsessions, all of which conditions are ultimately due to disturbances of emotional life. In the psychoneuroses the disorder is not primarily a disorder of structure, but of function. 'Organic' diseases on the other hand, as distinct from 'functional' diseases, are preponderatingly physical in origin, their cause being found in some defect of bodily structure.

It is a fact of common observation that emotional disturbances can produce physiological changes. A man is said to be, and may actually be, blind with rage, speechless with terror, dumb with grief, paralysed with fear, and sick with disgust. The psychoneuroses are of this character; they, too, are due to emotional disturbance. But whereas under ordinary conditions – when, for instance, a man is sick at a horrible sight – the symptoms are temporary, and normally pass off with the passing of the excitation – in the psychoneuroses the symptoms are more permanent, as though there were some foul spring of repressed emotion which continually discharges itself. Thus the 'shell-shocked' soldier continues to be ill long after the war is ended.

When we go deeper and investigate the origin of the psychoneuroses, we often find that they are concerned with problems essentially moral.

The breakdown of the shell-shocked man, for instance, is the result of the conflict between the sense of duty and self-preservation. Nervous pains, tics, terrors, phobias, paralyses, and fatigue are due to conflicts such as that between duty and fear, between moral sense and sex desire, self-display and modesty, between self-assertion and humiliation. The soldier's functional paralysis of the leg is due to the failure of will to control his repressed fear; a woman's pain in the back is found to be a manifestation of her repressed self-pity. In other words, these physical and mental symptoms are due to defects of character.

In dealing with the psychoneuroses the physician is thus compelled to face the moral problems which lie at the root of these disorders.

But not only is the physician called upon to deal with the moral problems which lie at the root of 'nervous' ailments, he is often called upon to deal *directly* with moral diseases, such as uncontrollable temper, sex perversions, stealing, cruelty, despondency, irritability, and vanity. Such diseases (which we shall later distinguish from sins) are not in any sense physical, for they are moral both in origin and also in their manifestation. Yet patients suffering from such ailments frequently present themselves to the physician instead of seeking the aid of the clergyman or moralist. Nor is this an accidental choice. They feel, rightly or wrongly, that the moralist will blame them or tell them to exert their wills.

They feel, rightly or wrongly, that they are *not* to blame for their condition. They have, moreover, already exerted their will to no purpose, they have turned their attention to other things, they have been blamed, condemned, threatened; they have been treated with sympathy and love, and all in vain. They then begin to realize that they are suffering from a 'moral' disease, and go to a physician, who will treat them as sick and not as sinful.

The psycho-physician is anxious to help the morally sick; he shrinks from nothing; he is shocked at nothing; and no word of blame ever falls from his lips.

In treating nervous disorders like 'shell-shock' or neurasthenia, the psycho-physician has developed a technique of his own, known as psychotherapy, which deals directly with the emotional conflicts from which they spring. But having learnt and developed this method of dealing with functional nervous diseases, the psycho-physician applies the same method to the treatment of moral diseases, bad tempers, sexual obsessions, and morbid fears. The method differs in many respects from that of the orthodox moral teacher, but it is one which has proved a most effective form of treatment for moral as well as nervous ills. It is the purpose of this book to give a brief account of this method and of the principles underlying it.

Several strong objections have been raised to this invasion of the physician into the sphere of morals.

(1) The moralist and the pure psychologist both maintain that the psychologist, as such, has no concern with moral questions.

It is true that the psychologist, as such, is not concerned with standards of right and wrong. Psychology is the *descriptive* science of mental processes – it merely observes, describes, and draws generalized conclusions; it does not consider what is right or what ought to be. Ethics, on the other hand, is a *normative* science of moral conduct; it has a certain standard; it seeks to define what is right and wrong, and how we ought to behave. But the psychotherapist finds he has to deal with precisely the same problems, though they manifest themselves in different shapes. In both, the essential conflict is between will and impulse, but whereas in the one case this results in conditions of bad behaviour, in the other case it produces neurotic disorders – the difference depending on the repression of the primitive impulses in the latter case. Thus the psycho-physician who deals with such nervous disorders is compelled to deal with moral problems, if he is to cure his patient. He seeks to apply a scientific method to the solution of these problems, and he aims at a certain standard of health for the individual.

The psycho-physician cannot, therefore, detach himself in a condition of splendid isolation from moral standards of life, whether or not they be the ones accepted by society as a whole. The psycho-analyst who says you 'ought not' to repress has at one leap sprung clean out of the realm of pure science. Unlike the pure psychologist the physician has a standard, namely, the health of the individual. If psychotherapy aims at curing abnormal individuals, it has already set up a standard or norm. For what is an abnormal individual? Before we can speak of the abnormal we must already have a conception of the normal.

The practice of psychotherapy, therefore, forms the connecting link between pure psychology and the science of morals.

(2) Another objection is raised to the psycho-physician dealing with moral problems. It is said that the physician deals only with abnormal men and women, and that to derive principles and form judgements by studying morbid cases will pervert and vitiate our conclusions. This is not as serious an objection as it at first appears. For, after all, who of us is normal? The greatest difficulty in studying the psychology of the normal individual is to discover him. From time to time we are called upon to analyse physicians and others who are considered to be, and consider themselves, perfectly normal, but who seek to be analysed in order themselves to practise psychotherapy. They may come as 'normal'

men, but they do not remain 'normal' for long! We find, in fact, that these 'healthy' people have complexes, repressions, and abnormalities of character, differing very little from those of patients; and, indeed, one soon forgets that they are not patients. The distinction between a sick man and a healthy man is a practical one, depending on how far he is able to meet the biological responsibilities of life.

Again, in further defence of the study of *morbid* conditions of conduct, we would point to the fact that in medical science it has frequently happened that the study of diseased conditions has produced discoveries, and added greatly to our knowledge of *normal* processes. The most notable case of this was the discovery of the function of the thyroid gland, the significance of which was unknown to physiology until it was discovered by the study of diseases traceable to this gland, cretinism and myxœdema – a discovery which has proved to be of immense value in the treatment of imbecility. So the study of abnormal people has helped us enormously to realize the underlying motives of conduct of normal people, and to discover the necessary conditions of healthiness of mind and strength of character. After all, it is only because of abnormalities of conduct that the subject of morality is of any interest at all, and only because every one is more or less abnormal that every one is interesting.

(3) Again, it is objected that the psycho-physician studies only the individual and his happiness, whereas ethics deal with an objective standard of right and wrong which should be applicable to all men at all times. It is said that one may find an ethic or mode of life which may be perfectly satisfactory for the health and happiness of the individual, but yet is out of keeping with the moral ideal, since this is essentially social.

We maintain, on the contrary, that the most effective way of solving problems concerning the health and happiness of society as a whole is by the study of the health and happiness of the individual. Man is not merely an individual; he is a world, a society, in miniature. He is made up of instincts and emotions, sentiments and complexes, which in no way differ from the emotions and sentiments which prevail in society as a whole. Society is but the reflection of the individual seen in a curved mirror, in which all the essential features are reflected, but in larger proportions, and with varied emphases. Even instincts like the herd instinct or maternal instinct, which are regarded as distinctively 'social', are really individual instincts, though they operate and manifest themselves in social life. Apart from the individual, they do not exist. The herd instinct is not the instinct of the herd, but the instinct in the individual which compels him to be concerned with the opinions and demands of the herd. The moral demands of society on the individual, which forbid him stealing, killing, or lying, would have little force were it not for this instinct which urges the individual to submission. It is true that we may learn a great deal about these instincts from the study of their operations in society and in family life, but we may learn a great deal more about them from the direct study of their sources in the soul of the individual, where we may observe all the seething ferments which strive and thrive in the life of the universe. The soul of the individual is the laboratory in which we may observe and even experiment with emotional forces of cosmic significance. The passions that sway the mind of the individual, avarice, vanity, ambition, sex, and fear, are the same as those which arouse the antagonisms of man to man and disturb the peace of society, and it is in the individual that they may be most effectively studied at first hand. We cannot adequately deal with revolutions until we understand the abnormalities and the psychology of the revolutionist: we cannot solve the problem of 'evil' in the world until we understand the impulses from which evil springs in the individual. On the other hand, the ideal which can produce happiness in the individual by harmonizing all his instincts and bringing them under his control will, at the same time, be the ideal which can produce happiness in the community. If by producing perfect harmony in his soul I could make but one of my patients completely happy, I should have the key to the problem of the world's happiness and goodness. Social and moral problems are essentially psychological.

The study of the individual is the most promising road to the solution of the problems of society. The plagues that ravage mankind can be fought only by their study under the microscope. We build our bridges by experimenting with models; we engage in sub-calibre practice before firing the big guns; so we should study the facts and problems of individual psychology before making laws for society or treating the ills of the race.

The purpose of this book is to approach the moral problem as a problem of the individual, to set out the psychological factors which constitute character, to study the causes of unrest of spirit, and to suggest lines along which ills may be cured, and the soul made free to realize happiness in a community of moral beings.

CHAPTER II

The Determinants of Character: The Hereditary Factor: The Environmental Factor

THE HEREDITARY FACTOR

It is generally assumed that the law of heredity operates as decisively in the mental sphere as in the physical, that the son inherits not merely his father's features, but also his father's traits of character and nervous habits. This is an assumption which is now largely discredited.

It is constantly said of some habit or trait of character: 'My father had it before me; I must have inherited it from him.' Or, again: 'He has had a cruel disposition, a vicious temper, a mean temperament, all his life; he must have been born with it.' But to say 'I have had it as long as I can remember' is no proof that a trait of character is inherited or congenital. Such an assumption was excusable before modern psychological methods opened up to us the earliest years of life. But many things may happen in the first four or five years of life, of which we have no memory, but which nevertheless may influence us for life. Since the development of methods of investigation like hypnosis and psychoanalysis, these early years of life are no longer hidden, but can be recovered to consciousness.

When the experiences of our earliest years are exposed, it is found that many of those symptoms and characteristics, which were previously considered hereditary, are in reality caused by early environmental conditions. Indeed, modern investigation encourages us to believe that few if any psychoneuroses and defects of character are inherited. Those who believe in the hereditary view have yet to prove their case. It is astonishing the way it is assumed in statistics of family traits.[1]

Two illustrations will make this clear. A man had since childhood a tremor of the hand, which came on after any hard piece of work, physical or mental. His father had had it before him, and it was therefore considered hereditary. Analysis of the origin of the symptom, however, brought to light an incident at three years of age, when the patient had a severe accident to his foot and he was held down by his father while the surgeon probed and cleaned the wound. The father's tremor was transmitted to the boy's hands, and became linked up and associated in the boy's mind with an emotional conflict, in which there was a futile struggle against insuperable odds. The incident was forgotten, but the association between this feeling of struggle against fate and the tremor of the hands remained, and in after life any occasion which demanded strained effort revived by association the tremor of the hand. His condition was not hereditary, although his father had had it before him, and he was said to have had it 'all his life'; it was found to be due to this early environmental experience.[2]

[1] We must exclude, of course, all conditions of 'mental deficiency' in which there is a defect of nerve structure such as an undeveloped brain or other organic disturbance. These conditions though styled 'mental' are really physiological and are usually hereditary or congenital.

[2] A man of about twenty-eight years of age had never been able to take milk as long as he could remember. It had always been attributed to a congenital idiosyncrasy of his physiological system. On analysis under hypnosis, it was discovered that at the age of three he was being given a powder (probably Gregory) in milk, which he found too horrible to swallow. At the sixth attempt as soon as he had taken the mixture into his mouth, the doctor seized his jaw and held his mouth closed, to compel him to swallow it. He choked badly, and was nearly suffocated. Thus, the taste of milk and Gregory was associated in his mind with this terror. The incident was forgotten, but the link of association remained and made it impossible for him to take milk. The morbid associations, being discovered, were broken, and before he left the room he was given a glass of milk, a meal he thoroughly enjoyed, remarking, 'It does not taste like milk at all.' The cause of his idiosyncrasy was not congenital, but environmental.

Traits of character, as well as nervous habits, are found to be due to similar experience of early life. A patient suffered from an overbearing conceit which he vainly attempted to overcome; he was 'born proud', with a lofty scorn of his fellows. This was found to be due to the fact that in childhood he was delicate and a 'funk', but he was encouraged by his fond parents to believe that this was because he was of different clay, of more sensitive breed, of bluer blood than the common herd, and therefore could not be expected to join in their rough games. This suggestion he absorbed and maintained unconsciously through adult life in order to excuse and hide his excessive but unrecognized timidity. He was not 'born proud', but had had pride thrust upon him by foolish parents.

It is true that such conditions may be *transmitted* from the parent, but when this is the case, the transmission is not by way of inheritance but by means of imitation or suggestion in early life, and the exact point of its development during life may be discovered by analysis. The same law seems to operate in this sphere as in a disease such as tuberculosis, which at one time was considered to be hereditary; we may inherit a predisposition, we cannot inherit the disease. The whole tendency, then, of modern investigation is to minimize the exaggerated importance previously accorded to the hereditary, and to emphasize the importance of the environmental as the important factor in the determination of character. It cannot be too strongly emphasized that we do not inherit bad temper, pride, meanness, alcoholism, or sexual perversions.

This principle is of the greatest practical importance. If the nervous or moral disease is ingrained, it leaves the patient in bondage and servitude to his disease, with very little hope of deliverance. Indeed, there is nothing more calculated to perpetuate such disorders than the false conviction that they are ingrained, and that we can be 'tainted' with them.

If, on the other hand, we establish the view here maintained, that the abnormal moral and 'nervous' conditions are the result of early environmental conditions, we still regard the individual as sick and therefore free from the full weight of responsibility, but since his sickness is no longer ingrained we can give him encouragement to hope for cure. The theory of 'original sin' has lost its prominence in the pages of theological writings, and it is time it took its flight from medical literature.

But, whilst emphasizing the fact that we cannot inherit diseases of a moral or psychological character, we must remember that there are important hereditary 'predisposing' factors which, though not themselves morbid, play an important part in the development of abnormal traits of character. These are (*a*) a 'nervous temperament'; (*b*) the instincts.

THE NERVOUS TEMPERAMENT

Nervousness runs in families; some people are born with a nervous temperament. But in the first place, nervousness is not a disease; it is only an ill if it is ill-used. Secondly, it is due to physiological rather than to psychological factors, and therefore does not contradict the principle that 'psychoneuroses and moral diseases are not inherited'.

(*a*) The nervous temperament or highly strung disposition depends on the high excitability of the nerves and is physiological in origin. The nerve impulse as it passes along the nerve meets with certain resistances, especially at the bridges or synapses, between one nerve and another. In some people the resistance is great, and it takes time for the impulse to pass along the nerve path. Such people are therefore slow in thought, phlegmatic in temperament, but steady and reliable in character. They are well-balanced people who never do anything *outré* – nor anything great. On the other hand, in nervous people, the synapses are 'open', and the impulse passes rapidly along the nerve paths. They are the rapid thinkers, in whom emotion is closely wedded to thought; they are sensitive but not always sensible, erratic and mercurial in disposition, unstable in character, revolutionary in politics – imaginative like Maeterlinck, witty like Wilde, impulsive like Peter. These, the people of nervous disposition, often draw round them a generous following but they cannot lead and the crusade degenerates into a cult. Such men of genius are predisposed to both moral and nervous disorders. Their genius easily turns into madness, for both are based upon the same instability of nervous constitution.

(*b*) In itself, a nervous temperament is not a disease; *everything depends on what we make of it.* Thus in a nervous family the father and mother are both highly strung; of the children, one becomes an artist, one a neurotic, another a poet who commits suicide, another an alcoholic, and another a great preacher. The man of nervous temperament may be over-sensitive to the hurts of life, but he is also more sensitive to the beauties and exquisite delights of nature, which the more phlegmatic can only behold with cow-like stolidity. If nervous people are the 'crocks' of the earth, they are also the salt of the earth. A neurotic is often a potential genius.

THE INSTINCTS

We also inherit the instincts. These are the chief raw material in the formation of character, for environmental influences would have no effect upon our lives were it not for the instincts which spring out to meet them. It is the fusion of environmental factors and inherited instinct which conditions experience.[1]

The most important of the instincts with which we shall be concerned are those of fear-flight, sex, curiosity, parenthood, the herd or social instinct, the instincts of self-display, pugnacity, self-assertion, and ambition. We do not propose to consider the nature of instincts, but in view of our further

[1] There is considerable discussion at the present time as to the nature and quality of the instincts; indeed, the question is raised as to whether there are any instincts as such, or whether we should speak only of instinctive activity or instinctive behaviour. For our purpose, I shall accept the view held by most psychologists, and assume the existence of innate instincts which give rise to instinctive behaviour; and, further, for the sake of simplicity, I shall follow in the main McDougall's classification of the primary instincts in his *Social Psychology*.

discussion, we must remind ourselves of certain characteristics of the instincts in general.

(*a*) The instincts are inherited and not acquired; this, indeed, is the one point of agreement in all definitions of instinct or instinctive behaviour. We therefore cannot be held responsible for having them.

(*b*) Every one, except the mentally deficient, has *all* the instincts. It is often said of some one: 'He is without fear'; of another, 'She has no sexual instincts.' It may be true so far that their instincts do not manifest themselves as such in conscious life, and may, therefore, escape recognition, but all the instincts are nevertheless present and operative in every normal life. Their influence may be detected in conduct in disguised forms, as when a man by his excessive bravado demonstrates the fear he represses, or when a woman betrays her sexual curiosity by her prudery. When repressed, the instincts may give rise to nervous and moral diseases. Their presence can then be demonstrated by mental analysis, which removes the repression and so permits their emergence into conscious life.

(*c*) Whether the instincts, though present in all normal people, are found in equal measure in every individual is another question. The question is of particular interest in the determination as to whether there is a difference in the balance of instincts between men and women, whether, for instance, men are 'naturally' and instinctively more dominating than women.

Even when a special instinct seems excessively strong in any individual, say, the pugnacious or the acquisitive instincts, it is often found that this preponderance of the instinct is due not to its having been more strongly inherited, but to the fact that the instinct was excessively developed in childhood. The acquisitive instincts of a Brighton boarding-house keeper and a Balkan brigand are probably equally strong; but the fact that the former has his social, and the latter his pugnacious, instincts more highly developed, is probably due to his early training and to the necessities of his calling. The conditions which develop one boy's acquisitive instinct and another boy's instinct of display, forming what we call the boy's 'bent', are largely fortuitous or suggested in childhood. But having once been so developed, it is most important that this instinct should be fully expressed and employed in the future career of the individual. The boy with the strong tendency to display would never be happy in an office, whereas to make the youth with a strong acquisitive instinct into an impecunious artist is obviously to court disaster.

On the other hand, and in spite of the specific development of instincts under environmental influences, it seems probable that as we are born with different temperaments, so we are born with our instincts variously developed. If pugnacity and anger are associated with the secretion of the adrenalin glands, and sex instinct with the gonads or sex glands, it would seem that these instincts would vary in strength according to the various endowments of these glands. There are certain types of men in whom the sex instinct, or pugnacious instinct, is *temperamentally* strong or weak, that is, dependent on their physiological organism; whilst in others the strength or weakness of these instincts depends on the development of these instincts by environmental conditions and early experiences.

(*d*) Each instinct is directed towards a certain biological end: flight towards self-preservation; sex towards reproduction; the maternal instinct towards the care of the young; curiosity towards the examination of any strange object to avoid danger. But it has been shown by McDougall that the instincts may be redirected to other and higher ends. (See later on Sublimation.)

(*e*) These instincts, though latent at birth, are not all active then, but emerge and become dynamic at certain ages. During the course of evolution of the race the instincts arose to meet certain emergencies, and in response to certain biological needs. Every individual develops as the race, passing from the speck of protoplasm through all the stages of evolution, until he emerges into independent life at birth, after which he passes through the later phases of evolution more slowly. In the individual each of the instincts remain dormant till the time comes for its emergence on to the stage of conscious life, when for its allotted span it actively dominates the conduct and determines the character.

At one phase the boy is possessed by the hunting instinct, at another time by the passion for pets, the instincts corresponding to the nomadic stage in the development of the race; this gives way later to the craving to collect and possess, corresponding to the stage of settled agricultural life. This year he is loyal to the gang of boys, next year he will abandon the gang to pursue a pretty frock. At each phase of life a new impulse springs up into activity.

But whilst each instinct in turn has its phase of activity when it dominates the whole personality, in childhood all the instincts find partial expression *in play*. Play is often explained as the outcome of exuberance of energy, but its function is to prepare us for life. Thus, hide-and-seek is a playful expression of the hunting instinct, and prepares for the nobler pursuits of later life; we play with dolls to prepare us for motherhood; we play at pirates to fit us for the battle of life.

To summarize: the instincts constitute the raw material out of which our lives and characters are built, the talents which are given us, useless in themselves, but useful in the purposes to which they may be devoted. Being charged with emotional energy, they are dynamic forces which not only give strength to the passions but power to the will.

NOTE – Various attempts have been made to explain life in terms of one or another of the instincts.

The whole emphasis of the Freudian School of psycho-analysis is placed on the *sex instinct*, the use of the term 'sex' being so widely extended that it includes almost all forms of gratification. Indeed, the term sexual is almost made synonymous with sensuous pleasure and gratification. We shall later discuss the meaning of pleasure, and shall observe that it accompanies the expression of any and every instinct, and not merely that of sex. But though the Freudians have over-emphasized the sexual element in life, it yet remains that sex is the primary function of nature as reproduction is her chief end.

The biologists of the last generation insisted so strongly upon the law of the 'struggle for existence' and the 'survival of the fittest', that we almost believed that *self-preservation* was the one law of life, and the one motive which dominated the lives and conduct of men. The insistence on the sexual or love principle in life was a natural reaction from the too exclusive views of the evolutionary biologists, from which the views of Freud have helped to deliver us.

Trotter has further demonstrated to us that our conduct is dominated by the '*herd instinct*' as effectively as Freud has argued that it is all sexual.

Adler, as though reluctant that any instinct should be left without its champion, has demonstrated that all nervous diseases are the result of the over-development of the 'masculine tendency' (or, as we should call it, the instinct of *self-assertion*), as a compensation for a physical inferiority.

The school of Jung lays emphasis on Archetypes which, like the Instincts, are innate, but which are primordial *images* or patterns of thought, such as the hero, the terrible mother, the shadow or hidden part of ourselves.

These attempts to find the key to life and its disorders in one or another of the instincts are destined to fail in theory and in practice. In theory, for the result of attempting to explain all the facts of life in terms of one instinct is that we distort many of the facts to fit in with the theory, as, for instance, when a Freudian declares that men fear the Zeppelins, not because of their danger to life, but because of their phallic symbolism representing sexual desires; or, when the self-preservationists says that the mother cares for her child because she recognizes her future dependence on her child in old age, and seeks to ensure that the child will protect her. In practice, we find that nervous disorders may result from disharmony in *any* instinctive tendency. The war, with its shell-shock conditions, gave support to the biologists, for these conditions were primarily concerned with the instincts of self-preservation and fear. There is, at the same time, little doubt that the vast majority of neuroses of civil life, especially of women, are due to emotional disturbances of the sexual instinct. This is due to its enormous strength, and because it is the most repressed of all the instincts. Nevertheless, we find that in the majority of men, as distinct from women, the conflict is concerned more with the self-assertive instincts, with ambition and power, which gives support to Adler's theory of the masculine tendency. Again, there is a sense in which the herd instinct is responsible for most nervous ills, since repression of the instincts is largely due to the conventions and injunctions of the herd.

MATURATION

Apart from the primary instincts and other potentialities, like suggestibility, we inherit *Patterns of Behaviour*. The child develops the capacity to walk at one period, to talk at another; to become self-conscious at another, to join gangs about the age of 13 and to fall in love about 16 or 17. All these processes, which I shall refer to later (Chapter XVI), are innate and emerge in every normal individual irrespective of environmental conditions.

This process is called Maturation, which I define as 'the emergence of innate potentialities in ordered sequence'. They are innate and they appear in the individual in a certain order or sequence.[1]

THE ENVIRONMENTAL FACTOR

We have already observed that individual traits of character, and in particular nervous and moral diseases, are primarily due to conditions of early environment. They may arise either from a single event or from a morbid atmosphere.

It is a matter of common knowledge that a *single experience* may change our whole attitude towards life, and make a complete change in our character.

Bitterness of character may be produced by a disappointment; a sexual assault may produce timidity, hysteria, or sexual frigidity. Such occurrences are particularly liable to cause permanent defects if they occur in childhood, and if they are repressed and forgotten.

But more important than the one definite event is the general *atmosphere* of childhood, consisting of a large number of trifling events, which may give the child a wrong attitude towards life or a wrong attitude towards itself. That is to say, abnormal conditions of mind are determined much more by the atmosphere of childhood than by any one shock. These influences usually work by way of suggestion. An attitude of defeatism for instance may result from constant frustration of the child.

Abnormal experiences of childhood, whether due to a single event or to an unnatural atmosphere, may have no immediate ill effect, yet the impression is made, and the complex produced lies latent until later in life, when some shock or strain, insufficient in itself to produce a neurosis, becomes active and lights up the complex into a definite moral or nervous disease. This accounts for the view held by most psychotherapists that all functional nervous disorders, even of later life, such as the breakdown of the girl of 18, the

[1] See my *Childhood and Adolescence*, pp. 43–68, Penguin, for a description of these phases.

woman of 30, or the business or professional man of 55, originate in childhood. It is the experiences of childhood which predispose us to the breakdown of nerve and character in later life.

Why should the earliest years of life be so important?

First, because in childhood the mind and brain are most impressionable, and the deepest impressions are the most difficult to eradicate. The child absorbs ideas by suggestion, that is to say, without criticism. He is especially impressionable to suggestions from his mother or father, adopts their mannerisms, and responds with the same emotions to the same stimuli. In the presence, say, of a sick man, a child watches the father, adopts his attitude, whether of pity or disgust, and will thereafter react according to this emotional response of his parent. Suggestion, however, may have either a positive or negative influence. The suggestion of hell-fire, intended to fill the child with religious awe, may succeed either in producing a defiance of religion, or, on the other hand, it may produce a punctilious and conscientious regard for religious exercises which is afterwards honestly but falsely mistaken for piety.

Secondly, in childhood we are as yet unadapted to life, and fail to react adequately to it. The death of a mother is an irreparable loss and irretrievable disaster to a child; later, he has learnt to react to such exigencies of fate, and can meet them with greater composure and self-confidence.

Thirdly, in childhood we form our general attitude towards life. It is in childhood that we form impressions of life, e.g. that life is easy, that people are hostile, that it pays to be good, that nothing pleasant ever lasts. We later undergo many new experiences and adopt many new ideas, but the general attitude we adopt towards life in childhood gives the tone to all our after-life. Our childhood atmosphere determines whether our later attitude to the world be pessimistic, confident, easy-going, stoical, self-assertive or antagonistic, 'inferior' or snobbish. In such cases, we carry into adult life an attitude towards the world which was perhaps natural and inevitable in the circumstances of childhood, but quite out of keeping with our later environment. So a man who has learnt to be antagonistic in childhood maintains this attitude even in an atmosphere of kindliness, and remains suspicious amongst the best of friends; his character is distorted.

Fourthly, in childhood we form our *attitude towards ourselves*, which is of much greater importance than even our attitude towards the world. It is in childhood that we first develop self-consciousness, and the impression we get when we first catch sight of ourselves is destined to remain with us through life and produce normal and abnormal conditions of character. To this we shall refer later in discussing Phantasy.

The environmental influences of childhood are very few and simple, and are almost limited to the members of the family and home surroundings. In support of the hereditary theory it is often maintained that we sometimes have children brought up 'under exactly the same conditions' and yet their characters are quite different. But the position of a child in the family, whether it is eldest or youngest, is most important, as we shall see later. Three children said to be brought up under entirely the same conditions may turn out entirely different in character, not necessarily because of any *inherent* differences but because their conditions, outwardly similar, are really entirely different. The mere fact that one is the eldest and plays the 'little mother' and the other the youngest and is treated as the 'baby' means that the environmental influences of their upbringing are poles apart. So too with sex: since a father is normally more devoted to a girl and the mother to the boy the girl develops an attachment to the father and the son to the mother. The Œdipus complex like all other complexes is the result of such environmental conditions.

Since it is the environmental conditions of early childhood which have given rise to our abnormalities of character, it is found that the simplest means of understanding the complexities of our adult psychology is to trace them back to childhood, where we may find the key to their origin.

CHAPTER III

Sentiments, Dispositions, and Complexes

WE HAVE DEALT with two determinants of human conduct – the instinctive emotions and the environmental influences. Every child, we have observed, is born endowed with a number of instincts – fear, anger, sex, maternity, submission, self-assertion, curiosity, self-display, and others, each of which is charged with emotional tone. When the instinctive emotions are brought into touch with environmental conditions, they tend to become attached to and grouped round the

SENTIMENT OF PATRIOTISM

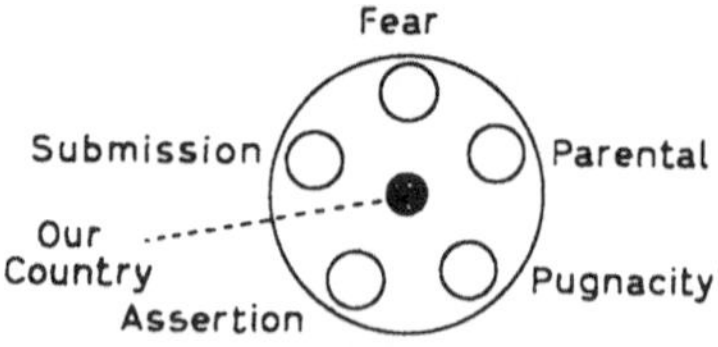

objects, ideas, events, or persons of the environment. These combine to form *psychological constellations*. Psychological constellations are composed of two factors, one from the *environment* – an event, person, or idea – and one from *heredity*, namely, the instinctive emotion.

Patriotism is a constellation in which the emotions are grouped round the idea of our country; we assert ourselves for our country, we fight for her, we feel tenderness towards her, we fear for her, we submit to her demands. The constellation, therefore, consists of the attachment of these instinctive emotions to this object.

The whole structure of our mind as developed may be considered to consist of such constellations, which are the true units of mental process, containing cognitive, affective, and conative processes in each.

Psychological constellations are of three forms: Sentiments, Dispositions, and Complexes.

The *sentiments* are those constellations which we consciously accept; the *dispositions*, those which are unconsciously accepted; and the *complexes*, those which are rejected as unacceptable, and tend to be repressed.

THE SENTIMENTS

A sentiment is a psychological constellation acceptable to the individual and with which he consciously identifies himself. Patriotism is a sentiment, the nucleus of which is our country, round which our emotions are constellated. Philanthropy is a sentiment in which the nucleus is our fellow-men. Religion, too, is a sentiment in which the idea or person of God is the centre round which all our emotions, whether of love or fear, are centred. The child has a mother sentiment, the disciple a sentiment for the master, the boy for his school, the philosopher for truth, the novelist for romance.

The most dominant of all our sentiments embody our ideals or aims in life, for it is to these that most of our emotions are particularly strongly attached, and is these that dominate our will.

We may have 'good' sentiments and 'bad' sentiments. They are 'sentiments' in so far as they are acceptable to the individual; they are 'good' or 'bad' sentiments as they are acceptable or otherwise to the rest of mankind. The revolutionary may have a sentiment for murder, and the sentimentalist for anti-vivisection. Both are acceptable to those who have them, and are therefore sentiments and not complexes, though both are sentiments which in the opinion of most others are bad.

PSYCHOLOGICAL DISPOSITIONS

Dispositions differ from sentiments in that they are *unconsciously* accepted. Their activities are spontaneous, so that to act in response to them is 'second nature' to us. A gentleman does not need to *think* whether he chooses to save himself, or his child, in a wreck – the decision is spontaneous; he has a disposition of honour. When we enlist in a time of our country's need we are actuated by a patriotic sentiment. But patriotism or philanthropy may be so part of our nature, ingrained from our earliest years, that all our work is *unconsciously* and spontaneously devoted to the good of our country or the good of our fellows, in which case we are said to have a patriotic or philanthropic *disposition.* So, too, one man may make religion his conscious aim, and possess a religious sentiment; another may actually think about religion very little, but he may have the greater religious disposition.

A disposition may be in conflict with a sentiment although both may be considered acceptable, as when a judge with tears condemns a man to death, or when we deliberately but with some shame do a spiteful act.

Dispositions, like sentiments, may be bad as well as good. As a man may have bad sentiments, so he may have vicious, careless, or cruel dispositions, which are acceptable to him but give rise to habits which are repellent to his fellows. A man's disposition is not, as such, inherited, but, like the sentiments and individual dispositions, is formed of emotional experiences in life.

Individual dispositions combine to form what we call a man's Disposition.

Psychological dispositions are to be distinguished from *physiological* dispositions, such as give rise to habits like swallowing, and from *psycho-physical* dispositions like the instincts, for they are formed of instinctive emotions attached to ideas or objects of the environment. I should venture to suggest that disposition should thus be distinguished from 'temperament'; since the term temperament (phlegmatic, etc.) has always been used of those psycho-physical conditions such as arise from disturbances of the endocrine glands like the thyroid or pituitary glands, which have a very marked effect on character.

The first object of all education, intellectual as well as moral and religious, is the formation of right sentiments and dispositions, that is to say, the attachment of emotions to the right objects, ideas, and persons. A liberal education will secure that our emotions are attached to ideas such as 'playing the game', 'loyalty', 'a sense of honour'. These qualities, adopted as conscious sentiments in schooldays, become the accepted dispositions of our manhood.

For whilst the first aim of education is to produce right *sentiments*, these sentiments can only become the basis of a strong character when they have become *dispositions*, the abiding spring of right habit and conduct.[1]

Our psychological sentiments, together with the dispositions – that is to say, all those constellations which are *acceptable* to the individual – are together combined and organized to form what we shall call the '*Organized Self*'. *Temperament* denotes the effect that the *physiological* make-up of the individual has upon his behaviour – like the 'nervous temperament'. Thus one person is sensitive *by nature* whereas another is stolid; one is temperamentally aggressive, whilst another is temperamentally gentle.

Disposition is developed as a result of *environmental* influences

[1] The purpose of education should not be to learn a subject, but to like a subject. In practice our educational system frequently succeeds in establishing a sentiment of hate towards many of the subjects studied, so that few boys continue, for instance, to take pleasure in the classics or history after leaving school.

But to say that we should like a subject does not mean that all our education should be 'simplified' and made easy. Indeed, the tendency towards 'easy' methods of study in schools deprives the child of one of the most important sentiments of all. The difficult task should itself be the nucleus of a sentiment stimulating determination and courage. There is no sentiment in life more valuable than that which sees in *difficulty* an obstacle to be overcome and mastered, and in which the hard task calls forth our courageous emotions.

– the way we are brought up – such as a kindly disposition, or a cruel disposition; and so are our *Complexes*, which are *morbid* Dispositions.

Character is the quality of our personality as a whole, *as determined by our aims and ideals.* True, these ideals are derived from our environment and upbringing, and so may be classed as dispositions, but they are unique in that we adopt them specifically as our conscious aims in life. So a man is of 'good character' if he has high ideals in life, which he lives up to, and of 'bad character' if he has low ideals, which he lives down to.

CHAPTER IV

Complexes

WE ARE CONSTANTLY forced to perform actions of a compulsive nature, or to give vent to emotional outbursts which are not only involuntary, but often antagonistic to the will. We are bad-tempered, shy, callously indifferent, when most we desire to keep calm, to be confident, and to display sympathy. Such morbid impulses, acting independently and in spite of the will, arise for the most part from *repressed complexes*. We must, therefore, study the origin, constitution, and effects of the complexes.

Complexes, like the sentiments and dispositions, are psychological constellations formed by the attachment of the instinctive emotions to objects or experiences presented by the environment, but which, owing to their painful or repugnant character, are *unacceptable* to the 'self'. Experiences associated with painful emotions, such as an act of cowardice, sexual assaults, wounded pride, frequently become the material for a complex. The thought of the war may be the nucleus of a sentiment to a man who was heavily decorated, a complex to a man court-martialled for cowardice. What at one age may be a mother sentiment, may at a later age be a mother complex. The complex is commonly named according to the dominant emotion contained in it, like a fear complex, sex complex, inferiority complex, or, at other times, by the name of the nucleus round which the emotions are grouped – a mother complex, or war complex, or religious complex.

It is important to remember that complexes may have been repugnant to us in the past and so repressed, whereas the same would not be unacceptable to us now. Nevertheless they remain as repressed complexes producing morbid effects, and it is only when they are unearthed that they are seen to be innocuous and acceptable. An insult at twenty is comic at fifty.

Complexes may be recognized or unrecognized. Acts of cowardice or humiliation may be recognized and remembered only too well, in spite of our endeavour to forget all about them.

But many complexes are unrecognized. As we may dissociate ourselves from friends who have insulted us, or refuse to associate with those who have disgraced our family, so we may 'cut' and refuse to recognize or identify ourselves with complexes which are repugnant. They then become 'dissociated', i.e. split off, forgotten, and we become quite unaware of their existence. This process of dissociation being an active one, the term 'repression' is found to be the more appropriate to describe it. The complexes themselves are called *Repressed Complexes.*

Sometimes all that is recognized of a complex is the *nucleus* or some accidental element in it. In a 'fixed idea', for instance, such as an idea that one is made of glass, or that the world is going to come to an end on a special date, there is an underlying emotional complex, but it is only the idea that emerges, whereas the emotional part may appear to be perfectly normal. The emergence of the nucleus without the emotion occurs also in cases of conversion hysteria like hysterical paralysis, in which the emotional part remains repressed. Usually, however, the fixed idea is associated even in consciousness with an emotion, so that the belief that the end of the world is coming is fraught with fear or evangelic zeal; and in the other case the emotion may burst forth in a hysterical attack. At other times it is the *emotional element* which is recognized, as in 'anxiety' states in which there is a fear but the object of the fear is unrecognized. When the complexes are recognized and are consciously inhibited from expression in *conduct,* we call it *restraint*: we speak of *suppression* when the complex is psychologically repugnant and voluntarily inhibited; when the process of inhibition is unconscious, we call it *repression.* It is important to recognize that repression is an unconscious process.

Emotional complexes are repressed in three ways. First, there may be a straight conflict between two instinctive impulses, resulting in the repression of one. A child's feelings of dependence and craving for petting may be repressed by its aggressive self-will. Being thwarted in its desire for love it may say, '*I* don't want to be petted', and assume an attitude of defiant independence, whereas it may be craving for the love which is denied. Again, a child's *self-will* and aggression may be repressed by *fear* of consequences, so that actually it becomes a timid instead of a self-assertive child. Secondly, as the individual develops, one phase may be repressed by the earlier persisting phase, as when the natural love impulses of a youth in later adolescence are denied expression because of his clinging to an earlier *self*-love phase characterized by masturbation. His self-congratulation that he has 'nothing to do with girls' is usually a self-condemnation of his egotism. Thirdly, and most commonly, the complex is repressed by our *self*, though it may be a self of a bygone day (see Chapter on Phantasy).

Complexes may thus be recognized or unrecognized; consciously restrained or unconsciously repressed. The former, the recognized complex, may affect our character and happiness; the latter, the repressed complexes, are alone capable of producing a psychoneurosis. Thus a humiliation which we remember may make us moody; it cannot of itself make us neurotic.

THE EFFECTS OF THE COMPLEXES

The repressed complexes, though themselves buried and forgotten, continue to have a baneful and morbid influence on life. They are charged with emotional tone, and force themselves into consciousness against the self as a whole.

Complexes denied direct expression manifest themselves in various forms:

(1) In dreams, which are the language of the unconscious.
(2) In nervous disorders – the Psychoneuroses.
(3) In abnormalities of conduct.

THE PSYCHONEUROSES

The functional nervous disorders described in our introduction – hysteria, neurasthenia, anxiety states, obsessions, phobias, and the rest – are the morbid manifestation of repressed complexes, which are otherwise denied expression. If a fear complex is refused normal expression, it achieves its end by paralysing the soldier. Sex perversions are the outcome of the repression of that instinct.

It will help us to understand the problem of moral conduct if we study some of the neuroses which result from these repressed complexes, because in psychological origin they are exactly similar to those moral diseases with which we are more particularly concerned. Most of us can recognize the various forms of neurosis: there is the type of patient with symptoms of anxiety, tremor, sweating, distress of mind, and terrifying dreams, who is a victim of '*Anxiety neurosis*'. Another is always tired: he sleeps profoundly, but without refreshment, and gets up in the morning more tired than he went to bed. This is the *Neurasthenic* proper. A third suffers from paralysis, blindness, headaches, or pain in the back, localized bodily symptoms – so-called *Conversion hysteria* – different in type from the generalized symptoms of anxiety neurosis. A fourth suffers from mental obsessions, like a fear of being alone or fear of crowds – called *Psychasthenia* by some and *Anxiety hysteria* by others. There are other forms, such as *dual personality*, with which we are not so directly concerned. There are also the *Psychoses*, or insanities, mainly organic in origin, in which the conscious mind is completely, and not merely partially, as in these other cases, dominated by the emotion or complex.

In origin the Psychoneuroses are due to repressed complexes: they differ from one another in *the disposal of the complex*. In *neurasthenia* the complex is deeply and effectively repressed, so deeply that there is no expression in consciousness of the repressed fear, sexual desire or ambition; indeed, these neurasthenic patients may be callous, indifferent, and devoid of feeling or passion. The neurasthenic is tired because he spends all his energy in keeping down or repressing the instinctive forces within him. He succeeds in his effort, but in doing so saps his vitality to such an extent that no energy is available for the ordinary purposes of life, and he becomes exhausted by the most trifling effort. Such a man frequently suffers not only from physical fatigue, but from mental depression.[1]

In the moral sphere the type is exemplified in the man whose 'morality' is preserved by the effective repression of all his passions: he succeeds in being moral but suffers from lifelessness and moral 'neurasthenia'. He has no temptations, and denies ever falling into sin; all these years has he served without breaking any commandment. Such paragons of virtue would be unable, even if presented with a calf, to make merry like the rest with music and dancing. They would solemnly propose the health of the host and hostess, and discreetly avoid all reference to the harlots: they are good but not happy, they have lost the capacity for cheerfulness. They are tired, neurasthenic, joyless. They end by being thoroughly weary with well-doing.

In *anxiety neurosis* the complex is not so deeply repressed, the fight between the 'self' and the complex being, as it were, *at close quarters*; the self is in imminent danger, and becomes anxious. When two opposing forces come into close antagonism there results a condition of tremor and strain. To take a physiological analogy; if I contract the flexor muscles of my arm, and at the same time the opposite extensor muscles, so as to make my forearm stiff, the whole arm is put into a condition of tremor. So, when two emotional forces fight at close quarters in my soul, a condition of *mental* tremor or 'anxiety' results. If my ambition is tense and eager, and at the

[1] See the author's *Psychology of Power*, published by the Macmillan Co.

same time I am obsessed by a fear of failure, there results a mental tremor. When I am roused with sexual desires, and at the same time attempt to maintain my moral character, again there is a conflict at close quarters which produces mental tremor like the physical: indeed, it is often accompanied by physical symptoms of anxiety, such as sweating, trembling, starting, palpitation, and general excitability.

There is, however, a distinction between 'anxiety' and 'anxiety neuroses': anxiety may result from an actual *recognized* conflict of instincts, such as we have illustrated. Anxiety neurosis, on the other hand, as distinct from mere anxiety, is occasioned by the fact that our fear is of something unknown, of which we get terrifying glimpses only in our nightmares, and which haunt our days with a pursuing horror. The patient is afraid not of any danger outside, but of an unrecognized impulse within which threatens to overthrow his dominant sentiments.

Conversion Hysteria. Perhaps the most interesting cases of neuroses are those which manifest themselves in a definite physical symptom, such as blindness, pain in the back, sickness. They are well called 'substitution' or 'conversion' hysterias, because a definite physical symptom is substituted for the mental and moral conflict. By the conversion of the mental disease into a physical, the mental condition of the patient is greatly relieved. A patient, for instance, who suffered from chronic vomiting, was found on analysis to have substituted this for a moral sickness at an act of cowardice which he could not bring himself to acknowledge. He was sick with himself; horrible as it was to vomit, it was preferable to be haunted with self-reproach. The hand-washing mania usually signifies a deeper but unrecognized stain of soul.

The complex, however, instead of reaching consciousness as a physical symptom, *may* emerge as a *mental* symptom. Such is a fixed *idea*, for instance, that one has made a mistake in the accounts, or an *emotion*, like a phobia or projected fear of open spaces, or a *moral* disease like a sex perversion or kleptomania.

A man, a male nurse, meets a lady of his choice, also a nurse, and as soon as he sets eyes on her has the almost irresistible impulse to punch her in the face. As such a symptom is hardly likely to further his suit he seeks for the explanation. Ultimately in analysis it goes back to a time when he was by underhand means ousted from his job by a female nurse. Meeting her afterwards on the stair he remarked, 'If I were a woman, I would punch you in the face.' The whole impulse was repressed, and the incident forgotten, but it formed a complex which emerged in this compulsive action.

The repressed complex was aroused by the appearance of a nurse, though under very different conditions. One may regard this as a neurosis or a 'moral disease' according to whether we regard it as an impulse or a perversion of conduct.

In neurasthenia, then, the complex is *completely* repressed; in Anxiety neurosis it is only partially repressed, and fights at close quarters with the self; in Conversion hysterias, obsessions, and moral diseases, the complex emerges by some back door in the form of a localized symptom, physical, mental or moral.

Several principles regarding the formation of the neuroses may now be defined.

(*a*) Every neurosis is the result of an unresolved problem. Because we cannot resolve it we repress it. Because it is repressed, it is dissociated to form a complex. Because it is dissociated it becomes beyond the control of the Will.

Because it is dissociated and beyond the control of the Will, it emerges in a substitute form such as a hysteric pain (to get sympathy), a phobia for open spaces (as representing a sense of insecurity), sex perversions (as a solace), and obsessional compulsions (as a propitiation for our feelings of guilt). Yet all this is quite unconscious.

(*b*) Every neurosis and nervous breakdown is thus the result of a *conflict*.

Complexes, like instincts, crave for expression, and they become repressed as the result of *conflict*. This conflict may take various forms. In its simplest form it is a conflict *between two instinctive impulses* or two complexes, like those of pugnacity and fear, the one urging to attack, the other to flight, resulting in paralysis. Again, the conflict may be *between an impulse* and *the self*, as when our moral self condemns our selfish greed. Finally, the conflict may be *between two phases of life*, e.g. the 'child' phase may refuse to give place to the puberty phase, which is therefore repressed and denied expression.

(*c*) This conflict is always *endo-psychic*, that is, a conflict of elements within the soul itself.

We frankly approach this subject from the psychological point of view. The attitude of the psychologist differs radically from that of the biologist. The biologist looks at life from the point of view of adaptation to environment. The psychologist interprets everything from the point of view of mental processes, and is interested in the events of the objective world only in so far as they give rise to mental processes. His view thus differs from that of the biologist. This difference of attitude is of the greatest importance, not only in the conception of the psychoneuroses, but particularly in their treatment.

It used to be thought that a nervous breakdown could be caused by an objective experience, like a 'shock', a fright, a sexual trauma, a disappointment, a failure. A man's main function in life, it was said, was to adapt himself to his environment, and a nervous breakdown was said to be due to man's failure to adapt himself to his environment. The soldier, it seemed quite obvious, breaks down because he cannot adjust himself to the strain and stress of war, the girl to the shock of the sex trauma, and the business-man to his failure in business. This is all perfectly true from the biologist's point of view, but not from the point of view of the psychologist, and it is an inadequate conception from the point of view of treatment. If a soldier's breakdown were merely due to his failure to adapt himself to his environment, he could easily overcome the difficulty by running away to safety.

Why does he not do so? Because there is something he fears more than the shell-fire, something in himself, namely, his own self-esteem. In other words, a man's nervous breakdown is not due to the failure to adapt himself to his environment, but *his failure to adapt himself to himself.* It is quite true that the shell-fire is the exciting cause, but it is effective only in so far as it arouses fear and gives rise to a mental conflict. The real conflict, a conflict more important than that between himself and his environment, is that between his honour, on the one hand, and his fear and desire for self-preservation on the other. He has failed to accommodate himself to those latent forces of fear, which his courage or sense of duty refuses to recognize. Running away or the ending of the war is no solution to such a problem, whereas it would be if it were merely a matter of adaptation to environment. He therefore has to resort to a nervous breakdown to deliver him from the conflict. The shocks which produce the psychoneuroses are always shocks we give *ourselves.* Stated in terms of psychotherapy, *the psychoneurotic symptom is always the result of an endopsychic conflict.*

Our problem is not primarily to fit a man to face his environment, but by discovering both elements in the conflict to fit him to face himself. A man is impotent to face the onslaughts of the objective world until he has restored harmony within the borders of his soul; only when he has resolved these conflicts in his soul is he fitted to face his environment. With peace in his soul he is capable of facing the most terrible experience, as has been proved by the war; without it he cannot face the responsibility of writing a letter.

(*d*) *Every neurosis is unconsciously desired.*

The purpose of every neurosis is to deliver us from a mental conflict. A gunner has spotted and is sighting a German submarine. Torn between fear and his sense of duty, he suddenly finds himself getting blind, but his blindness is purely psychic, there is nothing wrong with his *eyes.* Now, of course, he *must* go below, for what is the use of his remaining to sight his gun when he is blind? The neurosis is a compromise to deliver him from his mental conflict: his instinct of self-preservation and his sense of duty are both satisfied.[1] Denied normal expression his fear satisfies its impulses by a back door.

We may, then, understand why it is that psychotherapists say that every nervous and moral disorder is '*unconsciously desired*'. Not *consciously*, for no one who has had a hysteric pain, nervous indigestion, or a nervous breakdown would admit any pleasure in it. Not consciously, for so to *assume* an illness is malingering, and the neurotic is never a conscious malingerer. But he has an 'unconscious' desire for illness, in that it relieves him from an impossible mental situation.

There is no exception to this law.

It seems impossible that a symptom like the fear of madness should be desired; nor is it, if we take count of the conscious only. In one case the 'madness' was associated with an incident in which the patient, when a boy of five, was experiencing sexual delight in running about naked in his bedroom when his nurse came in, scolded him, and said, 'You must be mad to run about naked.' The unconscious response of the patient was, 'If this is madness, then madness for me!' The 'exhibitionist' tendency was thus repressed, but the unconscious desire for exhibitionism became so strong an impulse that it emerged into consciousness – not, of course, *as* a desire, but as a fear of the madness which would make it possible, without his being morally responsible. This, like most phobias, was the fear of something unconsciously desired. He feared madness only because he feared the desire associated with it. It is interesting to note that when this fear of madness comes on, he has an almost uncontrollable desire to tear off his clothes and run about naked. I have in mind three cases, one in which 'madness' represented a repressed desire for

[1] In the Neurasthenic Hospital it is very interesting to observe that patients may be divided at a glance into those who suffer from mental anxiety and distress, but without any localized physical ailment, and those who have such symptoms as blindness and paralysis, but are extraordinarily free from all mental distress. These latter, indeed, are often the life and soul of the party, getting up entertainments, and hobbling about the football field in perfect happiness. They have found a way out of their mental conflict.

exhibitionism; another a desire for sex licence; and a third, a repressed desire for unrestrained power.

In every case of neurosis, as of 'moral disease', we find that the symptom is designed to satisfy the desire of both elements in the conflict. Even the business-man's breakdown, commonly due to the conflict between a phantasy of power and a fear of failure, delivers him from this conflict, for he can still say, 'I *should* have succeeded, if it had not been for this physical illness.' He is excused for failing, and yet retains his phantasy of the great things he *might* have done.

CHAPTER V

Complexes and Conduct: Projection: Temptation and Conscience: Habits

EFFECT OF THE COMPLEX ON CONDUCT

From the illustrations already given, it will be obvious that the complex may not only produce nervous breakdown, but have a marked influence on character.

We shall observe its moral effects in –

(*a*) The projection or objectification of the complex; (*b*) over-compensation; (*c*) temptation and conscience; (*d*) habits; (*e*) moral disease.

PROJECTION AND OBJECTIFICATION

I knew a man to whom white spats were a 'red rag', because he was once humiliated by another in whose decorative scheme these were a characteristic ornament. The forgotten complex emerged in this dislike.

Repressed complexes which we refuse to recognize tend to attach themselves to persons and objects of the outside world. Thus, we condemn in others what we refuse to admit in ourselves. This is the principle of the objectification or projection of our complexes. The principle may be stated thus: '*Our relation to the outside world is determined by our relation to our own complexes.*' It is an extension of the endo-psychic principle.

A lady is consumed with irritation against another. There is no good reason for this, and therefore she finds a dozen. But why this anger? Because the other lady was sentimental. My patient is angry because she, too, was sentimental, but would not admit it, and repressed it. The hated complex was therefore projected on to the other, and she hated *her* because of her *own* sentimentality. The feeling was not really between my patient and the other: the problem was between herself and herself. Her relation to others was only her relation to her own complex; the conflict was endo-psychic.

It is a well-known fact that preachers are always preaching against the sins to which they are, unconsciously, most prone (and usually rigidly avoid those to which they are consciously addicted). Therefore, it is literally true that in judging others we trumpet abroad our secret faults. We personalize our unrecognized failings, and hate in others the very faults to which we are secretly addicted. We say their conduct is incredible, monstrous! We are annoyed with the incompetence of others only because we refuse to admit our own real incompetence. Most of our emotions are directed against ourselves. We are intolerant of the lazy, slovenly, 'footling' ways of others because this tendency is a constant temptation to us. We condemn the bigotry, meanness, or cynicism in others because we are potential bigots, misers, and cynics. We cannot bear conceited people because we are conceited without knowing it. Paul breathed out threatenings and slaughter against the Christians probably because he was three parts a Christian. On the other hand, an easy-going, tolerant spirit is often merely the projection of our tolerant attitude towards our own hidden faults. We forgive in others what we desire to forgive in ourselves, for by so doing we temper the sting of self-condemnation.

Allow any man to give free vent to his feelings about others and then you may with perfect safety turn and say, 'Thou art the man!'

The same principle applies to our love as to our hate. We love those who represent the things we have not. So the man who is not, but likes to think of himself as, a savant, an aristocrat, or a business-man, seeks to mingle in learned, aristocratic, or business circles. If he has the soul of a child and is timid of the world, he is constantly raising his voice in praise of courage, or seeking the company of courageous men. So, too, millionaires with little or no education often give great endowments to universities. Books on sex are sometimes written by those whose sex life is in some way or another abnormal. Advocates of universal peace are frequently those in whose souls harmony and peace are completely abolished by inner conflicts of soul; the unconscious craving for peace is projected on to the world outside. A projection of great importance is that which gives rise to altruism. Our sympathy for others may be a normal development of our sympathy for ourselves, or it may be a repressed self-pity. This gives rise to two distinct types of social worker whose work is quite different; that of the healthy reformer being characterized by a love for the oppressed, that of the revolutionary by personal resentment to the oppressor.

These illustrations help to support the principle that our relation to the outside world is largely determined by our relations to our complexes.

OVER-COMPENSATION

Another form in which the unconscious motive influences our life is by over-compensation. We over-compensate when, in order to hide our complex, we 'go to the other extreme'. A lady may spontaneously protest her devotion to her husband so strongly that one knows there is domestic trouble. The middle-aged man, who, at the beginning of the war, went about protesting that there was nothing he desired more than that he was young enough to go to the front was really displaying his cowardice, as was proved when men of his age were called up. The man who is always inviting frank criticism is excessively annoyed when you give him what he asks instead of the flattery that he really wants. The man who, being criticized, says 'I don't care a *hang* WHAT people say' shows by the vehemence of his protest how much he does care. The very excess of their protest is the strongest proof of their addiction to such failings. Over-compensation is the method by which we try to disguise our nature, but, like the lark fluttering with agitation over her nest, we exhibit most flagrantly the very thing we would hide.

It is wonderful in analysing the minds of men to discover how those with god-like qualities are found to stand on feet of clay. There are none so afraid of spooks as the rationalist; none so superstitious and terrified at omens as those who scoff at the supernatural; none have such a feeling of inferiority as the bravo; the 'hard' man, who can't stand 'sentimental rot', is himself a sentimentalist. Deference to others is often assumed by those who wish to avoid the humiliation of a snub; it reveals a phantasy of pride that cannot bear to be wounded, and therefore avoids the risk by an assumed humility. We often depreciate our work in some trifling point, in order to call attention to its otherwise perfect character.

The psychologist learns to read people's characters not by the person or mask that they present, but by the psyche or soul they unconsciously reveal by their projections and over-compensations.

TEMPTATION AND CONSCIENCE

So far as their purely psychological mechanisms are concerned, temptation and conscience are identical, for both are the voice of suppressed desires. Temptation is the voice of the suppressed evil; conscience is the voice of the good. When our impulses are aroused by the delights of evil, we are said to be tempted; when we awaken to the loveliness of the good, our conscience is aroused. Temptation is the voice of the suppressed evil when good is dominant; conscience is the voice of the suppressed good when evil is dominant. The 'good' man is a man who possesses sentiments such as kindliness, justice, and generosity: he suppresses cruelty, avarice, and injustice. But these suppressed desires crave for expression and therefore, in so far as he is good, these desires 'tempt him to evil'. On the other hand, the bad man is a man who has accepted as his sentiments selfishness, meanness, and vice, and suppresses all that is commonly regarded as good. In him the suppressed good craves for expression – and so the voice of conscience is heard urging him to be compassionate, courageous, and generous. The most hard-hearted criminals are sometimes moved with pity towards their victims. It is only if we are evil that we can be conscience-stricken, and only in so far as we are good in our dominant psychology that we can be tempted to evil.

The man who is perfectly bad could not be tempted, nor can the man completely good be conscience-stricken.

From this description it is obvious that conscience is not an entity any more than is temptation: they are functions rather than entities, functions of the complexes which are excluded from the self and which press their claims as impulses whether of good or evil.

It must be remembered, however, that this account deals only with mechanism, and not with values. 'Good and bad' are relative to an ideal, and as each individual has a different ideal, so will his conception of 'good' or 'bad' differ from that of another man. Thus, a man may be devoid of conscience when he burgles a house, but conscience-stricken if he commits a murder. Yet we would not say that his lack of conscience in the first place was an indication that he was good. He is merely a man with a low ideal. But the fact that he is conscience-stricken at the murder proves that he has some good in him, and conscience is the voice of this good.

On the other hand, the best of men are most conscious of wrong. This implies that they have indeed done wrong, and are so far bad, but bad only in relation to their own ideals, which may be infinitely higher than the burglar who has no sense of wrong. Further, when the self exercises its judgement upon itself and detects its own faults, the repressed wrong emerges into consciousness: it is performing the function of conscience. This function is most frequently and effectively performed by those who have high ideals, and therefore it comes about that to possess a 'sensitive conscience' is the mark, not of a bad man, as we implied above, but of one who is good.

Conscience and temptation may also spring from our *dispositions*, for, as we have seen, sentiments sometimes conflict with dispositions. The tender-hearted jury may be sorely tempted to acquit a wretched prisoner whom they know to be guilty of murder; and the dispositions of a lifetime may reprove us in some course of action which we have voluntarily determined upon.

Every temptation, like every neurosis, is, to some extent, desired; otherwise, why should it tempt us? We are always our own tempters.

The endo-psychic principle is as important for moral conduct as for the neurosis. We still speak as though temptation came from without, whereas no temptation would have the slightest effect were it not that it appealed to some desire within us, which normally we ourselves suppress. We are not tempted by the world, the flesh, and the devil, but by ourselves. Adam blamed Eve, and Eve blamed the serpent, but God was not deceived, and drove *them* out of the garden. They had not understood the 'endo-psychic' principle. In dealing with moral perverts, say, with the alcoholic, the point is not to remove his temptation, but to remove his desire.

GOOD AND BAD HABITS

The characteristic of all habits is that they are spontaneous and spring from unconscious motives. They are derived from two sources, dispositions and complexes. 'Bad habits', such as bad temper, perversions, a habit of contradicting, or of self-depreciation are due to repressed morbid *complexes*. 'Good habits', such as studious habits, generous habits, or courteous habits, are the results of accepted *dispositions*.

Behind and beneath every habit is an emotion, the arousal

of which determines the habit.[1] This is opposed to the commonly accepted view that such things as a nervous tic, bad temper, or a tendency to contradict are due to 'pure habit'. The conception of 'pure habit' is that an activity of body or mind tends to recur for no other reason than that it has occurred before. We maintain, on the contrary, that there is no such thing as a 'pure habit'.

James, in his deservedly famous chapter on 'Habit', takes as an illustration the fact that a piece of paper or suit of clothes, when folded, tend to recur to this 'habit'. But this is not true habit; it is merely a change of structure, not of function. When once folded, the paper does not continue folding itself, nor, unfortunately, do our trousers, once pressed, continue to crease themselves over-night.

It is true that when any function, mental or physical, has once taken place, there is a change of bodily or mental structure which *facilitates* the recurrence of the action. But this change of structure cannot *initiate* action or in itself constitute a habit.

As every physiological habit needs an external stimulus, so every 'nervous' or mental habit requires an emotion to set it in motion even though the emotion itself be in no way expressed. One proof of this conception of habit is based on actual experimental tests. A lady has a 'habit pain' in her shoulder. This was traced back on analysis to an occasion in childhood when she hurt the shoulder and was soothed by an unscrupulous nurse stimulating her sexually. Her sex feelings were later repressed; but when any stimulus came to arouse them, they did not emerge as sex feelings, but as the pain in the shoulder, through and by which she originally came to experience these pleasurable feelings. A man has a 'habit' of waking at three each morning. This dated back to a time when he wakened with dysentery and thought he was dying. The repressed fear of death lay behind this habit, and was

[1] I refer to psychological habits and habits of conduct, and exclude purely physiological 'habits', like that of reflex action of the knee-jerk in which there is obviously no emotional tone.

aroused by association every night when the hour of three struck. So it is with any habit of conduct or character. If one investigates the origin of any such habit it is always found that there was originally an emotion connected with it, and that it is the arousal of this repressed emotion which now gives rise to the habit. Even the habits of everyday life are the expression of latent desires, normal or abnormal.

This view of habit is of the utmost importance in the practical treatment of bad habits, and the formation of good ones. No good habit is worth much unless it be backed by a large and healthy emotional disposition. Good habits, if not inspired by healthy emotions, fall into disuse like diaries in the opening year.

It is also important for the treatment of bad habits. If they are looked upon as 'pure habits' they can be overcome and corrected only by prolonged training and the formation of opposing habits, as James suggests. If they are due, as we maintain, to complexes fed from an emotional source, they can be adequately and effectively removed only by eradicating the complex, the complete removal of which will immediately cure the habit.

All the rules in the world for forming good habits will not eradicate a morbid complex which lies at the basis of a bad habit. A lady of my acquaintance assiduously observed all the rules given by James for the formation of good habits, and ultimately succeeded in behaving nicely to her aunt. But when her aunt had the bad taste to die on a day fixed for a theatre-party, she could restrain her annoyance no longer: 'It's *so* like Auntie,' she said. The repressed complex was obviously still there.

In actual treatment, it is found that when the complex is completely eradicated, the habit ceases as immediately as the electric light disappears when the current is cut off. It does not require to 'take time' for the habit to pass. If it does take time, as indeed is commonly the case, it is an indication that the whole of the complex is not eradicated. It may pass as suddenly and effectively as the bad habits of the man who undergoes religious conversion; indeed, the experience of the cure of moral evils by religious means supports the theory of the emotional origin of habits. The cynic and the sinner, the roué and the self-righteous, the drug fiend and the intolerant, are as suddenly cured of their life-long habits by the emotional disturbance of 'conversion' as by the more specific eradication of the latent complex. All desire and all craving for the habit immediately and suddenly disappear, often never to return, as soon as the emotional life is reorganized. The process of discovering the complex may take weeks and even months, but when discovered, a readjustment follows, and the habit which sprang from it is immediately eradicated. This applies to nervous habits, pains, and phobias, as much as to moral disorders.

If recent psychology had done nothing more by exploring the 'unconscious' than expose the emotional complexes which perpetuate our habits of conduct, it would have put moralists under a lasting obligation.

CHAPTER VI

'Nervous' Disease, Moral Disease, and Sin

THERE IS, we have seen, a class of disorders of conduct – alcoholism, irritability, bad temper, cynicism, aggressiveness, despondency, and certain sexual perversions – which are beyond the control of the will, and for which, therefore, we cannot be held morally responsible. They are of the same nature and origin as functional nervous diseases, being derived from repressed complexes, and should, therefore, be treated as sicknesses.

It has been said that when men are up against life and find it too much for them, one swears, one gets a headache, one prays, and one gets drunk. This half-truth is nevertheless a statement of scientific facts.

We must clearly distinguish four main classes of disorder which may result from man's struggle with life:

(*a*) *Organic diseases* are those diseases which have physical, and sometimes mental, symptoms, and whose cause is physical.

(*b*) *Functional nervous disorders* are those which have physical symptoms, the origin of which lies in unconscious conflicts of the mind.

(*c*) *Moral diseases*, like the functional nerve disorders, are due to unconscious repressed complexes, but their symptoms are not physical, like paralysis, but disorders of moral conduct, such as an uncontrollable bad temper or a sex perversion. A 'moral disease' is a disease as judged by a standard of conduct, rather than, as in the neuroses, by a standard of individual health.[1]

(*d*) '*Sins*'[2] which result from a deliberate and conscious choice of the self, and depend upon the acceptance of a low ideal.

It is not maintained that these different conditions are always distinctly separable. In practice they are often almost inextricably blended with one another, but they are, nevertheless, to be distinguished, both in conception and in treatment.

The difference between these various types of disorder may be crudely illustrated from the instincts of fear, sex, and self-assertive ambition.

FEAR – (*a*) A soldier may be struck by a bit of shrapnel, which causes an injury to the brain. He consequently suffers from a paralysis of the legs, and may even go mad. This is an organic disease, the symptoms of which are both physical and mental. (*b*) Another is not hit at all, but owing to emotional conflicts, suffers from 'shell-shock'. He also develops a paralysis of the legs, but in this case the paralysis is purely functional. There is no disease of organic structure discoverable. (*c*) Under similar conditions he may, in spite of himself, become extremely pugnacious and aggressive towards his comrades, or he may do wild and reckless things which may endanger the life of others. His is a disorder of conduct, contrary to military discipline; he is suffering from a 'moral disease'. (*d*) Finally, he may deliberately abandon his post of duty and be guilty of an act of cowardice.

SEX – (*a*) A woman's sexuality may involve her, first in a venereal disease, physical in origin and in symptom, and also

[1] I recognize the liberty taken in using the term 'moral disease'. It may with justice be held that if it is a 'disease', it cannot be moral; and if moral, we cannot call it a disease. But I cannot suggest a better name to give to these disorders, which are disorders of conduct, but yet are due to causes over which we have little or no control.

[2] We do not use 'sin' in a theological or religious sense as a wrong against God, but in a more strictly psychological sense.

leading to insanity with mental symptoms. Both physical and mental symptoms must be treated as organic. (*b*) She may, on the other hand, have experienced some sexual assault in childhood, and suffer after marriage from severe physical pain in sexual intercourse – pain of an entirely functional nature. (*c*) Or she may develop a sexual perversion like homosexuality, as a result of that same experience, and unless restrained pervert others. (*d*) Finally, she may from weakness of character deliberately and voluntarily give way to sexual excesses and be guilty of moral wrong.

AGGRESSION – (*a*) May lead a man to run needless risks and expose himself to physical diseases – malaria, pneumonia, or heart disease; (*b*) an ambition complex may lead either to a nervous breakdown characteristic of the business-man and artist; or, (*c*) his masterfulness being repressed, it may manifest itself as morbid cruelty or sadism; (*d*) finally, to achieve his ambition, he may deliberately embezzle.

ORGANIC DISEASES

With organic diseases we have little to do in this book, except to say that in our present state of knowledge, being organic in origin and organic in symptom, they are best treated by physical remedies. This does not mean that organic conditions cannot be influenced by mental conditions; indeed, the reverse is proved to be the case. The state of one's thoughts, and especially emotions, affects to a large extent the metabolism (physiological changes) of the body. Hope stimulates the circulation and increases the rate of the bodily functions. The sight of food normally sets the alimentary glands in activity, increasing the saliva and digestive gastric juices, so that appetite is literally the best sauce. This power of the mind over the body has long been recognized by medical men in treatment. Encouragement will not cure an appendicular abscess, nevertheless the surgeon does not fail to encourage the patient, nor does he despise this as an aid to recovery.[1]

Inflammatory and other diseased conditions depend so much upon blood circulation, that if we can influence, by suggestion or otherwise, the blood supply to a diseased part of the body, there is no reason why the diseased condition should not be cured by such mental influences. There is no reason why tuberculosis of the lungs, aggravated by a patient sitting huddled up in despair, should not be influenced, and even 'cured', by hope and gladness which raise him up, stimulate his circulation and respiration, so that both fresh blood and fresh air are brought to the remotest parts of the lung. This accession of vitality may be just sufficient to turn the scale. Nor, *theoretically*, is there any reason why a cancer should not disappear when, in the struggle between the body and the cancerous growth for the nutritive powers of the body, the vitality of the body as a whole is so raised that these powers are wrested from the diseased cancer, which dies, whilst the victorious body continues to live.[2]

The medical man does not deny that mental conditions can actively affect physiological functions. But the fact remains that in the present state of our knowledge, the best remedy for tuberculosis is anti-biotics, open-air, and special diet; and for cancer, early operation. We do not deny, theoretically, that mental conditions influence organic disease, even to the extent of cure. We do deny that this is in the present state of our knowledge the best form of treatment. To treat such a patient solely by suggestion, unction, or prayer, is to deny him the best chance of recovery.

Further, organic diseases very often produce mental and moral symptoms as in certain forms of insanity, and particu-

[1] It has also been proved in experiments made by the present writer, in which the blood supply of an arm was so affected by suggestion that the temperature was raised to 92° F., and lowered to 68° F. (See *Lancet*, 1917, ii, p. 678.)

[2] Indeed, it may be that this is the process that takes place when, as sometimes happens, a cancer spontaneously disappears and is cured, such cures being attributed, rightly or wrongly, to the prayers of friends or to quack medicines.

larly in mental deficiency. The treatment of such patients must also of course be approached from the physical side.

FUNCTIONAL NERVOUS DISEASE

The functional nerve diseases resemble the organic diseases, in so far as their symptoms are physical – fatigue, blindness, trembling, headache, paralysis. They differ, however, in two respects: (*a*) The blindness and paralysis of the organic disease show a definite change of structure; in functional diseases there is nothing perceptibly wrong with the body, except that it is not working and functioning properly. It is not the body, but what makes the body work, namely, the mental and emotional life, that has gone wrong. (*b*) Not only in their origin do organic and functional diseases differ; they differ in their effects. The symptoms are only apparently alike, and an expert is usually able to detect the difference by definite signs on physical examination.

More important for our purpose is to distinguish between nervous diseases and moral diseases. *Moral diseases are diseases as judged by a standard of conduct; nervous disease, as judged by a standard of individual health.* Nervous diseases and moral diseases have similar causes, namely, repressed complexes, but entirely different symptoms, the one issuing in physical and mental conditions as in neurasthenia, the other in disorders of conduct and in our relations to others. Repressed fear may give rise to shell-shock or to aggressiveness of temper; repressed ambition to perverted cruelty, or to a nervous breakdown from 'over-work'; repressed sex to fetishism (the fixation of the sexual instincts upon some physical object instead of to a person of the opposite sex), or to a hysterical pain in the back. One man is aggressive, another suffers from a headache; one suffers from moral slackness, another from neurasthenia; one from a hysterical paralysis, and another from a sexual perversion.

MORAL DISEASE AND SIN

Finally, must we distinguish between moral disease and sin. There is a definite place in psychology for the idea of sin, as distinct from moral disease. The man who deliberately embezzles, gets drunk, gives way to his temper, gratifies his passions, is in a different category from the kleptomaniac, the alcoholic, or the victim of perverted sexual or angry passion. As organic and nervous diseases have similar symptoms and yet arise from quite different causes, so moral disease and sin may give rise to very similar conduct – stealing or lying – yet their origin is as different as in the other case. Perhaps the simplest case for illustration is that of the drunkard and the alcoholic: to the policeman and the magistrate they are simply 'drunks', and must both be punished. Yet the former may be drunk because of a depraved and brutish nature, whereas the latter may be drunk because of a nature so sensitive that it cannot bear the assaults of life. The drunkard maintains that it is the privilege of every free citizen, and of himself in particular, to get drunk if he wants to; and he does want to. An alcoholic, on the other hand, does not want to get drunk; but he is overwhelmed by an irresistible impulse to do so. The drunkard could stop drinking if he wanted to: there is no compulsion, except that of his deliberate choice. The alcoholic cannot, for his will is impotent to stand against the craving. The drunkard is deliberately sinning: the alcoholic is suffering from a moral disease.

What then is the essential difference psychologically between sin and moral disease? It is that sin is due to *wrong sentiments*; moral disease is due to *morbid complexes* giving rise to uncontrollable impulses. The full and efficient cause of a sin is a deliberate and conscious choice of the will moved by a 'false' or wrong ideal. The sinner and the morally diseased both see the ideal; but whereas the former does not, the latter cannot, under ordinary conditions, respond to it. As their conditions are different, so must their treatment be, that of the sinner being the persistent presentation of a higher ideal, whilst that of the morally diseased is adequate treatment by psychotherapy.

The difference between moral diseases and sins may be recognized, even apart from expert judgement, by the following characteristics: First, the moral disease has a *compulsive character* not characteristic of the sin, which is more deliberate. Secondly, sin is under the control of the will, whereas the victim of moral disease finds his will absolutely impotent to resist it. Thirdly, the sinner, as such, does not want to be cured, whereas the victim of moral disease, if he realizes that cure is possible, is anxious to obtain it. The psychotherapist as such rarely meets with 'sinners', and this for two reasons: first, because the sinner does not want to be cured, and therefore does not seek cure, and also because psychotherapy is not the appropriate form of treatment.

It will be recognized that a very large number of disorders at present considered sins really come under the category of moral disease. A reference to the three 'tests' just made will confirm this. Indeed, it is probable that most evil actions of everyday life – vanities, aggressiveness, evil obsessive thoughts, persistent habits – which are the despair of those who have them and those who treat them, are at least partially due to moral disease, and, if this is the case, our methods of treatment, whether on the religious and moral side, or on the legal, need very radical revision.

RESPONSIBILITY – The moral disease, in contrast with moral fault, is characterized by the fact that it is undesired, uncontrollable, and its cause is unrecognized. Just in so far as those characteristics are present, these disorders are outside the category of personal responsibility.

When a person does not do what he ought, we say sometimes that he is 'responsible' for what he does, and sometimes 'not responsible'. When 'responsible' we mean that he *can* do otherwise but he *will* not. He 'will not' because he does not want to, not because he can't. That is, responsibility is a matter of choice of ideals. We mean, he should have chosen the ideals we approve and not the ideals of his own – we must punish him because he holds, and follows, other ideals than those we approve. Our responsibility, then, is not so much for what we *do* as what we aim at, our ideals. We punish people for having false ideals, in order to induce them to abandon them.

But many of our actions are *not* directed by our ideals, good or bad, such actions being motivated by complexes in a man whose ideals may be perfectly right and good. In this case we do not hold him responsible. That is why in judging of a man's actions, and in considering whether we are to hold him responsible, we often ask, 'What is his ordinary character?' If this seems, as a rule, to be motivated by right aims – if he is a 'good living' person – we are much more inclined to set down his criminal action as an aberration for which he is not responsible. An instance in point is that of a woman killing her new-born child. If she was always a waster it will go much against her – for this crime, too, may be considered just another expression of her low aims and lack of ideals: if always a good mother, the crime is probably not the result of wrong ideals, but a mental aberration, for which she is not, therefore, held responsible. Her past conduct goes a long way, therefore, in helping us to decide her present responsibility.

To blame the victims of moral disease produces the most disastrous results. To blame a hysteric for his pains, a neurasthenic for his fatigue, a nervous wreck for his breakdown, or a victim of moral disease for his perversion, is to do him the gravest injustice. He is already fighting a losing battle; it flings him into despair, and adds to his distress the discouragement of blame. The failure of such patients is not that they cannot see what they ought to do, but in the impotence of will to do it. The weakening of moral responsibility in relation to sins is no more disastrous than the injustice of blaming a morally sick man for his perversion.

Is there then *no* responsibility laid upon the moral pervert? Surely there is.

(1) He is to be held responsible if, recognizing his condition, he does not seek cure for it.

(2) It is true that whilst the pervert cannot control his psychological impulses, he can frequently control the expression of these impulses in outward conduct. There are hundreds of homosexuals or exhibitionists who have never given way to their impulses in perverted acts. To that extent, therefore, the pervert may be held responsible. Nevertheless even in these cases there may come a point where the mind, constantly obsessed by an impulse, can stand the strain no longer and falls.

(3) Though it is admitted that the victims of moral diseases are not now responsible for their condition, were they not originally responsible? The alcoholic was surely to blame when he deliberately took drink to get rid of the feeling of failure; the snob should not have had such a phantasy of himself as a child; the hysteric's pain in the back, traced back to a craving for sympathy, was originally deliberately desired; and the victim of bad temper might originally have controlled it. All this is admitted. There was a time when the patient could have chosen otherwise; but the alcoholic chose to be drunk, the snob preferred conceit, the hysteric originally malingered the pain; before the experience became a repressed complex it was an accepted sentiment.

If then we are looking for an excuse to permit us to pass by on the other side, we may easily persuade ourselves that the unfortunate victim was at least *originally* responsible for his misfortune, and so comfort ourselves with self-righteous complacency. We are sorry for him, but, after all, whose fault was it? He had no right to be going down to Jericho when robbers were about. But this futile attitude cannot serve as more than excuse for inaction, for, in the first place, the responsibility usually traces itself back to a period in childhood so early that the patient can hardly be held to be responsible for his choice; in the second place, the original cause was of so trifling a nature that the patient with years of unhappiness and neurosis might be held to have more than compensated for his sin; finally, whatever the original responsibility might have been, the patient is at the present time the victim of a disease completely beyond his control, and he needs specific treatment as urgently as the man who is brought into hospital suffering from a street accident which may prove to have been originally due to his carelessness. The question of responsibility does not arise in the minds either of those who seek to help, or of those who have the power to cure. Blame is the expedient of impotence; helpfulness the expression of power.

But if the moral pervert, the victim of a moral disease, is not to be held responsible for his condition, is he to be left at large? Is the perverted homosexual, or the exhibitionist, or the sadist to be permitted to exercise his perversion unchecked? The case of the moral pervert is similar to that of the victim of an infectious disease. We do not blame those who suffer from scarlet fever or smallpox, but we do restrain them from spreading – we isolate them *and treat them.* As an individual suffering from a disease, he is not responsible. Nevertheless, society has responsibilities to its members, and must protect its moral life. The exhibitionist may not be responsible for his perversion, but he cannot be permitted at large to produce moral vices in others. Society owes itself a duty to keep its life natural and normal. It can no more permit such a pervert to practise his vices than we permit a lunatic to run amuck with a razor.

But it must also be recognized that society owes a duty not only to itself and its members, but also to the pervert, for he, too, is the victim of early environmental conditions for which other members of society are responsible. When I am consulted by a girl who has had a nervous breakdown as a result of the sexual exposure of a man, I am tempted to blame him for his wickedness. When my next patient is a man of otherwise high moral character, who comes with this very perversion, and despairingly cries for help to overcome impulses which he has daily striven to conquer in vain, and when I discover that he, too, is the victim of early conditions over which he has no control, I am moved towards him in pity and not in anger. Both he and his victim are sick. The exhibitionist or sadist or homesexual is often the victim of someone else's perversion. There is, therefore, an obligation laid upon society to cure such perverts, and not merely to punish them. The ends of justice will never be served by being unjust to the individual. This is becoming recognized by our magistrates and in our penal system, but there is yet a great gulf fixed between those who emphasize responsibility, and those who recognize and seek to cure the disease.

CHAPTER VII

Self-phantasy

THERE IS NO time in life more important for *psychological* development than that between the ages of three and four, when self-consciousness emerges; as there is no time more important for *ethical* development than the age of idealism in later adolescence. In the earlier period, as we have already observed, a child forms its attitude towards the world, whether of fear, pessimism or the feeling that the world is 'easy', 'hard', or 'unjust'. But what is of still greater importance is that at this age the child forms its attitude towards *itself.* At the age of three, a child first looks at itself, and this first impression of itself is destined to remain throughout life and determine the character of the individual. This early conception of ourselves, which tends to be of an extravagant nature, is therefore repressed, and forms a complex which we call a phantasy. Of all complexes, there are none more important than those which form themselves round the idea of the self, our phantasies of ourselves. Phantasies are of all degrees of consciousness and unconsciousness. In their most conscious phase, we speak of these phantasies as 'fancies' or 'day-dreams', such as that of the man who, owing to a latent feeling of inferiority, imagines himself as a great prize-fighter, an acrobat, an explorer, dreams of which he is perfectly and entirely conscious. We use the term 'phantasy' specifically to indicate those which are sub-conscious or unconscious.

I give some typical phantasies I have met. A man, as he walks in the crowd, feels himself to be an ordinary individual. But at the back of his mind is a more than half-conscious phantasy: 'I seem to be quite an ordinary man, but I am really a man of great importance. People take me just for one of themselves, dressed like anyone else; they don't realize what an extraordinary man they have in their midst. But let some emergency arise – a crisis, an accident to the King – I spring to the rescue, and everyone exclaims, "Who is this? A prince *incognito*, a genius in rags!" At last I come into *my own*!'

The characteristics of every true phantasy are these: it is extravagant, it is more or less unconscious, we identify ourselves with it as though we had already attained it, and, finally, it produces abnormalities both of character and also of nervous disease.

An artist suffered from a neurosis, the main feature of which was that he became unreasonably furious if anyone made the slightest criticism of his work, even when he had invited it. His phantasy, encouraged in childhood by a devoted mother, was this: 'There is nothing on God's earth perfect but me.' This phantasy was, of course, repressed from consciousness in later life, on account of its extravagance, but unconsciously showed itself in his character.

The conscious adult conception of oneself may be the exact opposite of the unconscious phantasy of oneself. A lady is overwhelmed by a feeling of worthlessness, of not being wanted. Beneath, I find she has a phantasy of herself as 'such a sweet, delicate little thing, with so lovable a disposition: nothing could be so exquisitely beautiful as I: how could anyone help loving me!' But some managed to do so, and because *everybody* did not flatter her, she felt '*nobody* loves me'. 'Self-conscious' people usually have such an unconscious phantasy.

The unconscious purpose of self-depreciation is frequently to persuade people to disagree with what we *say*, and therefore to agree with what we *fancy* about ourselves. 'How stupid I am!' a lady kept saying, till the cynic remarked, 'But why trouble to mention the fact?' Her anger at this remark revealed her true phantasy of herself as *really* rather clever. 'What a rotten shot!' said the golfer, unconsciously meaning, 'Please don't think this is my usual play. This is bad for me. I am really rather a good player.'

People are usually quite unconscious of the way in which they reveal their phantasies of themselves, often in amusing ways, in the ordinary course of conversation. 'I am really rather humble,' says one, defending himself from the charge of conceit; but this reveals his real phantasy – 'humble, compared with what I have the right to think of myself.' Says another: 'Oh, no, I do not think of myself as a genius: I consider both Prof. M. and Dr F. to be superior to me in their own line!' He failed to realize that even in claiming comparison with these eminent men he revealed an extravagant phantasy of himself. To a business-man, who feels that he is a failure, I remark, 'But you have been very successful.' 'Oh, but that is nothing – nothing, that is, for *me*!' 'That was a fine sermon you gave us tonight.' 'Oh, no,' was the reply, 'as a matter of fact, I spent only half an hour on it,' unconsciously meaning, 'Imagine what I really *could* do.' Probably my reader is thinking that he, at all events, has no such phantasy. Perhaps he may be like one patient whom I asked whether he had phantasies of his self-importance. 'Oh, no!' he replied, 'I think much less of myself *than I really am*!'

Extravagant phantasies of moral perfection are very common. A man is in distress of mind because, a few years before, he had swindled a railway company of a few shillings. In vain did I assure him that we have all done the same or worse. A priest might have commended him for his tenderness of conscience, whereas he would better have condemned him for his moral snobbery. For what lay behind this over-scrupulousness was a phantasy of moral perfection, which spoke in this wise: '*Others* may have such failings, but *I* – no, impossible!' and looking up to heaven —. 'True, it is not right to swindle even railway companies, but it is a lesser evil than self-righteousness. He made his sense of guilt a matter for moral pride. His self-condemnation for this trifling fault was an unconscious pose to emphasize his otherwise perfect character.[1] The psychologist who reads the unconscious motive will recognize that this pose was designed to hide much more serious moral failings. Phantasies of moral perfection are extremely common, and are least suspected by those who have them. The Pharisee was probably unaware of his characteristic self-righteousness.

But, we are asked, is it not right to have high ideals, to aim at perfection, to want to be universally loved, and to aim at doing great things? It is, but 'ideals' are quite different from phantasies, both in origin, nature, and effect, although they are constantly, and, from the point of view of character, disastrously confused, by none more than the so-called 'idealist'. The difference between the phantasy and the ideal must be more clearly defined.

The phantasy differs from the ideal in (*a*) exaggeration; (*b*) psychological origin; (*c*) identification; (*d*) effects.

(*a*) The phantasy is more exaggerated, being formed in childhood as the result of extravagant suggestions of our self-importance or intellectual ability. The phantasy tries to fly to the sun; the ideal is modest – it seeks at first to fly only a few yards. In the end, the airman soars in the heavens whilst Icarus lies broken on the earth. It is right to seek to do great things, but not to flatter our vanity by thinking we ought to conquer the universe.

(*b*) Psychologically, the ideal is part of a consciously accepted *sentiment*, whereas the phantasy is the result of a morbid repressed *complex*. The ideal is conscious. We say: 'That shall be my goal and aim!' It would be impossible consciously to maintain such absurd phantasies as we have illustrated. So we repress them.

(*c*) *Identification.* We unconsciously identify ourselves with our phantasies, but not with the ideal. A certain golfer remarked: 'I have played golf for thirty years, and have

[1] Gilbert and Sullivan have taken off characters of this kind in *Patience*:

'And every one will say,
As he walks his flowery way,
"Oh, what a very singularly pure young man
This pure young man must be".'

never been on my game yet' – he obviously had a phantasy of what 'his game' was, and actually identified himself with a certain standard he had never reached, calling it 'my game'. So, in phantasy, we take ourselves to be what we imagine we are – the phantasy is accepted for reality. In phantasy we *are* the sweetest, the most pious, the universally popular, the most important, the most angelic person in the world, and we break down because this phantasy conflicts with reality.

(*d*) The ideal and the phantasy differ in their *effects*.

It is interesting to observe how phantasies affect us.

(i) The phantasy may have a morbid effect upon our character; (ii) we may strive to live up to it, and, failing to do so, develop a nervous breakdown; (iii) the phantasy may be so extravagant that we may never start to reach it for fear of certain failure;[1] a large amount of aboulia or lack of will is due to expecting too much of ourselves.

(i) One of the most common phantasies of childhood is that of being God, with the attributes of omnipotence, omniscience, and perfection. Thus, a child, if it is always given its own way, with everyone waiting on it, may develop the phantasy of omnipotence, and its *character* later suffers from self-importance. Another, continually told how clever it is, develops a phantasy of being 'omniscient' and becomes dogmatic. Another, who constantly hears, 'What a perfect child!', grows up with a phantasy of infallibility, and is intolerant of criticism or blame.

A phantasy of superiority will lead to conceit, a cynical attitude towards our fellows, a domineering temper; a phantasy of being beautiful, to excessive self-display and jealousy; of 'being good', to self-righteousness, or being a censor of others.

If, on the other hand, the child is brought up with kicks and curses, his character is developed along the lines of inferiority; he suffers from timidity of character, servility, and self-distrust, having accepted the role of inferiority. Even when he achieves great things, he will still feel inferior.

[1] This was the case with the two brothers in Besant's *Golden Butterfly*.

(ii) If *one* phantasy is present it may only affect the *character* of the individual, but if there are two opposing phantasy complexes we have a certain prospect of a *nervous disorder*, which as we have seen is always due to the endo-psychic conflict between two repressed complexes. Neither of these by itself develops neurosis.

But if a child is subjected to *both* of these circumstances; if, that is to say, at one period of life (say 1–3) it is spoilt, and at another period laughed at; or, if it is simultaneously over-flattered by one of its parents and bullied by the other, then there is formed an endo-psychic conflict. The child is not sure whether it is a god or a worm, and this antagonism between two phantasies of itself persists into adult life and gives rise to a character which rushes from extremes of self-elation to depression, until the constitution can stand it no longer and breaks down. In all neuroses of this type one finds *both* elements of the conflict exaggerated. It is probably for this reason that it is the youngest child who so often breaks down with neurosis. It is a curious fact, that, although so much is said about the abnormality of the 'only child', in our experience we meet with very few only children amongst our patients. They suffer more from defects of character than from nervous disorders, for they have usually been brought up in one atmosphere, with one phantasy of themselves. Amongst private patients, mainly of the well-to-do, a large proportion of those suffering from nervous disorders are the youngest child, or virtually the youngest; that is, they were the youngest for three years, until they had passed the age for the development of self-consciousness. A youngest child is for a time the most important. It is petted by the mother, but pinched by the jealous elder children. To compensate for its inferiority to its brothers it indulges in a phantasy encouraged by the mother, and has dreams, like that of Joseph, of their sheaves bowing down to its sheaf, a dream rightly interpreted as a wish-fulfilment by the brothers, who very naturally put him into the pit.

On the other hand, in the army, with patients of the

working class there was a preponderance of the eldest child, apparently because in childhood they had responsibilities thrust upon them too early.

It is not difficult to see how extravagant phantasies lead to nervous and moral disease. If a man tries to conquer the universe, and succeeds in conquering only one hemisphere, he feels a perfect dud. This power phantasy is typical of the successful business-man who breaks down.

Others, again, pose before the world as martyrs, broken by the attempt to reach a great ideal. They imagine the world saying: 'See what a great man is fallen.' What the world is really saying is: 'Poor old So-and-so is getting done.'

The purpose of the breakdown is to preserve the phantasy.

I have in mind a man with a functional sciatica. If only he had not got that painful condition, what could he not do! He tells me he could be a fine athlete, horseman, and tennis-player, a brilliant conversationalist, witty in repartee, the soul of the party, a skilful bridge-player, one to rule and dominate others, a moral support of the oppressed people of the world, a spiritual guide to those in darkness – he could be all these things, *if* it were not for that pain! No wonder he developed a pain! The reason for his neurosis was obvious. Without that pain he would have been called upon to prove his greatness, and failing, he would have had to abandon any pretence to be a person of such extraordinary virtues and achievements: the bubble of his phantasy would be pricked.

It will now be obvious that the repressing forces, which repress the primitive instinctive tendencies and complexes, are these phantasies of the self. It is the 'self' that represses; but not necessarily our *present* self; it may be this self of a bygone day.

As we develop we have many 'selves': we have one self at 3, another at 8, others at 10, 13, and 18. At each age the self represses impulses repugnant to itself. Yet impulses repugnant to an earlier age may not be repugnant to a later phase. So it happens that there may be unwittingly repressed in us impulses which we *now* consciously desire to express, and yet cannot for they are repressed by some former buried self. This helps us to understand that repression is an *unconscious* activity: it also helps us to understand the nature of the 'censor' or 'censure' which Freud describes as a doorkeeper preventing impulses from entering consciousness. This 'censor' is the discarded self of a bygone age.

Further, it is becoming more and more clear to psychopathologists that it is not so much the repressed emotional complexes, like repressed fear or sex, which are the abnormal elements in us, but it is the self which represses them which is morbid. So that, as we shall see later, the symptoms come to counteract and correct our morbid self-phantasies.[1]

(iii) Phantasies inhibit moral endeavour. To 'aim high' may be merely the expression of an abnormal conceit by which we attempt to display our superiority over others. 'Idealism' is often merely a flattering name for indolence. There are thousands of people who are perfectly satisfied to achieve little, and excuse themselves on the grounds that at least they had high ideals. What virtue can there be in failing to achieve the impossible? Their 'idealism' is a cloak for incompetence – it merely ministers to a mind diseased and flatters a morbid conceit. The true ideal is a consciously chosen sentiment, a goal unattained yet relatively attainable, not the extravagant expression of a complex of morbid self-esteem. It therefore stimulates our will to endeavour, whereas with an extravagant phantasy with which we *identify* ourselves, we have no need to bestir ourselves. The main characteristic of the ideal as distinct from the phantasy is that it stimulates the self and arouses the will to moral endeavour.

[1] This is particularly the case in the obsessional neuroses in which a morbid egotism is the most characteristic feature; if the egotistic phantasy is of omnipotence we have obsessions of the 'fear of hurting' variety; if of 'purity' or 'perfection,' obsessions of the scrupulous 'hand-washing' variety; if of 'omniscience,' we have doubting manias.

CHAPTER VIII

The Law of Completeness

EVERY ORGANISM IS impelled to move towards its own completeness. Fullness of life is the goal of life; the urge to completeness is the most compelling motive of life. There is no motive in life so persistent as this hunger for fulfilment, whether for the needs of our body or for the deepest spiritual satisfaction of our souls, which compels us to be ever moving onward till we find it. Hunger, material or spiritual, is the feeling of incompleteness.

We see the law of completeness operating in physiology, in psychology, in morality, and in religion. In physiology we call this completeness 'health', in morality 'perfection', in religion 'holiness', in psychology we shall call it 'self-realization'.

So persistent and strong is this law that no organism can rest until it has satisfied its hunger by achieving its complete self.

Physiologically we may observe this law of completeness at work in every organism. If you cut off the limb of a newt, so strong is this impulse that the organism sets to work until it has grown a new limb and restored the newt to wholeness. If we inflict a wound on our body, immediately every part of the bodily organism sets to work to restore the injured part: the nervous system transmitting the signal of pain, the heart palpitating and driving blood to the wound to wash it clean, the glandular system actively producing white corpuscles and hurrying them to the spot to fight and expel in the form of pus the microbes which threaten the life; fresh blood is brought up to form new tissue, until, at last, the wound is restored and the organism is whole again.

As nature abhors a vacuum so every organism abhors incompleteness.

In religion the craving for completeness and the sense of incompleteness is well marked; indeed, it appears to be the basis of religion. Before the terrible thud of the cyclone the South Sea savage is awakened by the feeling of his own weakness and insufficiency, and falls down in worship before the power which moves the hurricane to his destruction. Did we feel no sense of incompleteness we should have no 'fear' of God, no need of God, no love for God. It makes the belief in immortality, with its promise of fulfilment, the most persistent of all religious beliefs. Such conceptions are reflected in our views of heaven. 'On earth the broken arc, in heaven the perfect round.' The injustices of this life will be rectified; those who hunger after righteousness shall be filled. Most people's dreams of heaven are, like other dreams, a complement or compensation: what we lack here we attain there. Thus, for the desert-tired Semite heaven was a paradise, a garden of fruitful trees and quiet waters; for the Mohammedan, exiled from home and family, it is the luxurious couch and dusky-eyed maidens; for Lowell's washerwoman, whose days were spent in toil, it is a place of perfect rest and idleness; whilst for the care-free Oxford undergraduate, heaven is a place of service!

Psychologically the urge to completeness is most clearly marked in the instincts. Every instinct actively craves for expression. If an instinct is given expression, it is satisfied; if it is denied this expression, its impulses, instead of weakening, become stronger, until it forces satisfaction in direct ways (as when we give way to passion) or indirectly as a nervous disorder.

Sentiments containing our ideals give rise to our conscious desires and wishes. The complexes denied natural fulfilment find their expression and attain their ends or unconscious desires by producing morbid nervous and moral conditions. As the instincts, sentiments, and complexes move towards their expression and completeness, so the individual self, like every organism, moves towards its completeness.

In spite of this strong urgency to completeness, there are, nevertheless, occasions on which nature fails of her purpose and produces organisms which are incomplete, mere fragments of a whole. Children are sometimes born without limbs, skull, or ribs, or suffering from abnormalities like microcephaly. These, however, rarely live, for nature has no use for her failures and, if they live, we hide them away as monstrosities. The comparative rarity of such cases tends only to emphasize the wonder of nature, which contrives so successfully to produce individuals complete in the most minute details of body structure.

Others are born lacking in the social or sexual instincts or wanting in some intellectual function. With these 'mental deficients' we have little to do in this work, for their defect, though mental in character, is physiological in origin.

But there are others whose incompleteness is purely psychological: owing to conflict and repression a large part of their personalities have failed to find expression and fulfilment. These are, according to Janet, the 'psychasthenics', the most characteristic feature of whose sickness is the feeling of incompleteness (*le sentiment d'incomplétude*). He feels something is wanting, he is at a loss, is timid in facing the world and its difficulties, or wanders as though he was in search of something lost. In practice he looks for a 'safe job', shrinks from anything venturesome, and is careful over his diet. He has failed in self-realization.

The craving of the self for completeness is shown in *dreams*, in *neurosis*, and in the conscious effort toward *self-realization*.

(i) The hunger of the soul for fulfilment is evidenced in *dreams*. We realize in dreams what we cannot realize in life: we complete ourselves in our dreams. Thus, the child of the slums dreams of gorgeous meals, because in reality it lacks food: on the other hand, the middle-class boy, with ample food, but dressed in collar and 'bowler' hat, dreams of being a pirate or Red Indian chief. One shudders to think of the terrible orgies little Lord Fauntleroy must have experienced in his dreams, dressed as he was in velvet self-complacency.

The dreams of adults follow the same law as the day-dreams of children, though they are more symbolic in character: they are compensating, complementary to conscious life. In them we give play to those impulses that are denied expression in waking life. The crude passions which the ascetic ruthlessly subdues make sport of him in dreams of wanton debauchery. Thus, ascetics spend their nights fighting their passions while normal men sleep the refreshing sleep of God in preparation for the duties of the day. The too-fanciful idealist, the poet and the 'highbrow', who have lost touch with earth in their philosophic or religious extravagances, are led in their dreams to dizzy heights and are then suddenly thrown down to earth with a crash. On the other hand, if a man dreams of climbing mountains and reaching the exhilarating airs of the mountain-top, we recognize that in his waking life he is too indolent and earth-bound, and needs to seek a sublimer atmosphere.

Thus, the mutilated soul strives to make perfect its imperfect life. Because they are the fulfilment of our unrealized self, dreams, rightly interpreted, afford a valuable clue to the psychotherapist in his endeavour to understand the character of his patient. By telling us what he needs they tell us what he is. Dreams are said to be repressed wishes: they may more perfectly be termed repressed *needs*, for what is repressed the soul needs for its completeness. The function of dreams, as we shall see later (p. 188), is to solve the problems of the day, and of life.

(ii) Paradoxical as it may seem, the *nervous symptom*, like the dream, is often an attempt to attain completeness. Many neurotic symptoms, as we have seen, are the expression of a repressed instinctive emotion. But as long as any emotion is repressed the self is incomplete. The function of the nervous symptom is therefore an attempt to complete the self by giving expression to the repressed emotion. Thus the man with a psychology characterized by extravagant self-importance, who represses his humbler submissive instincts, is made to suffer a nervous breakdown in which the sense of impotence and failure is the characteristic feature; the man who has too great ideas of himself as a hero suffers from fear; the man who is too intellectual, placing all the weight of his psychology on reason, is haunted by the fear of madness, in which the irrational and emotional side of his nature finds expression. Such symptoms as these come to restore the balance, to make articulate the silenced functions of the soul.

Even when the symptom is a physical disability, it stands as the representative or symbol of some repressed emotion: it is therefore an attempt of the organism to restore itself to health.

(iii) The completeness of the self can only be produced by the harmony of all the sentiments and complexes into one whole, the attainment of which we call *self-realization*, and the affective state of which we call *happiness*.

Self-realization – that is to say, the complete and full expression of all the instincts and impulses within us – cannot be achieved as long as there are elements in our soul that are repressed and denied expression. In a fully realized self there will be no conflict of purpose, no complexes, no repression, but the harmonious expression of all the vital forces towards a common purpose and end. That end, which is capable of so diverting the instincts from their original ends and redirecting them to a common purpose, we call the *ideal*; whilst the movement and activity of the self towards its realization we call *the will*. It is the craving for completeness and self-realization which urges us from the mere exhibition of our lusts and passions, and impels us to moral endeavour and the development of character. So, throughout the whole realm of organic life, in biology, psychology, morality, and religion, the craving for fulfilment and the urge to completeness is the most potent force which drives us to live and strive with persistent energy till the ultimate goal of self-realization is reached.

This Chapter published in 1923 was later confirmed by Jung who discovered in the *Mendala* the universal symbol expressive of the 'wholeness of the self' (1933).

CHAPTER IX

The 'Organized Self'

THE SELF, like every organism, moves towards its own completeness. The term 'self' may be used in many different senses. James says that a man's self in the broadest interpretation includes all that he may call his: indeed, noblemen and Scottish farmers often call themselves by the name of their property. In another sense, a man has as many selves as there are people who recognize him; he is one self to his wife, another to his children, another to his business partner, another to his God.

There is a 'self', however, which we normally recognize, and which we may call the accepted or '*organized*' self – the self that is 'us' for all practical purposes. As the instincts are organized round some accepted idea or person to form sentiments, so the sentiments are in turn organized round some ideal to form this *self.*

The 'organized self' may be defined as the organization of all the accepted sentiments and dispositions.

This 'self' consists of all the sentiments for home, family, and country, of the love of beauty, the love of the good, the love of the true, and such dispositions as sincerity, a tolerant and courageous spirit; or, on the other hand, the 'self' may consist of sentiments and dispositions of cruelty, licentiousness, avarice, and cowardice. It is this combination of constellations which we normally call 'ourselves'.

We must contrast this 'organized self' with the self in the sense of the whole psychological individual. When we say 'I restrained my impulses; I refuse to give way to my desires', we are using 'I', not of the whole psychological individual, but of a part which stands over against our impulses and desires. This is the self as organized, which is a very important conception of the self from the practical and moral point of view.

We might call it the 'accepted self', for it consists of all those thoughts and feelings, desires and aims which we accept as ours, and with which we identify ourselves as 'I'. 'I' consists of all that I accept in myself: this is my 'real self'.

We contrast it also with the profound ego. It is commonly held that behind all psychological processes must be an 'ego', a unifying principle, which takes all our sentiments and binds them together. The term 'self' is often used of this ultimate ego, of this unifying principle, not of that which is unified.

As a philosophic conception this may be true, but in psychology all we can observe is an organization of all the sentiments and dispositions.

But, it may be asked, if the 'self' is an organization of all the sentiments and dispositions, what binds them together? What is the unifying principle which organizes it? *It is that they are directed towards a common purpose.* We call it the 'organized self', because it is that part of our whole *individual* which, on account of having common interests and a common purpose, is organized into a whole. It is one because it functions as one. Every organism is an organism because the elements of which it is composed work together for a common purpose; it is, indeed, this which constitutes it an organism. So all the cells in organs like the heart and lungs perform one function, and all the organs in the body function together, and so form an individual organism. Further, when a large body of individuals, having interests in common, combine for common purposes to a common end, they form an organization we call the State. The State, like other organisms, is constituted of a number of individuals, and of them alone: nevertheless, it is not a mere accumulation of these individuals. The State is an organization of individuals functioning together. Again, they remain one only in so far as they contrive to function together; as soon as they cease to *act* as one they cease to *be* one.

So the individual 'self', psychologically considered, is constituted of a large number of sentiments and dispositions, each of which has its own life, and of them alone. But because they have interests in common, and work towards a common end, they form the organization which we call the self. It is only because the self works as one that it coheres as one; otherwise when it ceases to move towards a common purpose it disintegrates: this is the unifying principle. The 'self' is a unity more in function than in structure. *This function of the 'Self' we shall call the Will.* The Will is the activity of the self; it is the 'self' in function, the 'self' moving towards the aims and ends of the personality as a whole. The quality and nature of these aims and ends determines our character, good or bad.

All the accepted sentiments and dispositions combine to form the conscious self. Complexes are unacceptable and therefore repressed. But they and the latent instincts denied normal expression are abnormally expressed in impulses, dreams, and as neurotic symptoms, all of which are therefore in conflict with the organized self and the will.

The great endeavour of our lives is to build ourselves up into a well-organized personality, and to maintain our integrity. This urgency towards completion is part of our very nature, a compulsion from which we cannot escape.

CHAPTER X

The Will

The Will is the activity of the personality as a whole; it is the organized personality in function, moving towards its end or goal.

But since there are outside the organized personality many opposing factors, particularly the complexes and repressed impulses, and other potentialities emerging from the depths of the unconscious, there is inevitably a conflict within the personality which weakens the Will. That is why we must say that the Will is the activity of the personality *as a whole*, and not of the whole personality. This conflict creates man's chief problem in life.

This conception of the will, as the function or activity of the organized self, throws light on many problems of the will.

(*a*) The first point to be observed is that the will is not an entity in itself, but a *function* – the function or activity of the self. The Will is not an arbitrary authority which sits aloft and issues categorically commands for the self to obey: nor does it act independently of the self. It is a function – the function of the self – just as digestion is a function of the stomach. But it is a function that is vital to the self, for without the will the self would cease to be. It is only in so far as the self functions that it maintains its cohesion and existence. Like all organisms, the self is bound together only by a common purpose and activity. As soon as a man ceases to have a purpose in life the self begins to disintegrate and fall to pieces: our actions are at the mercy of our impulses and complexes. The exercise of the will is essential to a strong and healthy personality.

The self ceases to be a self as soon as the Will ceases to function. This explains why men have often identified a man's will with his character – a man of 'strong will' is a man of 'strong character'. The character is the *quality* of the 'Self', and the will is its *function*. In a hurricane, it is only by keeping your head up to the wind and waves that there is any hope of avoiding disaster. The will is the sign of activity and life, the life of the self. It is only in so far as a man exercises his will that he maintains his integrity.

(*b*) Further, the will is not the function of the *whole* individual; the will is the function of that part of us which is organized as the self, and of that alone. There are, therefore, excluded from the will those elements of the mind which are excluded from the self, namely, the repressed complexes and suppressed instincts. These are, nevertheless, charged with powerful emotional tone, and crave for expression, often in antagonism to the self, and they find expression in what we call 'impulses'. The will is the activity of the self, as distinct from impulses, which are the expression or activity of the complexes and instincts.

An impulse may spring from an instinct, as when we have an 'impulse' to steal, to be morbidly curious, or to take vengeance; or from repressed complexes, as when we have a compulsion to twitch the face, to throw ourselves under a moving train, to be cruel to our friends.[1] Augustine, the first of introspective psychologists, recognizing this dualism in the soul, described it as a conflict of two wills, maintaining against Pelagius that man's will was not free to carry out its desires because of a 'corrupt will'. This 'corrupt will' we see to be the impulses springing from complexes and instincts, and should not be termed 'will' at all – self-will, if you like.

This antagonism between the will and the impulses is bound to continue as long as the complexes and instincts are

[1] The term impulse is sometimes also used of the expression of individual *dispositions*; thus we speak of kindly impulses. I do not necessarily wish to exclude the use of the term 'impulse' from such a meaning, but, for clearness, I shall use the term in the more limited sense employed in the text, as the expression of repressed complexes and suppressed instincts.

excluded from the self, and until some way is discovered of liberating them and uniting them to the self by some common purpose. This is the task of psychotherapy.

THE POWER AND IMPOTENCE OF THE WILL

It is obvious that since the will is the function of the personality as a whole, the more our native potentialities, instincts and emotions are integrated into the personality, the stronger will be the will. The more these potentialities are repressed and bound up in Complexes, the relatively feebler will be the will, and the more be under the dominance of the impulses and compulsions springing from these powerful complexes.

In the ordinary affairs of life the will is supreme, for under ordinary conditions the will, being an organization of many instincts, and being impelled by the strongest motive of any organism, namely, the urge to completeness, has the power to dominate the instincts and impulses hostile to its ends. Further, the more we exert that will the stronger it becomes. But the will has its limitations.

It is generally recognized that there are external forces over which our will has no control: we cannot produce rain, change the course of the stars, bid the sea to recede, or otherwise command external forces of nature. What is insufficiently recognized is that the will is often impotent to control our emotions and desires. We are not masters of our fate, we are not even captains of our soul. This is most clearly brought out in moral and nervous disorders. One of the things that strikes us most forcibly in dealing with men with functional nervous disorders is the absolute impotence of the will. Here are men with paralysis, obsessions, fears, fixed ideas, pains, and blindness, conditions which are entirely due to mental causes, and yet the will is helpless in its effort to cure them. Indeed, it is usually found that exertion of will simply makes them *feel* worse, because each failure makes them more hopeless. Similarly, with abnormal moral conditions: one man has no control whatever over his sudden outbursts of temper; a woman simply cannot resist the temptation to sex, and is ready to be seduced by any tradesman who calls at her flat with the groceries. An adolescent suffers from blushing, another from self-consciousness and yet another from stammering, which their wills are entirely impotent to control, although the causes are obviously psychological, being due to a sense of guilt or shame of which they are entirely unconscious. So also the victim of traits of character like pessimism, or a perversion like fetishism, or a passion for drugs, cannot overcome these by the power of will. There is obviously a segment of the mind which is not accessible to the control of the will. We exert our will, but the impulse carries the day. This is one of the main characteristics of 'moral diseases'.

This impotence of the will cannot be explained as long as we maintain, on theoretic grounds, the absolute freedom of the will to determine all mental activities; nor can it be explained as long as we regard the will as the activity of the *whole* psychological individual. But as soon as we regard the will as the function of that part of the whole which is organized, the facts both of the strength of the will and of its impotence are adequately explained.

But in this conflict of will and impulse, what decides the issues? How are our actions and conduct determined?

Let us observe these conflicts in an illustration.

(*a*) A man lying on the seashore may have the impulse to bathe, and an impulse to continue to be lazy. It is a matter of indifference to the 'self' which he does, as he is on holiday. In such a case, when there is merely a conflict between impulses, it is always the stronger that wins: as the warmth of the sun is more 'attractive' than the cold of the water, he continues to be lazy.

(*b*) But suppose it is not a matter of indifference to the self, which is, shall we say, strongly imbued with stoical ideals. The conflict is then one in which the will and two impulses are involved. The will is no longer in abeyance, but active, and decides the issue. Since the self has identified itself with stoical ideals, and because bathing is a more stoical proceeding than slacking, we bathe. In such a case it is not necessarily the stronger impulse that wins, for the self has ranged itself on the side of the weaker impulse. It therefore often appears to be the weaker impulse that wins, whereas in reality our action is determined by the weaker impulse reinforced by the will working towards its end. This is the 'motive' of our action, the motive being that which actually determines the self to act in this way or in that.

To take another illustration. The sight of a criminal may stimulate our impulses either of pity or of anger, the stronger of which, say that of anger, determines our action. But instead of acting on our 'first impulse', we introduce the self and 'deliberate', ultimately deciding that after all he may be the victim of his early environment, and is to be pitied rather than blamed. The self ranges itself on the side of the weaker impulse, and we are 'moved' to pity and act accordingly, for pity is more in conformity with the ideals of the self.

(*c*) The conflict may be a straight conflict between will and an impulse. We may not be called upon merely to throw the weight of our will on the side of this impulse or that. Thus, the self may identify itself neither with bathing nor with being lazy, but assume a still sterner task, say that of taking an aunt for a row. Or, in our other illustration, we may reject anger as being unjust, and pity as being sentimental, abandon the role of judge, and devote our will to readjusting the social system which makes crime possible. Or, to take a still simpler case, the conflict may be a straight conflict between sexual desires and the self, or between an impulse to embezzle, to be angry, or to run away, and the self.

In such a case the question remains – how is it that sometimes the will dominates, whereas at other times the impulses overpower the will? In the conflict between the will and impulses, what decides the issue? What are the conditions under which the will is sometimes potent, sometimes impotent? This depends upon whether the self or the impulses are more strongly stimulated.

Impotence of will usually takes place under one of three conditions:

(1) When the complexes or instincts are excessively aroused, as when we are chased by a bull. In such a case the instinct is so strongly aroused by this stimulus that it overpowers the 'self', which is but feebly stimulated by its ideal of courage. On the other hand, in the trenches the sense of duty and the appeal to courage are normally so great that the will is dominant over the instinct of fear. But in that case the repressed fear may emerge in a substitute form as a paralysis, which achieves the same end as the fear, namely to get the soldier out of the battle.

(2) When the stimulus of the self and will is feeble, e.g. when, on holidays, there is an absence of any incentive to exert our will.

(3) This absence of an adequate ideal or stimulus to the will is characteristic also of times when we have undergone some great strain. In such times, whether of fear, of grief, of failure, or of the fatigue of war, our self is weary and powerless to make an effort, and tends to become disintegrated, and our actions are left to the mercy of our impulses. These are often therefore the *precipitating* causes of a neurosis.

Such disintegration may be prevented by the presentation of an ideal which has the power to arouse the will once more, and restore the power of the self, which is then able to rise above its misfortunes, weather the storm of its difficulties, and once more become master of its fate.

CHAPTER XI

Freedom of the Will

THE QUESTION OF the freedom of the will is for the psychologist essentially a practical problem; he is not interested in it as a purely theoretical speculation. For him, the problem would never have arisen if the will were perfectly and without question free, any more than we ask whether men can or cannot breathe air. Self-evident facts raise no problems.

The question which concerns the average man is whether he is free to pursue and achieve his ideal, or whether he must for ever bear the purgatorial torment of striving for fruit beyond his reach, dragged down by 'brutish instincts', circumscribed by the wall of environment.

Can we do what we want to do? It is in this practical spirit that we approach the matter.

Free Will. As we have seen, we cannot do whatever we like, such as changing the Seasons, or being in two places at once. But that is not what is implied in the phrase 'Freedom of the Will'.

By Freedom of the Will and Free Will, we mean that the will is free to make its choices and to pursue its ends *unhindered by our impulses and Complexes.* The obsessional patient, for instance, with his compulsions to make sure that the gas fire is turned off when he knows it is, or to wash his hands fifty times a day, is prevented by his complexes and symptoms from doing what he wants to do. He is

> '*Cabin'd, cribbed, confined*
> *Hemmed in by saucy doubts and fears.*'

Freedom of Choice. The will, we have observed, can be aroused by an ideal to pursue that ideal. There are thousands of aims presented to the mind every day, and it is out of these that the self 'chooses' those which it thinks potent for its purpose. What we call 'choice' is the judgement, after deliberation, as to whether this ideal or that will be most conducive to our completeness. Our choice is always determined by this end, but the deliberation and judgement as to the best means to that end gives us the sense of freedom. Choice is thus concerned with means to an end, which is an activity of the intellect. Choice is then primarily an activity of intellect, reason, and judgement, not of the will. It is our judgement that decides which of the multitudinous ideals, true and false, will provide us with the means to satisfy that craving for fulfilment which impels us, like every organism, to seek its completeness – our ultimate end. The self having deliberated and chosen, we are under ordinary conditions free to pursue our ideal. Indeed, this is the only thing we are free to pursue; it is the only thing that can stimulate us, for it is the only thing that ultimately appears likely to produce happiness.

But it is obvious that these facts can be stated as well in terms of determinism as of freedom. The will is free to seek its completeness, it is free and usually able to move towards the ideal by which it may achieve it. At the same time, it is determined by the ideal and by the craving for fulfilment and self-realization, which nothing but that ideal can satisfy. If the will is not aroused by such an ideal it falls victim to the dominance of the impulse of the moment.

Freedom of the Will as Freedom of the Self. Apart altogether from the freedom of choice, there is a sense of freedom enjoyed by the self when, by the release of all its complexes, it is freed from all its conflicts. When the self is free the will is free; freedom of the will is freedom of the self. But such freedom can only be obtained by the abolition of all conflict and hostility in the individual, and the formation of a complete harmony of all impulses. The completely harmonized self is the completely free self. Where there is conflict there can be no true freedom, for freedom means freedom to act, freedom to function. When we act according to impulse, we are not free, because there is always the antagonism between the self and the expression of the repressed complex or instinct. The lack of freedom is illustrated in those cases of neurasthenia when the will is so occupied in repressing the instincts and complexes that there is no will power left to devote to the ordinary affairs of life. Such patients characteristically suffer from symptoms of fatigue and a lack of will power. The freedom of the will is only progressively secured by the pursuit of an ideal capable of organizing all the instincts and leading to greater self-realization. This is the element of truth in the Augustinian paradox that we are only free if we choose the good.

When the self chooses rightly, that is to say, when it chooses what actually does make for the happiness and completeness of the self, it enlarges the freedom and scope of the self, and by so doing necessarily gives greater power to the will. So the freedom of the will is not static, but dynamic and progressive; it is dependent on the progressive attainment of this larger unity.

When, again, in psychotherapy, emotional complexes are liberated, whether of sexual emotion, fear, or ambition, the liberated instinctive emotions are brought under the dominion of the will and organized into a stronger self. There is, indeed, nothing so dramatically interesting in psychotherapy as to observe a patient under treatment pass through an emotional storm at the revival of some forgotten fear of sexual horror, and then emerge into the calmness of mind in which he experiences an extraordinary relief and freedom. Such freedom can be brought about not only by the liberation of repressed complexes and instincts in analysis, but can also be secured by the presentation of an 'inspiring' ideal able to produce such a revolution of soul that not only the sentiments, but those emotions that we attached to morbid things, are aroused to attach themselves to the new ideal. This is what normally takes place in religious conversion.

Nevertheless, there is nothing, not psycho-analysis nor even religion, which can exonerate a man from building up his strength of character by the exercise of will. Analysis must be fortified by synthesis, suggestion by determination, religion by moral endeavour.

CHAPTER XII

The Ideal

WHAT THEN IS the adequate stimulus of the will? What is it that has the power to arouse the will, the absence of which leads to impotence?

In psychology we use the term the 'adequate stimulus' of any sensation to describe the stimulus to which the sense organ is peculiarly adapted to respond. The adequate stimulus of sight is luminiferous waves of ether; of hearing, it is certain waves of air; of smell, it is certain odoriferous particles in gaseous form; of taste, substances able to produce a certain chemical change in contact with the taste buds on the tongue and palate. The same principle applies to the instincts: the normal stimulus of the instinct of curiosity is any strange object; of fear, any dangerous object; of the maternal instinct, any helpless object. Complexes also have their 'adequate stimuli', and may be aroused by special objects which in some way are associated with them. For instance, a red flower may produce a sick headache; the banging of a door may send a man into a fit.

Just as instincts and complexes may be aroused by special objects, so there are special stimuli which can arouse the organized 'self' to activity as will. But what is the adequate stimulus of the will? What is it that can arouse the will to activity? *The adequate stimulus of will, the stimulus which is peculiarly adapted to arouse the self into activity, is the Ideal, that is, the idea or object which leads to the complete realization of the whole individual.*

A man's whole life and character as well as his mental health and happiness depend upon his having the right aims, ends and purposes in life – in other words, the right ideals. By right ideals we mean those which by their nature are capable of mobilizing, co-ordinating and directing all the potentialities of the personality towards its completeness and integration.

We have observed that the self is composed of a number of sentiments and dispositions organized together for a common purpose and to a common end. The ideal is that the attainment of which will produce completeness and happiness, which is the aim and purpose of the self. If any idea or object is presented to the self which appears to contribute to its fulfilment and happiness, then is the self stimulated by it and the will moves towards it, even as a sensation or instinct is awakened by its own stimulus. In the absence of such an ideal, our actions are left to the mercy of our impulses.

If such an ideal is present, the will is aroused and dominates conduct; if it is absent, the will is in abeyance, and the impulses are aroused to activity. We recognize the potency of the ideal to move the will in ordinary practice, for when we make an appeal to a wrong-doer, we do so by placing before him higher ideals; we remind him of his family and how they will suffer, of his former ideals, of his self-respect; we try to show him that he will never achieve happiness except by courage and altruism. So we attempt to arouse his will to a new endeavour by presenting him with a new ideal.

If the will is the expression of the self, it would seem that the self can only choose in accordance with its own desires. This is to some extent true. The self cannot will to do what is contrary to its own nature. Ordinarily, a steady man cannot will to get drunk, nor an honest man to steal. There are many things that are so alien to our nature that we 'simply cannot do them'. Probably no reader of this book, by any exertion of will, could bring himself to murder: his whole nature revolts against it. His self can only act in obedience to *its own* nature and law. Normally, the will can no more be moved by an ideal alien to the character of the self than a heat-spot on the skin will respond to an odour, or the pugnacious instinct be aroused by a funny sight. If the self acts or chooses, it must choose only in accordance with one principle, and in one direction. That which determines the will to action is always the idea of the completeness and happiness of the self. The self has one end, one aim, and if it moves, it moves, as any individual instinct moves, to the satisfaction of its own end.

But the fact remains that a steady man sometimes gets drunk, a kindly man is sometimes cruel, and an avaricious man sometimes generous. Why is this? If the will can only be stimulated and aroused by the ideal which makes for self-realization, how is it that men choose to do wrong? It is because the self can be stimulated by so-called 'inadequate' as well as 'adequate' ideals.

This is analogous to what takes place in sensations and impulses. It will be recalled that every sensation has its own 'adequate stimulus' to which the sense organ is particularly adapted to respond. But a sense organ may sometimes be stimulated, and a sensation produced, by a stimulus other than the adequate one. Thus, while waves of ether are the 'adequate' stimulus for sight, sight may be produced by pressure of the eye-balls. So, whilst hot objects are normally required to stimulate the heat-spots in the skin, these may sometimes be stimulated by cold, and a cold bar of iron on a frosty day may feel hot. So, too, the self may sometimes be stimulated by 'inadequate stimuli'. Thus, a man may put his whole will and soul into embezzling, getting drunk, or obtaining a knighthood. This may be a 'wrong choice', for the will is aroused not by the adequate stimulus, that is, the ideal which actually produces completeness and happiness, but by 'false ideals' which appear to do so, but in fact do not. The morphia-maniac, for instance, is often credited with weakness of will. This is not the case, for in this pursuit of a few grains of morphia he will compass heaven and earth, and exhibit a determination of will and persistence of effort which would shame even a Scottish Canadian! But he pursues a wrong or 'inadequate' ideal. It is inadequate in the sense that it fails to satisfy the ends of the self.

We must to this extent modify our statement and say that the will is aroused to activity only by that ideal *which appears to the self* to conduce to self-realization and happiness. Whether the ideal actually does or does not in fact produce that happiness is another matter: sufficient that to the individual himself the ideal, whether of getting drunk or of philanthropy, appears to lead to that end. If it actually does lead to that end we call it a 'true ideal'; if it, in fact, does not, we call it a 'false ideal'.

The adequate stimulus is that ideal which can produce completeness and give happiness; the inadequate stimulus is that which appears to the individual to conduce to his happiness, but in fact fails to do so. This is a 'false ideal', and the man is said to have made a 'wrong choice'.

What, then, do we mean when we say that a man chooses rightly or wrongly? Psychology as such makes no pronouncements on ethics. To it the will 'chooses rightly' when stimulated by an ideal which in fact actually brings about happiness and completeness. It 'chooses wrongly' when it is stimulated by what appears to conduce to this result, but does not in fact do so, that is, by an inadequate stimulus. Nevertheless, to the man who so chooses, whether rightly or wrongly, such an 'ideal' appears to be what will give him happiness. The morphia-maniac, the *roué*, the miser, have all deliberately determined to pursue an ideal which does not in fact conduce to true happiness. They may know that it is a wrong ideal in the sense that they know it is an ideal of which society does not approve. But for them their own course of life appears to be the right one, that is to say, that which will bring them the greatest content. We can only deter them from this course of action by placing before them adequate ethical ideals and showing them how by the pursuit of these ideals alone will they be happy.

The ideal is the most potent factor in the determination of character and conduct, for the ideal alone is able to stimulate the will and so to organize all the instincts into one harmonious whole. Without it the individual is left to the chaotic influences of the conflicting instincts: with it the personality is welded together towards one common purpose. *The Ideal is that, the attainment of which produces completeness and self-realization.* It is at once that which stimulates the will to activity and that which determines the direction and character of activities.

But an ideal, we are told, is merely a product of the environment: have we any right to consider it as a third factor, distinct from heredity and environment?

It may be that every idea we possess is determined by some previous mental condition, that is to say, we may be compelled to believe in psychological determinism. In that case a particular ideal may be in a sense the product of environment.

But an ideal, if it is a true one, is an idea of a special character. It is an idea capable of satisfying the craving of the soul for completeness. The idea in itself is merely a psychological fact, the ideal is an idea possessed of a certain quality which corresponds with the nature of things in such a way that it can attach to itself all our emotions, and therefore contains potentialities for the soul's self-realization. We have millions of ideas, each of which has its influence on our character, but only a true ideal can lead us to the completeness for which we crave. Ideas are like pebbles which disturb the wave on the shore; the ideal like the celestial body which dominates the tides.

If, then, we look at the problem from the static point of view, we must admit that the ideal is only a factor of the environment; but if we consider life and conduct from the dynamic point of view – and life is dynamic, not static – the ideal which is alone capable of stimulating the will and achieving self-realization must be regarded as so potent a factor in the determination of character that it may properly be considered in a class apart from all other elements in the environment.

The introduction of this new factor into our life, in addition to the two factors already described, the hereditary instincts and environmental influences, changes the whole character of our activities. It changes our 'behaviour' into 'conduct', and our 'ends' into 'purposes'.

When an organism is motivated only by instinct and environment, we call the result its *behaviour*; when, on the other hand, the organism is not only influenced by these hereditary and environmental forces, but by a conscious ideal or end towards which it is directed, we call it *conduct*, for our actions conduce or lead to that end. So we speak of the 'behaviour' of animals, but the 'conduct' of men. Moreover, the 'end' assumes a different character. Every instinctive action leads to some result or *end*, but when that end is consciously conceived and voluntarily pursued, we call it a *purpose*. So we speak of the 'ends' of nature, for nature is innocent of any conscious aim, but of the 'purposes' of man.

What the true ideal is has never yet been determined. It is the search of all philosophies, ethics, religion, and psychology. No one ideal has yet been universally accepted. To the artist, it is to be found in the beautiful, to the philosopher it is truth, to the moralist the right or good, to the gourmand his stomach, to the faddist his system, to the religious man his God. One becomes an Epicurian, another a Stoic, another a Bolshevist, another a Christian. One takes as his motto, 'Liberty, Equality, Fraternity'; another, 'Frightfulness by blood and iron'; another, 'Love of God and man'. But whatever the ideal is conceived to be, it is chosen as that which will secure ultimate happiness. Yet only if it will really achieve that end can we admit that it is the true ideal.

As it is not part of our purpose to attempt to define what the absolute ideal is so we do not propose to judge of the moral value of the various ideals; but we may attempt to elucidate the principles upon which a right ideal must be determined, for there is a psychological value as well as what we term moral value, the psychological value being value for self-realization and happiness.

Psychologically the right ideal is one that can, by attracting all the instinctive emotions, bring harmony to the soul; by stimulating the will to a common purpose, weld the whole psychological individual into an organism; and by satisfying the craving for completeness, secure self-realization and happiness. What the will requires for its strength and development is not training but inspiration.

To possess an ideal or purpose in life is therefore the necessary condition of a strong will and of a stable character. Our character, as we have seen (p. 24), as distinct from our temperament and disposition, is the quality of the personality as determined by our aims and ideals in life, whether good or bad, whether adequate to bring us mental health and happiness, or inadequate.

CHAPTER XIII

Self-realization and Happiness

HITHERTO WE HAVE considered the *summum bonum*, the ultimate aim, of man as Completeness or Self-realization. The affective state which accompanies the sense of completeness and self-realization we call *Happiness*. The perfectly happy man is the man who finds harmonious expression for all his instincts.

PLEASURE: JOY: HAPPINESS

These are *affective* states. They differ from the instincts and emotions which are dynamic forces designed to produce effects on the outside world; they represent the effect these circumstances of life have upon *us*, the way in which we are *affected* by such – the way we feel. We feel pleasure; we feel joyous; we feel happy. They also differ from *sensations* which are the effect that stimuli have upon our special senses, like sight, hearing and touch, which are not necessarily unpleasant or pleasant, as are pleasure, joy and happiness.

Pleasure. Pleasure is particularly used of sensuous pleasure, pleasure in the bodily sensations, and the satisfaction of the bodily appetites. Thus we find pleasure in eating, in swimming, pleasure in sex feelings, in a walk over the Downs, or in basking in the sun.

There is nothing wrong in pleasure as such: it is harmful only if it detracts from the higher function of the personality such as ambition and responsibility, for man must pass out of this infantile phase, as the followers of Ulysses were urged to do, when basking in the land of the Lotus-eaters. Those who live for sensuous pleasure alone are such as are arrested in development, remaining in the infantile phase. They deny to themselves the exercise of the higher functions of achievement, by which alone they can find self-realization.

Far from being harmful in itself, sensuous pleasure serves a most valuable biological function which has not been fully appreciated; indeed it would not have persisted in the course of evolution, but perished long ago had it not done so. Bodily pleasure accompanies the basic physiological processes: it is pleasurable for the infant to suck, to urinate, to defecate, to exercise its limbs and its vocal chords. *The biological function of pleasure is to encourage and enhance these necessary processes.* If it were painful for the infant to suck, as it sometimes is when the milk is hard to get; or to defecate because of sores, this would discourage the child from these activities with the result that it would suffer from malnutrition and its health would decline. Apart from these specific functions, pleasure stimulates the metabolic processes of the body and the person who enjoys his food digests it the better, for the pleasure stimulates the secretion of saliva and the gastric juices, whereas if you are depressed or angry or afraid, this checks the gastric flow, and your health suffers.

Joy. Joy is of a higher order; it is associated not so much with the bodily sensations as with the expression of emotional life. A full life is one in which all the emotions can find expression, and this expression is associated with fullness of joy. Thus we speak of the joy, not the pleasure, of motherhood; the joy of success in our work. It is also more abiding than pleasure.

Happiness. Happiness has a wider scope still: it is the affective tone of the *whole* personality in the successful pursuit of its ends. The happy man is he who in the pursuit of his aims finds satisfaction and fulfilment in his life. It is a more abiding condition than even joy though less ecstatic, for even the joys of motherhood pass, and so does the joy of success, but the happy man is one who has this deeper and lasting satisfaction and peace of mind. Happiness is therefore closely associated with self-realization, with the fulfilment of the personality.

Happiness is not so much a state of mind; it is a state of mental activity, a condition of progress towards self-realization. Stagnation is the very antithesis of happiness; that is why so many men, when they retire without having any other aim in life, become unhappy. Their unhappiness depresses their metabolic processes and they pass to an untimely death.

The man who said 'Call no man happy till he is dead' was expressing the opposite of the truth, for it is only by living that we can be happy: the happy man is fully alive and active.

Nor is happiness, as the Hedonist says, the sum of all the pleasures, for you can devote yourself to all the pleasures of life and you will find no happiness in the end. If you sum up all the pleasures it ends in satiation, not in happiness.

On the other hand *asceticism* which eschews all pleasure is no answer; for in setting out to repress pleasure it must repress the natural functions which pleasure is designed to encourage. It is true that if the ascetic holds that by denying himself all the pleasures of this life, he has a better chance of happiness in Heaven, he may consider himself justified. He takes a sporting chance and is prepared to make the sacrifice; but, after all, is not that somewhat selfish, for it is himself that he is considering? But prospects of Heaven go far beyond the scope of the psychologist!

Asceticism can therefore never fulfil our criterion of a happy life. It is opposed to our ideal of mental health which is the full expression of all our potentialities in harmony. An ascetic ideal based on self-denial ends in self-annihilation; a stoical ideal which allows no place to the pleasurable principle in life justly deserves to meet its fate; a rationalism which seeks to rise above the instincts will achieve form without energy; an ideal without the instincts is an idea without power; a morality that sets itself against joy will achieve rectitude at the expense of life; a religion which rules out emotion blights the soul of religion, which is love. All such ideals, in so far as they involve repression, fail to secure self-realization and happiness, and are therefore false.

The happy man is he who finds in life a harmonized expression for all his instincts – for his self-assertive ambitious instincts in his profession, his sex instincts in marriage, his paternal instincts in his family or in benevolence, his curiosity in research, his display in speaking, writing, or painting, his pugnacious instincts and anger in defending his cause – these and other instincts directed towards some common ideal, such as living for his fellows, will make him infinitely happy.

HAPPINESS AND GOODNESS

The supposed antagonism between goodness and happiness is largely due to a wrong conception of either goodness or happiness. Those who seek to be good and not happy succeed in being neither. Goodness is the inevitable expression in conduct of a soul completely happy. An ideal of goodness is defective unless it tends towards happiness. Can we conceive of any ideal being the right one which makes for unhappiness? The common sense of the world, as well as psychological principle, condemns the piety which is morose. Psychologically, so true is this that we may take as a test of any ideal of goodness that its pursuit and attainment make men happy, such as in social service, business or profession.

But it will be found that this psychological ideal cannot be realized if ethical ideals are ignored. We cannot be happy without being good; for amongst the many instincts which crave for fulfilment are those essentially altruistic in their aims, such as the maternal instinct and the social instincts. In this respect happiness differs from pleasure, which can be utterly selfish, for it is the expression of individual instincts which may be entirely egocentric. We cannot be happy unless we have right relations to others, and such right relations imply goodness in conduct. The psychological ideal must exclude any conception of goodness which does not produce happiness, and also any conception of happiness which is antagonistic to the good.

HAPPINESS AND CIRCUMSTANCES

Happiness is largely independent of outward circumstances. There are, of course, certain circumstances more conducive to happiness than others. But it matters little what the circumstances may be as long as they call forth the harmonious expression of the instinctive emotions. Stone walls cannot imprison happiness, and iron bars cannot restrain the imaginations of love.

The crofter's wife may find full expression for all her instincts in the cottage, with her husband, home and children, and therefore may live an infinitely full and happy life. Indeed, such a woman, who with her husband was wresting a bare living on their croft, said to me, 'It's a hard life, but I would not change it for any other.'

A SENSE OF DUTY

Duty is the call that the ideal makes upon the personality.

We so often hear it said 'I do not *want* to do it! I do it only from a sense of duty' – say serving on a committee, or caring for an aged parent, or attending church; and feel very heroic in doing so.

This is a false antagonism. Do we then not *want* to do our duty? If not, why do we do it? Because it is right, we say. Then do we not want to do the right or do so only with reluctance? To say 'I did not want to do it, but only from a sense of duty' is to do ourselves an injustice because it means that we are identifying *ourselves* with our lower self, the self of inclinations, not with the *I* who prefers and pursues a higher ideal.

We follow our 'sense of duty' because *we* want to do so and for no other reason. Livingstone followed the path of duty when he explored Central Africa to discover the sources of the Nile in order to open up the country to civilization – and in doing so endured endless sufferings. He was doing what *he* wanted to do – and the difference between him and the changed; it becomes more spontaneous, more whole-hearted. I no longer keep saying 'Alas! for the sail!' but give all my attention to my patients, which is what *I* want to do. When we realize that in the choice of some line of action, which we may feel to be irksome, we have, after all, voluntarily chosen that path, then we lay aside the grumbling, and respond to it whole-heartedly – not because we must but because we will. Such service is perfect freedom.

HAPPINESS AS THE IDEAL

It has sometimes been suggested that we should aim at happiness as our ideal; that it should be the conscious aim which we pursue. Why should we not simply aim at being happy?

A subjective affect or state of 'feeling' can never be a right ideal, because as soon as we consciously seek it, it vanishes 'like the snowflake in the river'.

It is one of the many paradoxes of psychology that the pursuit of happiness, like the pursuit of pleasure, defeats its own purpose. We find happiness only when we do not directly seek it. An analogy will make this clear. In listening to music at a concert, we experience pleasurable feelings, *only so long as our attention is directed towards the music*. But, if, in order to increase our happiness, we give all our attention to our subjective feeling of happiness, it vanishes. A world in which everyone was absorbed with his own feelings would ultimately be an asylum in which shrouded figures sat emotionless and mute. The ideal sought must not be happiness itself, but must be conceived as having an intrinsic value in itself quite apart from the affective condition of happiness which it produces. In other words, *the ideal must be objective*. So such ideals as beauty, art, virtue, and religion are sought for their own sake, and desired as having an intrinsic and objective worth.

By thus directing our attention to an objective ideal, nature maintains the healthy balance between the subjective feelings in us and the objective world. She contrives to make it impossible for anyone to attain happiness by turning into himself, but only by moving into touch with the objective world. Thus, each man who succeeds in the search for happiness must needs add his quota to the world's progress.

It is at this point we are compelled to recognize as a factor of psychological importance the fact that men do estimate pleasures by the *quality* as well as *quantity*, and do prefer some lines of conduct to others on the ground of their intrinsic nobility.

THE OBJECTIVE IDEAL

But if the ideal is that which produces self-realization and happiness, this appears to leave right and wrong a matter of individual judgement.

The ideal of each man is that which seems to him to conduce to his happiness and self-realization. It is that ideal which can adequately stimulate the will, and it is his judgement as to which of many ideals he thinks will most conduce to his self-realization and happiness that constitutes his freedom of choice. But, admittedly, he may make mistakes, errors of judgement as to what are the most adequate ideals. The will, we have said, can be stimulated by inadequate stimuli which do not, in fact, make for self-realization and happiness. Is, then, every man to be allowed to follow the path which seems to him to lead to the ideal, and blunder through life only to find his mistake at the end? Ought we to stand by and see the Hedonist destroying his soul with pleasure? Is the superman to be permitted to pursue his ideal rough-shod towards its end? This would be in keeping neither with the interest of the individual nor those of the race: so the individual, seeking his own happiness, finds that he best secures it by making use of the experience of the race.

Is there no one ideal, an objective ideal, for all men? There is. In thousands of years of experience mankind has determined that there are some ideals which do, in fact, lead to greater happiness than others. Racial experience thus supplies us in a rough way with an objective ideal. It is this experience handed down from one generation to another that has given rise to what we call the moral code, and is embodied in such conceptions as honour, justice, altruism, generosity, liberty.

Such experiences of the race have been retained in moral tradition, and have been systematized in moral codes. The instincts themselves are 'racial' habits designed to save the individual from the mistakes that have cost the race millions of lives. The baby without a sucking or swallowing habit, the child without curiosity, the man without fear, are all potential corpses. We do not object to these reflexes and instincts on the ground that they are old-fashioned – which they are! The instincts have been learnt by painful experience of generations, and to act contrary to them is both foolish and dangerous to the individual. So, too, the moral tradition which sums up the experience of the race, though not so decisive as the instincts, is wisely regarded by those who seek happiness. The value of tradition is that it accumulates the experience of the race and offers it to the inexperienced individual. He who altogether rejects it, presuming that he knows best what is good for himself, is soon caught in his own snare. On the other hand, the individual who accepts such tradition as too authoritatively binding stifles his independent experience and development. Therefore, for society to make such a code compulsory is to deprive the individual of that free choice upon which his happiness depends: so it is embodied in public opinion.

The race has learnt that happiness comes more by benevolence than by meanness, by courage than by cowardice, by altruism than by selfishness. Moral conduct, therefore, whilst it must remain a matter for individual judgement, must consider in its judgement the accumulated experience of the race as it is expressed in a moral code, which warns one from false ideals and guides one to those which are found to conduce most to happiness.

Society claims the right, within wide limits, to press upon the individual the choice of the kind of ideal which experience has proved to be the most adequate; for if he chooses wrongly he brings upon both himself and others unhappiness. The criminal is a social danger, the bore is a social nuisance, and society gives a hint of its disapproval, and emphasizes the undesirability of his ideal, by punishing or ostracizing him, and so encourages him to seek another and a better ideal.

The question of right and wrong is not therefore purely, though it is ultimately, a matter of private judgement. There is, amongst the million possible ideals, an ideal which is the ideal for man's soul, which is capable of producing the greatest happiness. What this ultimate ideal actually is has not yet been determined, or generally agreed upon by all men. But that there is such an ideal seems scientifically probable. For in all nature there is no need but has the means to its satisfaction, for a craving cannot persist eternally without satisfaction. As there is food for hunger and as the sense of sight presupposes light, so there must be an ideal the attainment of which brings fulfilment and happiness to the soul.

THE FUNCTION OF LOVE

The true answer seems to be in the principle of love.

The term 'love' is rather unpopular in psychological writings; it is hardly spoken of; hardly decent. This is not surprising for it is capable of such a large number of meanings. It means one thing to an archbishop, another to film stars, and another to Freud, who identifies it with sex. He says that he means by sex 'all that is included in the word love' – which virtually means abolishing the word love and substituting the word sex. Rarely he makes the distinction, as when he says the boy is more actuated by sex, the girl by love.

The truth is that love is not a simple instinct like sex or anger or fear, but a sentiment (see page 20), namely, a group of emotions created round an object or person. Patriotism is, as we have seen, a sentiment, in which all our emotions are centred round our country. So love is a sentiment in which many emotions – devotion, respect, sex, aggressiveness in defending the loved person, and tenderness, especially of the love of the mother to her child, submission to the wishes of the loved person and admiration. The meaning we give to the word love depends on which of these components of love we emphasize. To the Freudian and to Hollywood it is the sex aspect which is dominant, but that does not exhaust all that is meant by love; to the mother it is the tender aspects; to the archbishop it is the devotion to a high ideal. 'Falling in love' occurs when all these are activated – we fall in love with the whole of us and with all of us.

One of the practical difficulties encountered by those of us who regard love as the paramount virtue and the fulfilment of the law is that it is capable of such varied interpretation to the man in the street; thus a man may say he is actuated by love when he seduces an unwilling girl.

The essence of true love is *concern for the welfare and happiness of the person loved*, even to the sacrifices of our own pleasure. It is 'devotion' to another, 'affection' for them: that is the dominant feature of love. Even when a man seduces a willing girl it is not necessarily for her happiness.

Love is essentially a positive and active motive. It is one thing to avoid doing anything which will hurt another; it is quite another to give him help. It is one thing not to take revenge; it is quite another thing to show mercy.

In love there is no question of a 'sense of duty' in the sense of doing something irksome and against our inclination, for what we do out of love is never irksome. Even the hardships and deprivations we are called upon to undergo are readily and willingly undertaken.

There is no antagonism between love and moral behaviour; for we do not steal from those we love, nor cause them harm, nor speak ill of them behind their backs, nor even hurt their feelings. Love is in fact the fulfilment of the law, for it involves honesty, goodness, justice and mercy. Those who love have no need for rules and regulations. Indeed it is justifiable to break the moral code of the community (like breaking the Sabbath in the olden days) if our actions are done out of mercy. Doctors on the field of battle have often given badly wounded men an overdose to put them out of their misery and pain; nor is it unknown in civil practice. They break the civil law: they are obedient to the law of love.

In the experience of love, personal considerations vanish; the man who loves cannot be conceited because conceit is concern for himself; nor self-opinionated, for love 'vaunteth not itself, is not puffed up'. Love cannot be bad-mannered, for love 'doth not behave itself unseemly' – it is in fact polite, for politeness is in essence consideration of others.

We find love in all communities of the world, even the most primitive. It is not a specifically Christian virtue, for we find the golden rule, 'Love thy neighbour as thyself', in at least a dozen religions of the world. The commandment 'Thou shall love the Lord thy God with all thy heart and with all thy soul and with all thy mind, and thy neighbour as thyself' existed before Christianity. But the Christian religion adopted it as the *basic* principle in life.

It is obviously the solution of the world's problems, for only by good will can the peace of the world be achieved. All the Conferences in the world will fail, as indeed at the present time they are failing time and again, if they meet in an atmosphere of suspicion, threats and fear. Only by 'good will amongst men' can the peace of the world be restored.

Love is also the basic need of the child. The child given protective love can exercise freedom in its activities in that atmosphere, whereas the child who is deprived of protective love is in a constant state of anxiety and insecurity, and is a candidate for a later neurosis (see p. 178).

In the pursuit of love – whether for our family, our country or our fellow-men, or in religion, the love and service of God, we have an ideal which appears to satisfy all the demands of an adequate ideal. It is capable of giving expression to all our emotions; it is *practical* in that it calls us to *do* things for others; it is *objective* in that it presents us with a pursuit outside ourselves; and by directing all our energies to a common end, it *harmonizes our instincts* and so brings us peace, happiness and health of mind.

Love is said to be the most selfish and the most unselfish thing in the world; selfish because we find our greatest happiness and self-realization in the exercise of love; unselfish because our *conscious* aim is the welfare of others, which takes precedence over our well-being and happiness.

CHAPTER XIV

Libertinism and Self-realization

WHILST SOME PEOPLE maintain that the pursuit of happiness should be our aim, others maintain that the pursuit of pleasure should be our main endeavour. This is libertinism as distinct from self-realization and happiness.

Libertinism is the expression in conduct of our crude instinctive desires and impulses. It is the denial of *restraint*, choosing pleasure as its ideal.

What are we to do with our instincts when we have accepted them? If repression is bad should we give full and free *expression* to all our instincts?

The problem arises in a very practical form in the treatment of the neuroses. There are some physicians who do not hesitate to advocate the free expression of the sexual instincts as a cure for neurosis.

The argument seems so simple. If the neurosis is due to sexual repression, the obvious cure is to go and give free expression to our sexual instincts in whatever way we like. The advice is bad, for it fails to distinguish between self-realization and self-expression. The term 'self-expression' is taken to mean the free and unrestrained expression of our instincts. 'The instincts were given us to use, not to repress; therefore, why should we set any limits to their expression?' This is the policy of the libertine, and one which attracts the youth of every age. On the other hand, self-realization is used in the higher sense of a harmonious expression of the whole self.

If the ideal of libertinism worked, it might be worth pursuing. But it does not work. The libertine principle fails both in theory and in practice.

(1) It is socially impossible.
(2) It is bad psychotherapy.
(3) It is opposed to biological principle.

(1) SELF-EXPRESSIONISM IS SOCIALLY IMPOSSIBLE

The argument of the self-expressionist is often put in this way. We must live according to nature; it is against nature to restrain our instincts. The man is to be commended who dares to follow nature and stand against the prudish conventions of a foolish society.

But if this principle holds good with the sexual, why not with the other instincts?

The soldier, at the first burst of a shell, deserts his post and runs away. He is tried by court-martial and pleads 'natural instinct'. On hearing his defence, the Brigadier rises and shakes hands with him, saying, 'I congratulate you, my dear fellow, on having the courage of your convictions in resisting the foolish conventions of this mid-Victorian sergeant-major.' Another man, annoyed at being pushed in a crowd, is repressing his anger when he suddenly remembers the teaching of the very new psychologist. He strikes the most innocent passer-by to relieve his pugnacious instinct. The rest of the onlookers take his side and praise him for daring to be natural in giving vent to his feelings, one being heard to remark that 'our instincts were given us to be used, not to be repressed'. Again, the known thief who is found in a bank at night is exonerated from all blame, and receives the apology of the bank manager, on the ground that he was exercising his instincts of curiosity and acquisition. What a world we should live in!

(2) SELF-EXPRESSIONISM IS BAD PSYCHOTHERAPY

From the point of view of cure, the advice to go and 'express your instincts' is only one degree more foolish than the antiquated advice which used to be given to every neurotic girl: 'All you need is to get married.' In actual experience I have never known a true neurosis cured by marriage, still less by sexual libertinism. But I have personally known many neuroses precipitated by marriage; indeed, I am sometimes tempted to think that half my patients are neurotic because they are not married, and the other half because they are!

The psychological reason for the failure of libertinism is obvious. If there is a psychological repression, the instinctive emotion is attached to this complex, and the mere expression *in conduct* of an instinct does not mean that it is *psychologically* liberated from that complex. It does not solve the problem because the repressing forces of fear and guilt, themselves unconscious, may thus be aroused and activate a worse conflict. I knew a lady of mild disposition who was found to be suffering from repressed pugnacious instincts, which manifested themselves in an impulse to stab people. She was advised by an analyst to give expression to this repressed instinct by being more assertive in ordinary conduct. She compelled herself to do so with an effort, but got more miserable, as we should have expected. The experiment completely failed, because her pugnacious complex was still *psychologically* repressed, and any expression of this instinct in *conduct* was, in the nature of her case, abhorrent to her. This produced a severe mental conflict, for she was forcing herself to do what psychologically she hated. Before she could express her pugnacious instincts naturally and in harmony with the rest of herself, the repressing force had to be discovered and the siege raised.[1]

In such cases, to advise expression in conduct only aggravates the condition, for whereas before sex was repressed and the moral sense dominant, now sex is dominant and the moral

[1] What was repressing her pugnacity and self-assertiveness? As a child she was self-willed and assertive, but this was later repressed, because on several occasions she was terribly humiliated as a result of it; she therefore decided to be 'nice' and gentle, and became excessively so. It was this morbid gentleness which repressed the pugnacious instincts which were only buried, not dead, and appeared in the obsession. When she recognized that her assumed gentleness was a hypocrisy, she was less reluctant to allow her pugnacious instincts more natural and sublimated expression – no longer in the impulse to hurt but in greater confidence and strength of will and purpose.

sense denied and repressed. This does not solve the problem; it merely substitutes one form of repression for another, and a worse one, for it is one in which the self as a whole is overpowered by one instinct. The experience simply makes a man sick with himself. The physician who advocates sexual indulgence as a cure for neurosis simply proclaims himself incompetent to deal with the psychological situation. It is not only bad morals, it is bad psychotherapy, as Freud said.

(3) SELF-EXPRESSIONISM AND BIOLOGICAL LAW

But the libertine may answer, 'Why worry about the moral sense? Let it go and there is no conflict.' The girl who acts on the principle of the 'right to motherhood' is acting contrary to social and moral sense, which will not permit her to be happy under these conditions. But why not defy society? Why be bound by the opinion of others? Why heed the voice of the herd which imposes such demands? Abandon moral scruples and there would be no conflict. This argument is based on the idea that morality is only an imposition of a conventional society upon the individual, an imposition society has no right to make.

As long as we hold an objective view of morality as an imposition from without, this argument may have some justification, and moral laws may be called into question as the dictates of convention. This is a view of morality held by many – the divine law is written on tables of stone in terms of 'Thou shalt', and 'Thou shalt not'. But, as we have seen, the call of duty is the demand that the ideal makes upon the self to seek its complete happiness and self-realization, and 'right' conduct is that which conduces to this end. In other words, the law is not an imposition from without, but is a demand of our own psychology – it is written on the tables of the heart. Morality is in essence the enunciation of higher biological laws of nature. Society, in upholding moral laws, is fulfilling the laws and end of nature. It rightly condemns and ostracizes those who act contrary to these laws.

CHAPTER XV

Biology and Morality

IT IS NOT generally realized that many forms of behaviour like altruism or marital fidelity, which we regard as having a moral or religious origin, have their roots in basic biological principles.

It is sometimes assumed that the law of nature is opposed to the moral law, which is conceived to be derived from some source outside nature. Nature, it is said, is selfish, whereas moral law is altruistic. This is due to a misconception of what we mean by 'nature', which must be taken to include the whole of nature, including man and his social, psychological, and moral functions. The basis of modern science was laid in the study of the laws of the *physical* world, but the scientific method of study must extend to the higher functions of the mind and soul, for they, too, are subject to law, and their laws are as natural as the laws which govern the movements of the stars.

There is no fundamental antagonism between biology and morality. *Moral laws have their basis in biological principles*, using the term biological in the broad sense of adaptation to life.

We may illustrate the intimate association between biological laws and moral principles in several examples:

(*a*) The principle of *Sympathy*, with care for the young, the sick and feeble.
(*b*) The natural development of *Conscience.*
(*c*) The principle of *Altruism.*
(*d*) The principle of *Marital fidelity.*
(*e*) The *Natural development* of innate tendencies, instincts

and patterns of behaviour into higher forms – dealt with in the next chapter.

(*a*) *The Law of Sympathy.* There are those who, seeing in nature no law except that of the struggle for existence, have blamed Christianity for maudlin sentimentality, in that it has advocated the care of the sick, the unfit, and the feeble, and encouraged a principle so opposed to biological law as that of sympathy. Why should we maintain hospitals to keep alive people who will never be of any biological use? Why should we keep alive the aged, who are only cumbersome? The law of life is the struggle for existence and the survival of the fittest. In the interest of a virile race we should kill off the sick, the aged, and the unfit, and keep alive only the strong. It is true that in animal life they tend to kill off the wounded; and primitive tribes go farther and kill off the aged and unwanted infants. But in the course of evolution there is gradually developed another principle, which is no less concerned with the preservation of the race, and does it more efficiently and with less waste, namely the development of sympathy, tenderness and care, most effectively expressed in the maternal instinct. This appears to be an inborn and physiological process depending on the lactogenic hormone which provides not only milk, but the milk of human kindness.

Suppose, then, we were to put the more primitive principles into practice. Our hospitals would become lethal chambers for putting to death the incurably sick, and we should have attached to each school a room for the administration of over-doses of chloroform to the congenitally blind or mentally deficient child. We should quietly do away with the clergy at fifty-five years of age, drown university professors at sixty, and hang lawyers, say, at forty!

We are told that such a practice would preserve the strong and develop a race of supermen. Let us examine the validity of the argument.

What is it that makes us keep alive the aged and sick? It is the maternal instinct. This instinct sprang into existence in response to a definite need, which was the care of the offspring, as long as it was unable to care for itself. But this means the young of any species was developed in strength and virility. Without this care the young were exposed to danger and death. The maternal instinct was therefore necessary to the survival of the race.

But nature tends to 'overdo' instincts like the maternal and the sexual, which are indispensable to her ends. The surplus of the sex instinct goes into art and music, whereas the surplus of the maternal instinct, originally contrived for the care of offspring, becomes attached to anything that is weak and helpless.

The maternal instinct, originally directed to the care of one's offspring, later becomes directed to any helpless object. The instinct is, then, sublimated into activities like that of nursing the sick. There are two kinds of nurses – the nurse and the 'born' nurse – and the born nurse is the one with the maternal instinct. They may be equally efficient, but the nurse with the maternal instinct has a 'touch' which the other can never cultivate.

The maternal instinct, necessary to the continuance of the race, is that which compels us to keep alive the aged and the sick.

Suppose, then, in the interests of a virile race, you killed off the sick and the old. You cannot destroy the unfit without doing violence to the maternal instinct upon which the fitness of the race depends. *If you killed off the sick you must first have stifled the maternal instinct, and if you stifle the maternal instinct you would kill off the race.* If we killed off the sick, far from having a virile race, we should have no race at all. The expression of sympathy and pity is not the outcome of maudlin sentimentality, it is the expression of a biological fact necessary to the preservation of the race. It did not originate in Christianity, although it is to Christianity that we owe the wide and conscious acceptance of it as a leading principle of life. In caring for the sick, Christianity is not going contrary to biological law, but is giving expression to its more fundamental principles.

Indeed, there can be only one possible justification for the killing of the sick, and that is when it is done, not in the interests of a virile race, but as the expression of pity. This might induce a surgeon on the field to put out of his misery a soldier lacerated beyond hope and suffering agonies of pain. It is questionable if even the legal penalty of death for murder does not do more harm to the sentiments of the people who are collectively responsible, than to the victim, by blunting their sense of pity upon which the welfare of the race depends.

It is sometimes forgotten that this 'biological' principle is no new doctrine: it has been tried and has failed. In Sparta infants were exposed to the night cold to weed out the weak. It is the common custom amongst some savage tribes deliberately to kill off the aged and also the superfluous infants. But we have yet to learn that Sparta survived as a great nation, nor does the example of savage races encourage us to take them as our model of biological efficiency.

(*b*) *The Development of Conscience.* Most people have a sense of right and wrong; it may be lax; it may be so severe as to make the individual's life a misery with constant self-condemnation and guilt. What is conscience? How does it arise?

Some people regard conscience as implanted by God to act as a guide in the affairs of life. If so it must become very much besmirched in the process, for people, especially in religious persecution, curiously enough, have done the most cruel things, prompted by conscience.

In analytic treatment, especially in tracing back the origin of over-conscientiousness, over-scrupulousness and obsessional propitiatory compulsions and rituals, we have discovered the psychological origin of conscience in general.

Everyone is acquainted with the phase in early childhood, about the age of three, when the child identifies itself with those round about: 'I am Daddy going to work; I am Mummy doing the cooking; I am the milkman; do you want any more milk today?'

This is not mere imitation of action; for the time being the child is impersonating the others, and in doing so takes over their personalities, including their standard of behaviour. (These phases I have described fully in my *Childhood and Adolescence*, pp. 115–41, Penguin.)

So the boy says, 'I'm a brave man like Daddy', and adopts his father's courage; 'I'm polite like Uncle John', and opens the door for you. Or 'Mummy says it's wrong to steal or to tell lies.' Thus conscience is developed.

For by this incorporation of the personalities of others into his own, he establishes a *duality* in his personality. On the one side there is the Ego or natural self, consisting of the innate instincts, innate patterns of behaviour and their impact with environmental conditions to form our dispositions. On the other side there is the Ego – ideal, Super-ego or moral self, formed of the incorporation of the personalities superimposed on his own.

Depending on the kind of people presented to him, with whom to identify himself will largely depend his character. That is why a good parent sees to it that a child has good companions, although the child must learn also to resist bad influences.

This process of the formation of the Super-ego, and of a duality in the personality, takes place about the age of three, and is a most momentous event in the life of the individual. Consider the results of this duality.

In the first place it means the development of *self-consciousness*, which signifies that one part of the personality is conscious or aware of the other aspect of our dual nature; the natural self is aware of, and largely dominated by, the strict demands of the moral self or Super-ego; whilst the Super-ego is aware of and is often ashamed of the activities and desires of our natural self. Self-consciousness is not only the power to see ourselves as others see us, but to see ourselves as *we* see us. It is probably this self-consciousness which distinguishes man from the lower animals, and constitutes moral behaviour, for out of this self-consciousness spring other attributes of human nature.

Arising out of, and as a consequence of self-consciousness is the power of *self-criticism*, the power we have of judging our behaviour not only in the light of what others expect of us, but also in the light of the standards of behaviour we have adopted by the process of identification, and expect of ourselves. That is the basis of *conscience*, for conscience is the judgement which the moral self, or Super-ego passes on the behaviour of the natural self or ego.

The formation of a conscience is inevitable in every child, because the process of identification is inevitable; so that if you never gave a child a single moral maxim, he would still develop a conscience of some sort. If the mother with whom the little girl identifies herself is easy-going, the child will become so; if very strict and severe, the child may be so strict with herself that she becomes over-conscientious and over-scrupulous, and is likely to become an obsessional with compulsive propitiatory acts.

If on the other hand a boy identifies himself with a merciless hero, he may later feel very ashamed if he has shown pity to someone, and blame himself for what he regards as softness or sentimental weakness.

Arising further out of self-consciousness and self-criticism is *self-control* – for seeing his behaviour as undesirable and unworthy of the standards he has set himself, the individual sets about rectifying it. If the will has been well developed, co-ordinating a large proportion of potentialities, he is able to do this; if less well developed, so that the balance between the impulses and the will is less marked, he will have difficulty in controlling his impulses.

Combining these three functions into one illustration: if the boy who has identified himself with his 'brave' father shows fear at a barking dog, he is *self-conscious* of this fear, *criticizes* himself in the light of the standard of courage he has set himself, and sets about developing, by *self-control*, a more courageous attitude towards danger. This is the beginning of true moral conduct.

The development of conscience is therefore a natural

biological function, innate in every man: but the *form* that conscience takes depends on environmental conditions, especially that of identification, and differs with every individual. Conscience therefore needs to be developed like every other quality in human nature. A healthy conscience must act as a guide to co-ordinate the various potentialities in every man, utilizing all but repressing none.

(*c*) *Altruism* means a consideration for others and a concern for their welfare. It is generally thought to be the product of a high degree of moral culture; but in fact has its roots in biological development.

We find altruistic *behaviour* even in animal life. Sitting at my window, in the country, I one day saw only a few yards away a contest between a pheasant and a fox. The fox of course wanted to get the pheasant; the pheasant on the other hand, in spite of great danger to herself, was guarding her nest and her brood. Each time the fox advanced on her, she flew up a yard or two out of his reach. This contest went on for ten minutes or so until at last the fox gave up and made off. We cannot of course read the mind of a pheasant; she was no doubt acting instinctively, but in her behaviour she was altruistic, with little concern for her own safety, which would best have been served by flying away altogether, but her whole concern was with her brood.

In human beings altruism is developed at a more conscious level. In the first place it is the result of sympathy or fellow feeling. If we have ourselves suffered, we 'feel for' others who are undergoing suffering, and this greatly enhances social life. Sympathy is a natural innate development. In any large nursery of children, if one child starts to cry others begin to howl. This is not mere imitation, for the other children *feel* sad because of their fellow feeling; and they will sometimes comfort the misery of the first child by giving it a toy – not because they have been taught to do so, but because of natural sympathy and pity.

Altruism is still further developed by identification. When the little boy is playing at Red Indians, he for the time being *is* that Red Indian, with all his courage, his fears, his adventurous spirit. In fact, *for the time being he is more that Red Indian than he is himself*. This not only develops his conscience, as we have indicated, but it enables him to put himself entirely in the place of others and therefore *he will do good to others as though it were himself* – but without any thought for himself. He literally 'loves his neighbour as himself' – except that for the moment he is entirely concerned with his neighbour without a thought for himself.

This natural capacity of thinking ourselves into the personality of other people is the basis of the highest altruism, for it means that we are concerned for their welfare, feel their suffering, share their misery as though it is our own; because for the time being it *is* our own: it is ourselves projected into theirs; it is their experience of joy or sorrow introjected into our own personality. For the moment we are more them than we are ourselves. We may have no sorrow of our own, yet we can be sad with them; we may ourselves not be sick or suffering, yet we can feel and partake of their suffering; we may have no success to our credit, but we can rejoice in their success and happiness, as though it were our own. This natural development of altruism comes about as the result of sympathy and identification, both of them natural and innate aptitudes.

(*b*) *The Law of Marital Fidelity*. Let us pass to another illustration of considerable moment, that of sexual morality. We have looked at this problem from the psychological and social point of view; let us now observe it from the biological attitude. The advocates of 'free love' and sexual licence base their claims upon the argument that they are 'acting according to nature'. 'Man,' we are constantly reminded, 'is a polygamous animal.' They gibe at sexual morality and marital fidelity as 'mid-Victorian'.

What is the chief end of nature? I intentionally do not say the 'purpose' of nature, for nature is not conscious of these ends, nor does she deliberately pursue them; but there are, nevertheless, actual ends towards which nature is moving by the law of struggle for existence. It is generally agreed that the chief end of nature is the reproduction of the species and perpetuation of a healthy race. Nature has various means of securing this. In the earlier stages of evolution it was secured by the reproduction of large quantities of the species. The struggle for existence secured that only the strongest and best survived.

In the earlier phases of evolution man and the animals were polygamous, for at this phase the greatest urgency was the production of large quantities of species, since so large a proportion were exterminated. A cod has thousands of eggs, but owing to the ravages of enemies, only a few of these eggs ever achieve what we might term 'adult cod-hood'. The perpetuation of the species, therefore, could best be secured by promiscuous and polygamous practices. But the mere production of large quantities was not an efficient means to the end. In the later stages, therefore, not quantity but quality was emphasized, so that whilst in the later phases of evolution fewer offspring were produced, they were better able to defend themselves and survive. The most important contrivance for procuring this end was the maternal instinct, which secured the protection of the offspring, and prepared the young for the emergencies they would later meet in life. The higher in evolution we go, the more strongly is the maternal instinct developed, and, therefore, the fewer the offspring necessary to each mother.

But, as we have observed, this end was, in the later stages of evolution, more economically and effectively attained by the *development of family life*, which secured protection for the mother during her reproductive period. For the establishment and maintenance of family life monogamous instincts were developed. It is true, then, that man is a polygamous animal, but it is just as true that *man is a monogamous animal.* The one represents an earlier, the other a later, phase in evolution.

Monogamous impulses are found even amongst animals, like the lion, who is faithful to the lioness during the period of reproduction, and sometimes, I am told, throughout life. In nature we find no race of men where sexuality is absolutely promiscuous; even in the lowest we find marriage laws which, although they are primitive, are often maintained more rigidly than the marriage laws of civilized communities.

Monogamous impulses are developed in the process of evolution. They are the results not of social necessity, although they are in fact upheld by this, but are embedded in man's physiological constitution, part of his constitution as developed in the process of evolution.

As we have seen (p. 115) monogamy is an economy of nature so that fewer offspring are required and there is less waste.

But the monogamous impulse, together with the development of the maternal instinct in the higher animals, is also responsible for family life; for they are the means of the establishment of the home, even if it is only a nest or a lair; and that means greater care of the offspring.

Birds like the robin and the gull are not only faithful to their spouses during the period of reproduction but both parents take a part in building the nest and in feeding the fledglings. The establishment of a family means that the mother is protected and helped by the father, so that she may give better attention to the young, to their great advantage.

Moreover, monogamy provides for the development of a better order of species; for it provides the young with an atmosphere in which they can develop higher qualities.

In an atmosphere of security the young can experiment and be adventurous; play in ways that will prepare them to meet the actualities of later life; they can develop conditioned reflexes which enable them to cope with situations for which no specific hereditary instincts are provided; and by imitation they can pick up from their parents habits of life, such as the avoidance of danger or getting on with their fellows, which serve them in good stead in later life. The very young rabbit which you meet in the woods does not run away when you approach it with a gun; then it sees its mother run away and by imitation follows suit and that becomes a habit, saving its life.

It is for these practical considerations of survival that monogamous impulses have developed or are in the process of developing; and it is for these basic biological reasons that society encourages the process of nature by upholding the principles of monogamy.

Since monogamy is the trend of this evolutionary process towards a higher form of living, it is up to those who consider both the present welfare and the future happiness of the race to encourage that process and neither so to act nor to advocate opinions which are detrimental to these higher standards of life.

There is no doubt that polygamous impulses survive in man and very strongly, but they belong to the earlier phases of evolution which gradually are giving place to the monogamous. Promiscuity is outmoded; so, for the firmer establishment of family life with all the advantages it brings, will extra-marital relations come to be outmoded.

Polygamous tendencies in man and woman still exist, of course, as is instanced in the case of a patient of mine whose mother as a young woman went with a girl friend one night for a walk in Finsbury Park, met two young men, had intercourse with them and was delivered of a baby by a strange man whom she had never even seen. It is not surprising that the child became a neurotic, a cost to the community as well as a burden of unhappiness to himself.

But monogamous impulses are just as innate as the polygamous, although being a later development in evolution they are not so strong, and therefore need to be fortified by the moral injunctions of the community.

The fact that many animals are polygamous is no reason for our imitating them in accordance with the 'go back to nature' school of morals. If we acted consistentlv on this principle we should meet with some surprises The female 'praying mantis', for instance, during the process of mating eats up the male bit by bit, starting at the head; and she is half-way through his body before the mating ceases. It is not the only instance of a female using her sex appeal to get her 'bread and butter'! There is a lot to be said for it – from her point of view. The empid fly is more cautious: he discovers a dainty morsel, wraps it up in silk and formally presents it to the female. He then takes the opportunity of quickly mating with her while she is preoccupied, absorbed in admiration of the gift. He thus avoids the misfortune of being eaten as is the male mantis. This method of reproduction is not unknown among humans. But we can hardly take these lower creatures as examples to us as to how we should conduct our love-making in civilized life!

In the individual the sexual development follows that of the race. Polygamous tendencies arise with the hetero-sexual impulses at sixteen to eighteen, and then the monogamous tendencies emerge. The boy of sixteen falls in love with several girls at once, and his polygamous tendencies are naturally expressed in 'flirting', which may be a valuable activity, if it enables him to discover the right partner in life. Having chosen the partner, the monogamous impulse emerges towards the one and only woman, and seeks to find expression in marriage; family life establishes itself, and the fidelity of husband and wife secures the ends of nature.

The youth, however, who, in his polygamous phase, expresses these tendencies in licentious practices, mortgages the future happiness of his married life, so that this phase of life, instead of preparing him for marriage, unfits him for it. The polygamous impulse should be the hand-maid (expressed in 'flirting'), and not the rival, of the future monogamous impulse. Again, the grown man who continues in the flirtatious stage appropriate to the adolescent degenerates into a foolish 'philanderer' and is recognized by women of sense to be a case of arrested development. As in the individual, so in racial evolution, it is interesting to observe the monogamous tendency displayed side by side with the polygamous. Even men of polygamous and loose tendencies show the monogamous impulse in remaining faithful to the one woman for a longer or shorter period. This loyalty, though temporary, is the manifestation of the monogamous impulse.

The problem of 'free love' and 'marital fidelity' is not, therefore, a question of nature against moral convention. The real conflict is between an earlier phase of evolution and a later phase, the polygamous and the monogamous, both of which have left their impression in our psychology. It is a conflict between different forces of nature in ourselves, and it is for us to decide along which line lies our happiness. The man who lives polygamously is not living 'according to nature', as he imagines: he has simply failed to keep pace with nature. He has been arrested in his development, which should have progressed from the polygamous to the monogamous, and from this to the paternal phase. If, then, an appeal is made to nature, it must be to the whole of nature, and not merely to its lower and earlier manifestations. It will then be found that natural law and moral law are but two phases of man's development towards self-realization. The savage, in his state of nature, is not the last word in nature's speech. It is true that by reducing ourselves to a state of psychological savagery we may rid ourselves of neuroses; although even the savage is riddled with neuroses in the form of taboos and other obsessional acts and superstitious fears associated with guilt. But the matter cannot rest there, for in so far as he is a savage, man fails to achieve happiness, for he lacks unity and harmony of mind, and fails to achieve the purpose of man's evolution towards that organization of human society we call civilization, and the organization of the instincts we call the moral self. This need has become part of the psychology of civilized man, and it is impossible, however much he may desire it, for him to find happiness by a return to the chaotic condition of soul typical of the savage. The life of the savage is often called 'simple'. In outward organization it may be, but psychologically it is far more chaotic than the ordered life of civilized man, whose instinctive forces are directed to a common purpose. So it is with the individual who permits unrestrained expression to his impulses, for he finds no peace in life. Every organism, the human mind included, is working towards a synthesis, and not merely for expression. Any system of conduct or of psychotherapy which neglects this in practice is neglecting a fundamental psychological and biological principle, upon which rock it will be broken to pieces.

CHAPTER XVI

Psychological Development and Self-realization

INNATE PECULIARITIES, whether the instincts or patterns of behaviour, tend *of themselves* to develop to higher forms, given ordinary conditions of life, and to attach themselves to new interests.

NATURAL DEVELOPMENT

Man's life consists of a number of phases, each of which rises to fullness of development and then dies away, to give place to the next phase. Infancy, childhood, puberty, adolescence, manhood, middle-age and old age – each has its own distinctive psychology, which rises, like the wave, to the height of its crest and then sinks into its trough in sacrificing itself to the succeeding wave.

Each of these phases makes its distinct contribution to the full development of the whole personality and to the attainment of self-realization.

In the evolution of the race each of the instincts arose one after another to meet the special emergencies of life. In the individual, every instinct is present at birth, but lies latent until there comes the call for it to play its part on the stage of life. During its phase of dominance, each period of life is characterized by the emergence of some instinctive tendency which dominates the life of the individual. At the end of its period, whether it has been successfully developed or whether it has been only partially expressed, it must give place to the next emerging instinct which claims the stage. Between each phase of life there is a *re-birth*, at which the old dies and the new springs into life, and at each re-birth the soul is rejuvenated like the faded blossom that turns to tender fruit. But the passing of the old phase in favour of the new is not necessarily by way of repression, for during its phase, each instinct, normally expressed, becomes incorporated into the self to the healthy building up and *organization of the self*. In this way each instinct becomes *transferred* to an object worthier of the developing self. But at every period of transition, when one phase passes and the next arises, there is liable to be a disturbance in the psychology which, if unsuccessfully accomplished, may in later years cause a breakdown, or neurosis, which requires specific treatment by *analysis*, *re-association*, and *sublimation*.

RE-BIRTH

The mysteries of psychological re-birth are as strange as those of natural birth; we know not whence it comes nor whither it goes. It has attracted and fascinated the imagination of man so that we have it reflected and constantly reiterated in custom, dream, and myth. For the persistence of any myth or custom is always an indication that it appeals to some deep-rooted and persistent psychological experience.

The most familiar of such *myths* is that of the phœnix. The phœnix leaves its temple and wanders the world for a thousand years; at the end of its age it returns to the altar, whereon it is burned in flames, and out of its ashes there rises resplendent the young phœnix, itself to roam the world for its allotted span. Psychologically, such a myth represents a re-birth, the passing away of one psychological phase and the emergence into life of another.

In *custom* we also have the symbol of re-birth. When the aboriginal Australian boy is initiated into manhood, he is made to pass through the hollow trunk of a tree, and emerges a man; he is buried and is dug up again to take his place as an adult in the council of the tribe; he is dipped into water, and emerges a new creature. Or, again, a tooth is knocked out to indicate the passing of the old self, the sloughing-off of childhood.

Our *dream* psychology, in one interpretation, is full of these re-birth phantasies, as we should expect. A woman, recovering from a neurosis, sees herself dying on a couch; when she dies, she, the onlooker, feels a sense of great happiness and exhilaration. A patient dreams of two men, who are really one, waiting on a platform about to catch a train (which represents psychological progress and advance). One of these men seems to be dying; the other struggling to come to life. They are both himself. The patient wakes in fear: for the labour of birth is difficult, the re-birth is not yet fulfilled.

A girl of sixteen dreams of coming to a pool of water, dives in and emerges naked and clean, to find awaiting her an entirely new set of clothes. She sees herself struggling with her father, breaking free and escaping with a young man: it is the re-birth from puberty to later adolescence.

But while the idea of re-birth is thus universally portrayed in myth, custom, and dream, it was not intellectually conceived as a psychological fact until Christ insisted that there was not only a physiological birth – born of water, but a psychological re-birth, born of the spirit.

This is what Nicodemus could not understand; he could not rise above the physiological level: birth to him meant physical birth, and nothing else – 'How can a man enter the second time into his mother's womb?' As a man of the world he does not believe one can change human nature, forgetting that human nature does nothing but change. In reply, Christ insists that psychological re-birth is a reality. He contrasts physical birth, born of the waters, that is the uterine waters, with psychological or spiritual re-birth. The importance of psychological re-birth, nowadays virtually lost by the Church, is being rediscovered in psychology.

RE-ORIENTATION

The process of re-birth implies that new potentialities arise in the course of maturation of the individual. By re-orientation we signify that these potentialities and emotions attach themselves to new *interests*. The boy of 3 directs his energies to very different interests from the boy of 13; the girl of 11 is a very different person to the girl of 17. A man may transfer his affection from sport to his family: from his family to humanity: from his country to the country of his adoption: from self-pity to altruism, or from a gay life to one of ambition: new sentiments are formed by the attachment of the emotions to new objects. At one time it is rabbits, at another a lover, at another religion, at another putting, which absorbs his attention.

The myths of metamorphoses, in which animals turn into men, and men into gods, is psychologically, if not objectively, true: the self is constantly changing its form. The theory of the transmigration of souls is metaphorically, if not metaphysically true, for our self is constantly passing, to emerge into a new form – in the midst of life we are in death; indeed, life can only persist by death.

When a healthy transference takes place, as, for instance, when the boy transfers his love from his mother to his lover, most, but not all, the emotions are transferred. The emotions which were previously attached to the mother, such as admiration, tenderness, protection, fear for her safety, anger on her behalf, are transferred to the girl to form a new sentiment: the mother sentiment gives place to the lover sentiment. But the mother may still be the object of affection, gratitude and respect. On the other hand, there are attached to the girl certain emotions (notably, of course, conscious sexual desires) which did not belong to the mother. Thus every phase represents not merely a transference of the old emotions, but the attachment and development of new ones.

Where do these new ones come from? They are the instinctive emotions whose day had not yet dawned, but which have now emerged to claim expression. Thus, with the emergence of the instinct, the need for its expression and the object of its attachment present themselves.

SACRIFICE AND RE-BIRTH

(*a*) The idea of re-birth suggests *the place and function of sacrifice.* At every phase of life the old has to be sacrificed for the new: the old phœnix must die, the blossom must pass to permit of the new life. The mother sacrifices the school-girl complexion for the tenderness of mother love. At every re-birth the instinct that has dominated the last phase must give place to the instinct uprising. Every transference involves a sacrifice of the old love to the new love, of the old ideal to the new ideal.

The law of sacrifice is one of the earliest of biological laws. We find it operating even in one-celled organisms, which, when they reach a certain stage of growth too cumbersome for self-preservation, surrender a part of themselves. This broken-off piece forms a new organism, and we thus have the earliest form of reproduction by fission. The 'mother' cell has to sacrifice a bit of itself to live, and that sacrifice forms another individual. From this early phase to that of the highest psychological organism, the individual must constantly make sacrifices for a freer and fuller life. Sacrifice is involved in the very idea of progress. Sacrifice is the surrender of the old for the new: it is necessary to biological development and to psychological and moral progress. Without sacrifice we should never slough off the old, and therefore never emerge into the new life.

(*b*) *Sacrifice and Self-realization.* The ideal of sacrifice is not hostile to the psychological principle of self-realization. Indeed, it is necessary to psychological progress. But it is frankly opposed to the principles of asceticism, in so far as these lay stress on the negative aspect of sacrifice. The ascetic who makes much ado about that which he is sacrificing pays a poor compliment to the good for which he finds it so hard, yet considers it a virtue, to make the sacrifice. The ideal of completeness is inconsistent with the repression of the instincts which is characteristic of the ascetic ideal. Self-denial, if it means the denial of the whole self, is obviously antagonistic to the principles of self-realization. But if it means that the self must deny, say 'No' to, those false ideals and desires which threaten its life, then self-denial is akin to true sacrifice and necessary to progress.

The life of the ascetic is not necessarily a life of sacrifice. Indeed, he may be suspected of shirking his true responsibilities, if instead of throwing himself into the stream of life, battling with his hardships, and undertaking the responsibilities of business and family, he prefers to choose for himself what discipline he will undertake. Even when he has succeeded in finding artificial means of self-discipline he is still innocent of life's real discipline. The man who accepts the ordinary responsibilities of life and seeks no sheltered life, has, in the course of fulfilling those responsibilities as worker, husband, and father, ample opportunities for the exercise of his self-denial. It is admitted that whilst the responsibilities and hardships are much greater, he also experiences the greater joys, and it is for these joys that the sacrifices are gladly and joyously made. His joys and his sorrows are both more intense – he lives a fuller life.

But to leave our emotions attached to morbid complexes and then spend our time in striving to repress them is a hopeless misadventure. Religiously, such a man may be considered a saint; psychologically, he is often neurotic, for he has not yet learned how to utilize his impulses, and the monastery must needs be to him a perpetual nursery.

(*c*) It follows that *sacrifice should always be for the sake of a greater good.* If sacrifice is a re-birth from the old to the new, we must emphasize not the negative aspect but the positive good; not what we surrender, but that for which the sacrifice is made. To pride ourselves self-complacently on having made a sacrifice is to misconceive the function of the sacrifice. Unless the sacrifice we make is for a greater happiness, there is no justification for making it. The man who sacrifices affluent circumstances for a life of heroic hardship chooses between two functions of the soul, and rightly chooses that which appears to him to produce the greatest self-realization; otherwise, he is not justified in making it. It was *for the joy* that was set before him that Christ endured the Cross. The cutting-off of the hand, the plucking out of the eye, are only justified as expedients to permit us to enter into life. Martyrdom for a right cause is gladly and willingly undertaken, and the soldier has greater happiness in dying than in being a coward. But to flog ourselves to show our devotion to religion, to incarcerate ourselves and voluntarily deny ourselves to prove our piety, is as foolish as it is to kill ourselves to prove our love of our country.

Thus, far from self-denial or sacrifice being *in itself* good, it is frequently an evil. The man who sacrifices his home and family for his business, or sacrifices his ambition for popularity, the woman who sacrifices her 'life's happiness' in marriage to look after her mother, are often making false denials. Although they may eulogize themselves for their nobility in sacrificing home, ambition, and prospects of marriage, it is not necessarily virtuous, for they are making sacrifices of a good to gratify what may be some morbid impulse. The fact that they are 'sacrifices' does not justify them.

If sacrifices are for a better good, why praise the man who makes a great sacrifice? The only justification for such praise is to encourage others who shrink from making such sacrifices. The man himself who makes the sacrifice aright seeks no commendation. He could do no other, and is happier so.

As our life progresses, then, new potentialities and emotions are brought to the surface of consciousness, and new interests are developed in conformity with them, each phase making its distinctive contribution to the development of the whole personality. In their contact with life, right and good sentiments are formed, leading to complete happiness. As each phase passes the old must be sacrificed to the new, and be transformed into the new that we may achieve a higher self-realization.

THE ORGANIZATION OF THE PERSONALITY

When by the process of identification the individual incorporates the ego-ideal or super-ego into his personality, he establishes within himself a guiding principle in life. This guiding principle is then capable of harnessing all the natural forces of our lives, instincts and patterns of behaviour alike, and directing them towards a common end. In this way the personality is organized and all its potentialities harmonized.

This *process* usually takes place about the age of 3 or 4, by which time, as we have seen, the child has developed its own standards of behaviour by which to guide its conduct, its own conscience and sense of guilt by which to correct its conduct and its own self-control by which it can change its conduct. It is, *psychologically speaking*, an entity in itself, self-governing, independent and self-sufficient.

But as we have seen the personality is constantly changing according to the process of maturation so that the personality is confronted with new problems at every phase of life. The problems of the married man of 30 are very different from his problems at the age of 13. Not only so, but he is constantly changing his standards of behaviour in conformity with his changing responsibilities.

This means that his normal standards are constantly changing. For the boy of 13 to 14 the paramount virtue is loyalty to those of his gang; for the adolescent concern for his mate; for the adult, his family and the community.

This re-orientation of his ideals is particularly marked in later adolescence, when he is confronted with the task of being a grown-up person with new responsibilities.

The age of 16 to 18 is the *age of idealism*, when the self is so organized as to seek definitely for that ideal through which it may be made complete.

The idealism characteristic of this age enables the second-year university student to settle all disputes, solve all social questions, and form the perfect Utopia merely by prefacing his remarks and suggestions with the phrase, 'In a properly constituted state of society —'. He fails to see that the difficulty is to achieve the properly constituted state in which his admirable theories could be applied. Yet it is right that he should indulge in these idealisms at his age, for without the image of the ideal his life would be sordid. Nor should any youth of this age be discouraged by his matter-of-fact parent or teacher. Psychologically speaking, he is seeking for that ideal sentiment which can harmonize all those instincts which, in the course of the years, have been emerging in him. He seeks for the unifying principle of his inner life. It is, therefore, an age in which the feeling of incompleteness and depression is very marked, this feeling being largely accentuated by the need of sexual completeness in marriage. Failing this psychological completeness, the need of an ideal is projected and objectified in all those social, intellectual, and religious idealisms so characteristic of later adolescence. Feeling the need of self-mastery, he seeks to master the forces of nature, and pits himself against his fellow-men: feeling the need for psychological harmony in his soul, he throws himself into movements for universal peace. But sordid facts of reality constantly intrude and spoil the vision. He cannot find the ideal, his impulses are left chaotic, and from the heights of idealism he falls to the depths of despondency, the only escape from which often seems to be in death. This phase of life, commonly regarded as the happiest period of life, is in consequence also characterized by the greatest number of suicides.

In later adolescence, the self, having found some ideal of stable value for completeness, settles down to the effort to attain it, and so starts the process by which the self is built up into a strong character.

(*d*) An age of idealism is followed by the age of the *development of character*. During all the years from infancy to adult life instincts have been emerging and developing. In the full development of character every instinct plays its part and becomes incorporated into the self, and so the character is built up. This process of development is, therefore, exactly the opposite of repression. The old phase is not repressed by the new but, having fulfilled its function and made its contribution to the building up of the self, it passes, like the blossom, to the fruit of the next. Its death is but a transition. Thus, in the perfectly developed character, there is no repression but continual progression.

In adolescence the youth was concerned with ideals; in this later age he should be concerned rather with the achieving of some small fraction of his ideals; but what he achieves is solid and real. The ideals of the youth move him to enthusiasm; the ideals of the man move him to endeavour. His ideals are less extravagant, but those he retains are more stable. No man of 35 has any right to be dominated by the fantastic idealism of youth; the middle-aged 'idealist' may fail because he lacks realism to carry out the reforms he earlier dreamt about. The holding on to the old, and refusing to integrate the newly developing life into consciousness results in a conflict which is a common cause of breakdown. If middle age is characterized by some loss of idealism, it gains in strength of character.

ARREST OF DEVELOPMENT PRODUCES NERVOUS BREAKDOWN

Amongst our acquaintances there are men and women of great intellectual ability and artistic taste who, in their emotional life, are yet children. In intellect they are often beyond their fellows – I think of a university lecturer and a man whose name is famous in literature – but look into their souls and you find they are children of four or six: their emotional development has been arrested. And since the emotions are given us to enable us to meet emergencies – courage to face danger, fortitude to withstand difficulties, confidence to meet anxieties – these grown-up children fail to adapt themselves to life. Thus, there is a conflict between their grown-up selves, which need to meet their responsibilities, and the child, which shrinks from the task. They are timid, find life too much for them, they are unable to face a crisis, are nonplussed in an emergency, run for port when the wind rises. Men of this type often marry motherly women to act as a bulwark against the world, or develop a neurosis which excuses them from facing their responsibilities. Such people have been arrested in development, and, delightful and charming as they may be, their character is never formed. They start by being the happy Peter Pan, they end by being the distraught 'Mary Rose', living in a world of ghostly unreality.

It is quite possible that people who suffer from arrest of development of this kind may show very little sign of it for many years. They may advance, but they advance timidly, and the development of each phase is feeble and incomplete. Then suddenly they are brought face to face with difficulties such as those presented by the war, or have an unfortunate love-affair, and inevitably they fall back into childhood from which they have scarcely emerged. This is psychological 'regression', and is analogous to the 'throw back' in biology. The cause of such regression is incomplete progression. One cannot make a man of an individual emotionally a child by telling him to 'be a man'; he is lacking those qualities that make for virility. He can be cured only by dealing with those factors in childhood which produced the arrest.

But why, it may be asked, does arrest take place? Excluding, of course, arrest due to defect of brain structure, such arrest in development may be the result of: (*a*) the overstimulation of an instinct in childhood, of self-display for instance, which makes it persist as the dominant force in the psychology; (*b*) the suppression and starvation of some instinct craving for rightful expression; for instance, if any child is starved for sympathy in childhood, it tends to crave for it morbidly in after life, and becomes a 'hysteric'; (*c*) the premature stimulation of an instinct which tends to fixate it on some abnormal object; for instance, when a child experiences an assault, by which its latent sex feelings are precociously aroused. In any of these conditions the character is dwarfed and stunted.

Those who suffer from arrest of development must be treated in the same way as any other neurotic, the conflict in their case being between the earlier phase which persists and the later phase which struggles for expression.

In treating patients who have suffered from arrest of development, we often observe the process of re-birth in their dreams. Let me give two: A married lady with an unwanted child clings to the phase of sexual gratification and fails to develop her maternal instinct. She dreams as follows: 'I am at home in my drawing-room, and you and my husband are there. You are speaking to my husband, and as you speak he gets smaller and smaller until he sinks back into a grease-spot on the couch. Then I am in bed, and I notice my left breast is getting larger and larger, and then the right breast gets larger, and I am surprised that they remain large.' The first part of the dream may be interpreted as representing the passing of the sexual phase (her husband) and the emergence into power of her healing forces (represented by her doctor). The second part of the dream represented the birth of the maternal instincts (symbolized by the breasts), which till now have been repressed. Nor is this emergence a temporary, but a permanent condition. This dream *may* be interpreted as a transference of her libido from her husband to the doctor. But if so, the latter part of the dream sets that right by its immediate re-transference to her maternal instincts.

A patient of 50 years of age is sick with a neurosis: he has lost all interest in life. In his day of prowess he was a famous rowing-man, and he said to his soul in effect: 'I shall never do anything as great as that again', so he clings to that age, and lives upon his reputation – his development is arrested and he becomes neurotic. In the course of treatment the re-birth takes place, as illustrated in this dream: 'I was back in

Oxford, at Folly Bridge, to take the crew out. But the boatman says the boat is out of repair and I cannot take it out. Then I go on to the landing-stage, and you meet me and say, "There is an abundance of coal, and now is your opportunity."' His association with coal was 'the crude material of fire, life'. This dream tells him in symbolic language the uselessness of looking to his age of prowess: it is out of repair, out of date, and he must give it up. As soon as he abandons that, there comes the great opportunity, an abundance of crude material, of life and power within, which awaits development.

(1) Failure to pass on from one phase to another produces moral and nervous breakdown, for it produces a conflict between the old and the new. At the moment of re-birth we are 'between two worlds – one dead, one powerless to be born'. The new phœnix cannot be born before the old dies: the old blossom must pass before the fruit can come: the emotions cannot be transferred to the new ideal so long as they remain attached to the old.

It is a significant fact that the ages at which nervous breakdown most commonly takes place are these times of re-birth – 13, 18 to 20, 28 to 30, 40 to 45 in the woman; 50 to 55 in the man. The breakdown of character and nerve at these ages is frequently due to a failure to progress to the next age. To illustrate:

The married woman who refuses to have children, in order that she may continue to have full expression for her self-display or sexual instincts, finds herself becoming peevish and irritable. This irritability is caused by the suppression of her maternal instinct, by the dominance of the earlier sexual phase. The expression of the sexual instinct is closely followed by the emergence of the maternal instinct. If this latter is suppressed, a conflict ensues between the sexual and the maternal, with consequent breakdown and unhappiness. The man of 60 must surrender power to the younger man. If he nervously clings to his 'power' he pays the penalty in a breakdown, usually ascribed to 'over-work'.

(2) Thus the first condition of mental health is to advance with every phase of life, for at each re-birth there springs forth new life. Those who strive to 'remain young' merely succeed in becoming stale and fossilized. They become 'old fossils', a fossil being the petrified remains of an earlier phase. The man of 50 who tries to be a 'gay young dog', and 'one of the boys', is dominated by a psychology characteristic of the age of adolescence, and presents one of the most pathetic sights that the gods can behold. The woman of 50 who dresses like a flapper, and who fancies herself 'girlish' and 'fascinating', or loves to sit on a footstool by the fire, may fondly imagine that she has succeeded in keeping the blossom of her youth. She has, indeed, kept the blossom, but what a withered thing it is! The old phœnix refuses to die, and fancies itself young, but what a jaded bird!

The secret of perpetual youth is to grow old. The fruit of the new phase is always fresher than the withered blossom: life can only keep young by always advancing. The man of 30 keeps fresh by surrendering his athletic championships to develop his individual power and character: the healthy young mother is infinitely younger than the 'girlish' spinster of the same age. The woman of 45, whose interests have been for twenty years centred in her family, will remain young only by advancing to the phase in which she lets her interests spread to the wider concerns of human life around her. The man of 55 need never be 'on the shelf' if he voluntarily leaves the struggle for power to younger men, and is content to contribute to society the wisdom gained in the ripe experience of years. There are fresh instincts ready to spring forth at every re-birth of life, like the young phœnix, from the dead ashes of the old. By welcoming these we remain young, by advancing with age we achieve perpetual youth.

(3) It follows from these principles *that every age has to some extent a distinct moral standard.* Different countries different customs; different ages different ethics. So what is right for one phase and for one age is wrong for another. Pugnacity may be smiled at in a boy of 12: condemned in the man of

30. It is right for a man of 40, in the interests of justice, to speak the truth even against his best friend; the cause of truth must take precedence even over the interest of individuals. For a boy of 14 it is better to withhold the truth than to betray his comrades, for that is the age for the development of loyalty to the herd; the boy who will sneak at 13 will later in life basely betray his cause and country.

Since every age has its distinctive psychology it is very necessary not to impose a false standard at any specific age. To lay responsibilities on the child of 4, to expect a boy of 6 to be an 'example' to others, to compel a boy of 13 to read poetry, or to prevent him from writing it at 18, to ask a girl of 19 to accept the disillusioned view about marriage of her mother of 45, all these are attempts to impose unnatural standards upon those unfitted at their time of life to bear them.

So in different ages of life we should be judged by different moral standards. But the question arises: Is there, then, no one standard of morality for every age? There is, if not one standard, certainly one principle of morality for every age; the morality proper to every age is the fullest development of the emerging psychological functions and instincts characteristic of that age. When, for instance, the desire for display emerges in the girl of 15, its expression should not be discouraged, but directed to the formation of good taste. To repress it will deprive the girl in later life of that natural desire to please which gives charm to life and grace to conduct. Its repression may also mean that the cruder sexual desires are forced into too early prominence.

CHAPTER XVII

Individual and Social Morality

SO FAR WE have described the goal or end towards which all organisms are tending as completeness and fulfilment. In man we call it self-realization.

But such self-realization can come about only in a community: only in a social environment can a person find this fulfilment and happiness, and realize himself to the full.

The man who lives in isolation, as a hermit, whether in a desert, forest or lonely island can never have his personality completely fulfilled.

Such a man is subject to all kinds of dangers from wild animals, from storms, from famine in bad years, from diseases for which he has no remedy and no one to help; and it takes him all his time to scrape a miserable living from the soil. Without the companionship of others, his mental capacities and culture are extremely limited. Fear dominates his life and fear paralyses his soul.

In a community we have numerous privileges – armies to protect us against our foes, police to protect our home while we sleep peacefully or are away on holiday; when we are ill there are doctors at hand to minister to us and hospitals where skilled surgeons can operate on us without pain.

There are also the cultural amenities, clubs, pubs and churches, where we can meet our fellows to discuss the problems of the day and have our vision enlarged; concert halls and art galleries where we can hear the best of music and feast the eye on beautiful things – or unbeautiful ones according to one's taste!

But if we are to enjoy all these privileges, they bring with them certain responsibilities, in particular that we should permit others in the community to enjoy the same freedom. If we do not want others to steal from us, we must not steal from them; if we do not want them to seduce our wives or entice our husbands we must not seduce and entice theirs. If we want to travel in peace and safety on public roads, we must not endanger the lives of others by reckless driving and so deprive them of the same freedom we ourselves wish or enjoy. That is the social basis of morality. Morality in essence is common sense.

These obligations we owe to the community are therefore laid down in customs or embodied in laws, to be obeyed by all in the interests of all. So it is laid down that we must not steal; we should drive on our side of the road; we must not cross the traffic lights.

Laws are made for the freedom of all; they are not mere restrictions to our personal liberty, as so many think, but that all should enjoy greater freedom, ourselves included. What would happen if there were no regulations for traffic in Piccadilly Circus? The whole of the traffic would be jammed, and no one, including the man who tries to dash through, would be free to get through at all. As it is, by conforming to the law the traffic flows fairly evenly, and if there are slight delays, we know that *it is the restrictions that enable us to pass in good time.*

Some of these obligations are so necessary to the full enjoyment of the whole community, such as the laws against stealing and murder, that the breach of these regulations are regarded as *crimes* and severely punished.

Others are breaches of *good manners*, like telling tales, gossiping or yawning with open mouth in another's face. These are not punishable by law; but we dislike people who gossip or swank and brag, and simply do not invite such boorish people back. *Politeness, in essence, is simply consideration for others.* The punishment in these cases is merely social ostracism.

There are other forms of behaviour which are not absolutely forbidden nor yet in themselves punishable; but are definitely disapproved as being harmful to the community. These are *vices*. Thus in a civilized community prostitution is a vice, detrimental to the community in the spread of venereal disease, in the break-up of families and as a degradation of human nature. Gambling is considered a vice by many, because a man may gamble away all his money and leave his family destitute. A woman may be incited by the man at the back door to put her money on a 'certainty', and loses the money put aside for the mortgage – so that, as not infrequently occurs, the family has to lose their house and home. The clerk has a little flutter, loses, and ultimately has to resort to embezzlement to pay off his gambling debts. Over and over again in Courts, the youth charged with embezzling will explain that he lost money on the horses and had to embezzle to pay his debts.

Gambling is not prohibited by law: but it is discouraged to this extent that a man cannot recover gambling debts in Court – just as the law does not forbid prostitution, but it says you must not flaunt it in the streets to the annoyance of others.

The argument against gambling in principle is as follows: there are four ways of getting possession of things such as money: one is by gift such as birthday and Christmas presents; another is by trade where we exchange money for bread, meat and books to the mutual satisfaction; thirdly, by stealing, where one benefits and the other loses; and gambling where although the arrangement is mutual, say at cards, the loser is distressed. The essence of the matter is that the first two, gift and barter, make for good will of both participants; in the latter, stealing and gambling, one party is satisfied but it makes for distress and often ill-feeling between them. Minor forms of gambling, however, such as putting a half-crown on a horse every week, is perhaps worth it for the excitement of anticipation it gives, even if one loses. To some people it is the one excitement of the week.

Or take sex perversions: at the moment the authorities are at variance as to whether homosexuality in private with both parties consenting should be punishable or not.

Everyone now recognizes that a man is not responsible for being a homosexual: he has become so as a result of childhood experiences over which he had no control. That they are not innate is shown by the fact that many of them can be cured by discovering and dealing with these unconscious causes. (See my Article 'The Cure of Homosexuality', *British Medical Journal*, June 7th, 1958, p. 1323.) But though the community recognizes that the homosexual is not responsible for his being a homosexual, he is held responsible if he seduces and so perverts other people, especially boys – for *society must protect its members not only from the thief but from the pervert* (see p. 168). So in the army a soldier can be court-martialled for tuberculosis: not that he is in any way responsible for it, but at one time men who found themselves with tuberculosis would join up so as to live an open-air life. But in acting to their own benefit they were endangering others who lived in close quarters with them. The community cannot allow that.

The road hog cuts in and makes other people brake to avoid an accident. He gets in first and that is all he cares about. But the community of drivers condemn such a person as a pest, and cutting in as a dangerous vice, although it may not be punishable by law. But if it amounts to dangerous driving and not just discourteous driving, and particularly if it causes an accident, then the community steps in and says it must be punishable by law. Indeed, in repeated offences it takes away his freedom to drive, because he himself is in the habit of taking away the freedom of others to drive in peace. A law-abiding community, say in the matter of rules of the road or in queuing in shops, is one in which the individual has the greatest freedom.

What I am trying to say here is not *what* the community ought or ought not to approve or disapprove, but to establish that society, because of the privilege it bestows upon its members, has the right to insist on conditions and restrictions upon the individual which will safeguard the freedom and privileges of all in the community including himself, and protect them from those who will deprive them of their privileges.

Those who disobey such laws, and thereby endanger the lives of others, society claims the right to punish; those who would deprive us of our freedom must be punished by being deprived of their own freedom, and of the privileges they so lightly abuse.

Codes of behaviour vary according to the community. Boys in the gang period (13–14) have a code of honour very different from the adult. In a past generation the standard of moral behaviour of many was that of a 'gentleman'; a breed that is fast disappearing. They would do nothing but what befitted a gentleman. So strong was this motive that Dean Inge stated that if you told a bishop he was sinful, he would be unconcerned, but if you told him he was not a gentleman, he would be furious! It was said of the Kaiser that he resented most of all that the British did not regard him as a gentleman. Nor was he! He was far too self-opinionated and bombastic, lacking in that consideration of others, which is the essence of being a gentleman. So when a doctor falls in love with an attractive girl patient and has an affair with her, the community in the form of the General Medical Council strike him off the Medical Register, for it considers such conduct, if generally permitted, detrimental to the effective treatment of patients in the community – and irrespective of the fact that the young woman may have been quite willing and acquiescent. For him to plead that it is quite a natural thing for people in love to do impresses them not at all. 'You can do that sort of thing,' they say, 'but not, in the medical profession, with your patients.'

So, when an Oxford undergraduate has a girl student sleeping with him in his rooms in college all night, he may claim that it is a perfectly natural thing to do, but the community in the form of the College authorities say: 'We have no concern with your morals in general, but that sort of thing is not what you came to the University for, nor for which the country gives you grants and financial aid. For if that kind of thing became general so that men and girl students spent their nights in each other's rooms, and their days spooning in a punt on the Cherwell, there would be little work done. So you are forbidden to do that sort of thing here, but can do it elsewhere as far as we are concerned.' So they rusticate him elsewhere.

Such people, the doctor or the student as well as the road hog for whom good roads are supplied, are given great and special privileges by the community, and it is for the community to see that they do not abuse these privileges.

All such matters are not merely matters of individual judgement; the community, because of the privileges it bestows, has a say in the matter and the right to put its point of view which does not always coincide with that of the individual, but is for the freedom and benefit of all.

Moral principles. Having established by experience that there are certain forms of behaviour that are necessary to the life and well-being of the community, society embodies these in the form of moral principles. If it finds that stealing is detrimental to the community, it makes a law to that effect. Thereafter honesty is elevated to a moral principle, being regarded as 'right' and stealing as 'wrong'. Lying itself is not forbidden by law but it is considered a vice, and is punishable by law if by the lying another's character is defamed. The customs (mores) of the community are thus transformed into moral principles, and come to be regarded as right or wrong *in themselves.* Lying is 'wrong' in itself; stealing is 'wrong'; infidelity is 'wrong'.

Motives for moral living. We may then roughly describe the various phases in the development of moral behaviour, according to the stages of culture reached by particular individuals. For morality is progressive.

Group I. In the first place there are those who, usually on account of their up-bringing, flout the laws and customs of the community if they can get away with it. They do not subscribe to the moral code, and their only deterrent is fear of consequences. Why should they not do as they like, drive recklessly as long as there are no police traps; tell lies if they are not likely to be found out, or if they are, they brazen it out; have promiscuous sex relations as long as they can avoid the inconvenience of being landed with a baby, and if they do produce one, disclaim all responsibility? Such people are the rebels; they are *immature*: they have not yet grown up to their responsibilities as members of a community. For them street regulations are required in the interests of the community. But rules and regulations are not all that successful, for the simple reason that there is an obstinacy in human nature which makes us want to break rigid rules with which we are confronted. St. Paul said in a striking phrase, 'The law *made* sin.'

Group II. In the second group are those who do obey the laws but only because they must. They also are deterred by fear of punishment, but at least they are deterred. They conform to the habits of good taste because if they don't they will be ostracized by their fellows as outsiders, and are not asked back. They are outwardly polite, but they have no real consideration of others. In the religious sphere they are 'moral', but only for fear of Hell; or possibly the hope of Heaven, which is hardly less selfish. They conform, but their heart is not in it. If they are honest it is because it is the best policy. This group probably comprises the majority of people.

Group III. Then there are those – the more intelligent members of the community – who do not accept these moral principles on compulsion nor from fear of punishment, but readily and willingly adopt these principles and live up to them because they realize their reasonableness, and that these laws are necessary to the welfare of the whole community. Or they adopt them as their own guiding principles in life, even though in some cases they don't like them very much. They drive carefully on the roads, not only in their own interest nor as some irksome duty, but as a reasonable and necessary standard of behaviour. They respect the laws of marital fidelity, because they realize that to behave otherwise leads to trouble. Like everyone else they might like to tell lies to gain some advantage; but never in fact do so. They are honest and expect others to be so. In such cases the individual's conscience is almost identical with the social conscience. They have adopted moral principles as right *in themselves* and do not question every act.

If they diverge from the principles it is because they realize, like the prophets and seers of old, that there are moral principles of justice, honesty, truth and mercy which are higher than those at present adopted by the community, but which are for the higher welfare of all.

The fact that such a man may at times fail and fall from grace does not mean that he is any the less sincere.

It is the fashion in these days for those who belong to the first two groups and have little regard for moral principles to taunt this group as being 'hypocrites' and 'self-righteous'. Indeed the parable of the Pharisee and the publican has gone into reverse: instead of the Pharisee thanking God he is not as other men, it is the 'Publican' who thanks God that he is not a hypocrite like the Pharisee, or 'self-righteous' like those church-going people. This of course is only another form of self-righteousness, it is snobbishness in reverse.

Hypocrisy is vice pretending to be virtuous, which is a very different thing from a man sincerely and intelligently adopting moral standards and trying to live up to them. He recognizes his shortcomings only too well. There are of course numerous cases of true hypocrisy in which the taunt of hypocrisy is justified, where the vicious pretend to be righteous, but make no effort to be. For as the Marquis de Rochefoucauld said, 'Hypocrisy is the homage which vice pays to virtue.'

Group IV. Further, there are those who are actuated not so much by the acceptance of moral principles but by love of their fellows. They do not need to be told to be honest and not to steal, for they would never think of stealing from those they love. They do not need to ask whether an action is 'right' or 'wrong', for if they act for love of their fellow-men they will do nothing that will harm or hurt them. Thus it is that some people regard love as the basic principle of life. They do not need the law, for love is the fulfilment of the law. They are not bound by the law, and are even free to disobey the laws, such as the law of the Sabbath, if it is called for in the interests of love for their fellows.

The difficulty in practice is that so many meanings are given to the word love, from that of sex-gratification to the highest forms of spiritual love, that it will still take years, perhaps centuries, before the motive of love can be generally understood and practised by ordinary members of the community. But that is no reason why others should not believe in that form of love that considers only the welfare of those they love. In time the yeast will leaven the whole lump. Such people are often found amongst the religious but as often not.

Group V. The fourth group consists of those who are religious and accept moral laws as 'the Will of God' – that is to say they accept them as 'eternal principles' of the Universe, which hold good at all times, in all places and on all occasions. This rests on the belief that God, the ultimate Principle in the Universe, is Himself righteous and good. Many pagan gods, even the Greek gods on Olympus, leave much to be desired, according to our way of thinking, not only in their love-affairs, but also on account of the dirty tricks they played on people. Like God, like people: people cannot be expected to be moral if their gods are immoral; and the reverse holds good, that a belief in a moral and righteous God will mean that the people will be like their God.

Religion and Morality. It will be observed that in discussing the source of moral principles I have refrained from mentioning religious principles. If I seem to ignore the place of religion in moral progress it is because I wish to emphasize that the basic standards of morality are founded on social convenience and social necessity. That is not to decry religion as a great force in the upholding of moral principles. For the Church, in which I include all denominations and not only Christian, is in fact the only organization in the country that deliberately and systematically upholds and teaches morality as a necessity for social living and to full self-realization of each individual in the community. The State does so, but in a negative way, by means of inhibitions and threats of punishments: many school-teachers who consider the development of the child's whole personality, including character, do so, while others regard it as not their job. In ancient Greece it was the philosophers like Socrates, Plato, and Aristotle who taught men in the streets and in the market place how to live. But philosophers of the present day, secluded as they are in their colleges, have very little impact upon the community as a whole. The Churches alone are the only organizations actively teaching and upholding moral principles.

I cannot therefore agree with the 'humanists' of the present day who regard religion as a set-back to morality.

But it is true that there are certain aspects of its teaching, which I outlined in my Presidential Address before the Conference of Educational Associations some years ago, which deserve criticism. I refer principally to the claims of some Churchmen that morality without religion is of no worth: that the only true motive of morality should be devotion to God, who is regarded as righteous. If that is held, then those who do not believe in religion will find good reason to throw over morality altogether. They may argue, 'If religion is the only source of morality, as I don't believe in religion, there is no need for me to be moral.' That I believe has been taking place in the community: as people leave the Churches they tend to abandon moral practices. My thesis throughout this chapter – obvious as it is – is that morality is a natural ingredient of communal life, fortified by religion, but not dependent upon it.

Moses found it of great value to preface his Ten Commandments with the statement 'Thus saith the Lord', and this acted as a strong incentive to moral living. But the fact that religious people support their moral living on the grounds that it is the Will of God does not detract from the fact that it is necessary for those who do not believe in religion to maintain these principles, for they are necessary for the welfare of the community.

CHAPTER XVIII

Individual and Social Conscience

THIS BRINGS US to consider an important distinction which I have not seen in any book on Ethics, although it must have been noted – the difference between the individual conscience, and what for want of a better term we shall call a social conscience.

A simple illustration will make this clear. A boy goes robbing an apple orchard. He himself has no conscience about that at all, and the more apples he gets the better. He knows however that other people would consider it wrong and that he will be punished if found out. Therefore he takes all necessary precautions to avoid detection. This distinction is of great importance in Courts of Law and constitutes the difference between the medical and the legal professions when the plea is one of insanity. According to the McNaghten rules to prove non-responsibility it is laid down that the accused 'did not know what he was doing was wrong'. The medical profession takes this to mean that he was deficient in that he had no sense of right and wrong – as so often with a mental deficient. The legal profession interprets the phrase as meaning – Did he know that what he was doing was wrong *according to the law*? A person suffering from psychopathic personality may be totally lacking in a moral sense, as indeed are some who have suffered from sleeping sickness, affecting the brain. If such a person after committing a murder late at night puts up a ladder to get into his room at his hotel, the law takes it to mean that he must have known that what he was doing was wrong. Not necessarily: all he did know was that others would consider it wrong and that he could be hanged if discovered, as he was in the case I have in mind. So a woman suffering from involutional melancholia (a form of insanity) might kill her child to save him from all the distress of life. She considers that she is doing quite right in doing so; she has no conscience in the matter; but she also knows it is against the law, and is quite prepared to accept the penalty. Should she be hanged?

There are cases like the obsessional individual who may have a morbid conscience and severe sense of guilt regarding his behaviour which is based on a stricter moral standard than those of the community. There are also the prophets and seers who have higher standards than those of their fellows.

But usually the community has a higher sense of moral values and a saner judgement than most individuals. The reasons for this are interesting.

The main differences between the individual conscience and the social conscience are:

(*a*) The community has a *long-term view* of things. The experience of the individual, say the adolescent, is very limited; he may think a course of action is a good one, but he has never tried it before and he cannot be sure of its results. The experience of the community is vast and from its observation of human nature it is able to prescribe with some accuracy what is a satisfactory line of conduct and what is not. This experience is embodied in what we call, in minor forms, *convention*; in more important matters, *tradition. Tradition is the embodiment of the experience of the race.*

Conventions and traditions should therefore be respected for they are probably right as they are based on such wide experience of the community.

But they are not always right; for circumstances change and the reason for behaving in a certain way may no longer hold, as we shall later show in regard to polygamous practices. The fact that something has always been done, like certain ways of farming or of bringing up children, or of conducting a church service, in a certain way may still be right, but it may be quite wrong under modern needs and conditions. In that case it is necessary from time to time to study and revise these traditions, discover what were the original reasons for them, which were probably good reasons, but which may be outmoded, and determine new laws and customs if they do not still hold.

But simply to flout convention outright because it *is* conventional is stupid folly and itself proves the individual who does this to be incapable of forming correct judgements. Where the experience of the individual is limited he is well advised to listen to the opinions of others of wider experience and then himself decide on his course of action, for the final decision must always be his.

To her first adult party goes a girl of 16 who does not know that wine has the effect of removing inhibitions which would make her less capable of refusing wine, until she may do something really foolish which she regrets. It is surely common sense that she be warned by those of wider experience; and recommended to take one glass only at this first party.

Neglect of such advice often ends in disaster. A patient of mine, a girl of 16 at a boarding convent school, was seized in the night with a severe abdominal pain in which she felt her whole abdomen coming out. She was in fact getting a baby, but she had no idea that she was pregnant nor how she had become pregnant.

It was traced to an all-night party on a Destroyer nine months before where they were all having a good time, and in which the wine removed both her inhibitions and her memory of the event.

Is it not right that the community here, in the form of the parents with their wider experience, should warn a girl of the consequences of such behaviour, in her own interests as well as those of others?

(*b*) Another great difference between individual and social morality is that the individual is so often *swayed by passion* which affects his judgement, whereas the community is more dispassionate in the way it draws its conclusions and makes its judgement. A girl may know that it is stupid to give way to her sexual impulses, but in a moment of passion she is swayed by the immediate gratification of her impulses. The community, drawing upon its past experience, can pass on its deliberate judgement that it does not pay in the long run. Which is likely to be the better judgement is not difficult to see. In a fierce argument it is natural that a man should lose his temper, as every schoolboy does; but experience shows that the man who restrains his anger is more likely to achieve his ends. Hence the moral principle handed down by tradition urges us to keep our temper, to control our passions. A boy or girl should have learnt this long before puberty.

(*c*) A further characteristic of the social conscience as against the individual conscience is that *the social conscience can go on principles only*. It has to deal with people in the mass, and what is best as a whole; and because it deals only with principles, it can take little notice of individual cases – for hard cases make bad law!

Yet it does concede exceptions, and this in accordance with the general principle of maintaining the life of the community. 'Thou shalt not kill' is a hard-and-fast principle, yet the law exonerates you if you kill in self-defence. In war you are *expected* to kill, but still in self-defence of homes and families.

There is a law against crossing traffic lights – and yet both fire brigades and ambulances constantly do so, and they are not brought to book – unless they are involved in an accident in doing so. It is illegal for a doctor to produce an abortion; but he is never prosecuted if he does so to save the mother's life, for it is considered that the mother's life is worth more than the child's.

Exceptions do not invalidate the general principle. Even the ambulance men and the fire brigade are taken to task if they cause an accident, though probably this would be dealt with leniently. But this does not mean that anyone can go dashing across the lights in order to get first on the golf club or to meet his girl friend.

For the trouble is that, human nature being what it is, if

any form of behaviour is condemned, but allowable in certain cases, everyone will of course consider his own case an exception which is permitted. In the long run the exception would become the rule! If therefore we break the rule or flout tradition we must have very good reason for claiming to be exceptions before the community will accept our plea.

Let us then apply these principles to one or two present-day issues.

Divorce. Why on earth should the community interfere in so personal a matter as whether or not two married people wish to live together any longer? What business is it of the State to lay down laws about it and make it difficult? After all people voluntarily enter marriage; why should they not be able to break it voluntarily? It is surely a private matter. But is it?

If we are Roman Catholics we oppose divorce of any kind on religious grounds (although they permit of separation), since marriage is a sacrament, and as such is life-long and indissoluble. The Anglican Church is divided on the subject; some priests consent to re-marry people who have been divorced while others refuse to marry even the innocent partner. Most Nonconformist ministers would consent to marry divorcees, even the guilty partners, provided they are satisfied that there is real repentance for past misdemeanours, but would refuse it in other cases, for Nonconformists are more concerned with the moral as distinct from the sacramental view of marriage.

According to the Law, as Lord Jowett, the late Lord Chancellor, once said to me – marriage is merely a contract, like making a contract for a sack of potatoes: but, he added, the only difference is that if the sack of potatoes turn out to be rotten you can return them!

There are however other psychological and social problems involved beside the purely legal.

The Russians after the First World War tried the system of allowing free divorce; a man or woman need do nothing else than go into the appropriate office and declare his marriage was at an end. He was asked why, but at the same time told it was not necessary for him to give a reason. That was found not to work; it disturbed communal life too much.

Our community does not forbid divorce altogether, but it discourages people from playing fast and loose with marriage by making it difficult to break a marriage.

On the whole it is probably the women of the country who are most strongly against divorce, for no woman wishes to be discarded at her husband's will and humiliated as soon as he finds someone more attractive – although nowadays, as women are more economically independent, it is commonly the wives who take the initiative and break the marriage, even abandoning their children.

The reason why in this and most civilized countries divorce is discouraged and the reason for maintaining the stability of marriage is two-fold. First of all if men are allowed a free-for-all to seduce other men's wives, or wives to entice other women's husbands, this often leads to bitterness, anger, strife, violence and not uncommonly murder. The community takes a poor view of this. It is a nuisance to the community when the enraged husband shoots the co-respondent. It makes a mess, the police are called in, and it disturbs the life and peace of the community, which therefore clamps down on it. It denounces the seducer as a sex hog, for the same reason as we denounce the road hog, because he deprives others of their rights.

The second and to many the more cogent reason is that divorce breaks up our family life and is therefore bad for the children, who thereby suffer from insecurity, which is a common cause of delinquency and of unhappiness in the child. This applies even when there is no bitterness and resentment between the parents, for the children are still deprived of a stable home and family life. The child who loves both parents is distressed at the separation and cannot understand it. It is not so harmful if the children are grown up or even adolescent for they are independent of their parents psychologically.

Society claims to make these strictures against the break-up of families because it takes a long-term view of these matters, and is not motivated by passion in the same way as the participants. It is concerned to see that the children who will constitute its future citizens have the opportunity of health and happiness.

Therefore the community does not look with particular favour on a woman who produces three or four children, gets bored with them and with her husband, and makes off with a man who will give her a 'good time'. Having had a 'good time', the man often returns her like a sack of potatoes gone rotten. Such parents are lacking in concern for their children; the community is concerned because it is saddled with the responsibilities which the parents cast on them.

These are good reasons for the community discouraging divorce.

Nevertheless, the community, as represented by the laws of the country, does not forbid divorce altogether, for being of a practical turn of mind, and keeping in mind its ultimate aim, it realizes that the retention of a marriage which is a series of quarrels and bickering is worse for the child than for the home to be broken, though that in itself is a hazard.

The community also realizes that in some cases it is the nagging of a wife that drives the husband away; or that it is the cynicism and scorn of a husband which becomes unbearable to a wife who therefore finds more sympathy and love in another man who may also be kinder to the children. Therefore, the Court, in the interests of the child, may give the custody of the children to the so-called 'guilty' partner. It is all practical, common sense and done with a purpose.

Divorce then is obviously not a purely personal matter, for the parties concerned to decide. It affects the whole community especially in regard to the effect upon the children who will constitute the community in the next generation.

Pre-marital and extra-marital relations. A kindred subject to that of extra-marital relations is pre-marital relations, which in recent years has been regarded with a more indulgent eye, and has given rise to a great deal of controversy. Why does society, still, regard it with disfavour?

The problem is contained in the phrase 'Is Chastity outmoded?'

When it is asked, 'Is Chastity outmoded?' this term 'outmoded' is capable of two meanings which are often confused. It may mean that it is no longer the custom or mode in the community as a simple statement of fact: or it may mean that it is now old-fashioned, to be discarded, and no longer to be expected of our young people – which is not a mere statement of fact, but a moral issue.

On the question of fact there can be little doubt that extra-marital relations are far commoner than in previous years as evidenced by the fact that one out of every four births are conceived out of wedlock, and from the statements of adolescents themselves. The headmistress of a school in the United States, when asked how she regarded adolescent schoolgirls who got pregnant, replied simply that they didn't know their job!

This of course is obviously not a new problem. In a village near where I live there is a tombstone which says:

> '*Here lies ——'s daughter Charlotte,*
> *She was born a virgin, she died a harlot,*
> *For fifteen years she kept her virginity*
> *Which is pretty good going for our vicinity.*'

Chastity is certainly not old-fashioned; promiscuity is far more old-fashioned, for instance amongst aboriginals, although even they have their tribal rules and taboos. But promiscuity is outmoded in civilized countries.

At the same time chastity is not something new, developed by the Puritans and promulgated by Queen Victoria. Chastity was far more strictly observed amongst such tribes as the Red Indians before they were depraved by the 'civilized' white man, for a Red Indian father would put to death a daughter who was guilty of unchastity.

Why is it then that the community regards with disfavour

such pre-marital relations. The fact that it does so is proved by the fact that society is shocked when it reads that at Oxford University chastity is quite outmoded (which is by no means the case, but newspapers must have something spicy to fill their pages), and also from the fact that those who believe in free love are so anxious to prove that what they are doing is acceptable.

When people ask 'Is Chastity outmoded?' the emphasis is usually in the affirmative: they seem to argue that as 'everybody's doing it' (from the first definition) that it is right (according to the second definition). But suppose 90 per cent of girls had pre-marital relations (which personally I think is far in excess of the real number, for many adolescents boast of affairs they never had), that would not mean that the community is not justified in condemning a practice which results in so many disasters to social life and to its members. It does not *forbid* pre-marital relations or regard it as a crime, but it condemns it as a vice, as it does prostitution, which also it does not forbid. Such disapproval is not puritanic; it is simply common sense.

What then are these consequences which compel the community to take note of a practice which appears on the surface to be so innocuous? The consequences are personal and social. Let us look the facts in the face.

Take a common illustration: Here is a girl who is persuaded by a man to have sex relations: she is reluctant to do so, for every normal girl has hesitation in committing herself to its consequences, but he assures her that he loves her, and as love is what she is wanting, she allows herself to be carried away and acquiesces. After the man has gratified his passion, he leaves her, disclaims all responsibility if she becomes pregnant, and has no more use for her. It is the end for him; for the girl it is only the beginning. The psychological effect on her is that she is disillusioned about love; that 'that is all he wanted'. She feels cast aside, depressed and anxious. In other cases she becomes hard-boiled, and having once had sex relations, and having lost her virginity, she says 'What does it matter?' and has other affairs without love. Many prostitutes start in that way – after a seduction.

Or it may be an engaged couple, who, they declare, cannot get married yet. That may work out quite well and if pregnancy occurs they get married. But it very often does not work out so happily. The engagement may be broken off, usually by the man, as engagements often are, and the affair ends in anti-climax. The fact that the girl has committed herself so completely, body, mind and soul, makes such a break far more devastating than a break of an ordinary engagement.

Suppose the girl becomes pregnant and the man refuses all responsibility perhaps because he is married. What is the girl to do?

She can go to the woman round the corner and get an abortion. Apart from the fact that this unskilled surgery often ends disastrously to her physical health, what is the effect on her mind? The first effect is relief at her escape from her immediate problem; but what should be the happiest event of her life, the supreme joy of motherhood, is transformed into a secretive, sinister and sordid experience.

I once had a young woman patient, the daughter of a distinguished man, who became pregnant. Because they were Roman Catholics, she did not have an abortion, but had the child adopted immediately after birth; without her even seeing it. She was later sent to me for kleptomania – compulsive stealing – though she had no need of what she stole. And why stealing? Because although she had fully acquiesced in the adoption, she subconsciously suffered from a deep sense of loss; she was missing something. Her stealing was the symbolic representation of a compulsion to get something – although she did not realize what it was. It was a hunger of the soul for her lost motherhood.

People talk a lot about the repression of sex: what of the repression of motherhood in such cases?

There is a physiological basis for such a disturbance.

It is one of the miracles of reproduction that the physiological processes in the woman follow a certain sequence, regulated by the endocrine secretions: first the ovum is produced, discharged, meets the spermatozoa. When it is fertilized another group of processes takes place in the womb to nourish the fertilized ovum, until the birth of the child; whereupon another set of processes takes place, the lactogenic hormones get to work producing milk and the milk of human kindness, tenderness and love, the expression of which is the mother's greatest joy.

If a woman interferes with nature's process by an abortion or by giving away the new-born child, she represses that maternal instinct, with unhappy consequences to herself and to the child.

It is for that reason that some girls finding themselves pregnant elect to have and to keep the child whatever the consequences. They are to be admired, for thus they are following nature's plan. If they happen to be well-to-do, it is not so disastrous; as in a patient of mine who delivered herself of a baby at the age of 42, the father of the baby being her father's best friend (though her father was unaware of this liaison). He had a wife and family and he did not want to risk his reputation as a 'respectable man', or as he put it, he wanted to 'do his duty to his family'. But as he often visited his friend he often saw his friend's daughter – his lover – and the child. In spite of these most favourable and affluent conditions the boy grew up anxiety-ridden, a hopeless neurotic, for a child soon senses the anxiety surrounding his home and the mystery about his birth.

Apart from the contribution a father makes to a child's upbringing, children who have no father grow up feeling 'different' from other children, and to feel different is one of the worse experiences for a child, for children are very sensitive about their parenthood. It is quite different where in a family the father is, say, killed in war. That loss of the father is bad enough, but the child had a father and can think of him with pride and admiration; whereas the illegitimate child has no father. There are other instances of children, the result of 'free-love' of well-known people whose names I will not mention, who have turned out hopelessly neurotic.

But in most cases, the mother, unmarried and not well off, has to go out to work, parking the child out often in unsuitable conditions with people who have no particular love for the child. The child develops a feeling of inferiority, of not being wanted, a feeling he may maintain all through life, robbing him of all real confidence and happiness. Years ago I had a patient of this sort. The mother was a school-teacher and lost her job on account of this child. She was penniless (for there was no public assistance in those days), and so tried on two occasions to stifle the child, but could not bring herself to do so at the last moment. The child became a homosexual for which he came to me for treatment and of which he was cured by the discovery of its cause. Why homosexual? Because this early experience gave him a fear of women and therefore his only resort was for men and boys.

The final option of a girl who finds herself pregnant is to make the man marry her and 'make an honest woman of her'. What chance has such a marriage got of being a happy one, when the girl marries a man whom she would not otherwise want to marry, and the man marries a girl with whom he is not in love, under compulsion? Not a hope! And what chance have the children brought up in a loveless home?

Another ill consequence of extra-marital relations is the spread of venereal disease. The present-day promiscuity amongst the young has led to a great increase of venereal disease which is devastating in its results if left unrecognized or untreated. It is stated that there are more deaths from venereal disease than from tuberculosis and polio put together. Gonorrhoea can produce life-long ill-health in a woman. Syphilis, if not adequately treated, and often it is not, may lead not only to insanity but to the transmission of the disease to the innocent children. One of the saddest cases I have ever had to deal with, years ago, concerned a man who brought his three daughters, exceptionally handsome and beautiful girls. In a passion during the war he had contracted syphilis, and knowing the consequences, had treatment before marrying, until he was declared free from the disease. He then married – and *all three daughters had congenital syphilis as a result.* The distress of himself and his wife and the bewilderment of the girls, who found themselves the objects of a concern they did not understand, can well be imagined. Was it worth it?

Apart from individual cases, *the effects on the community* are disturbing. I have known a case of syphilis caught by a person as a result of someone with the disease coughing in his face. Kissing, especially with cracked lips, can have the same result. But by far the most common cause is sex relations with an infected person. Medical officers do what they can to stop the spread of this disease, but in spite of the propaganda it increases.

The community is naturally concerned about this spread of disease amongst its members.

It is no argument to say that these people should take precautions against such diseases and get adequate treatment. Many do, but the fact is that although such treatment is available and has been for many years venereal disease is widespread, and on the increase.

It is also pointless to argue that there are contraceptives to prevent unwanted births and those having pre-marital relations should take these precautions. Some do: but contraceptives have been in existence for many years and the *fact* is that one out of every four births are conceived extra-maritally, and numerous illegitimate children are thrown upon the community to care for at great expense.

The community has after all some say in the matter. It objects to a girl spawning infants all over the place and then leaving it to the community to clear up the mess, in the same way as it objects to the litter-bugs who visit seaside resorts, take advantage of all the amenities, including life-saving devices, and then leave their litter about for the local council to clear up. The community argues in both cases, 'Why should they have all the fun and leave us the mess to clear up?'

These cases, but a few out of my experience, are by no means exceptional and may be multiplied without number. Far from being unique, they are common experience.

In view of all these disastrous results – psychological distress, venereal disease, this begetting of unwanted babies, compulsory marriages – it is not surprising that the community does not look with particular favour on the results, and also on the promiscuity which is the circumstance of these results. Moreover with its long-term and dispassionate view of such consequences, it feels it necessary to warn its daughters against being led away by their passions. If it is claimed that there are exceptions which work satisfactorily, the answer of the community is that it deals with principles; that it has its own interests to serve apart from those of individuals; and that hard cases make bad law.

It is said that promiscuity before marriage does not preclude a happy marriage later. I have had two patients who married prostitutes in the course of their amorous adventures. One of these marriages was quite happy, the woman being sick of her previous life and nauseated by it. In the other case the wife had developed extravagant tastes and when his considerable fortune had run out, left him for a rich master-builder, who incidentally became insane. In any case pre-marital relations make it far easier for each party to have illicit affairs which tend to the break-up of family life and is bad for the children. Such relations are therefore generally and justifiably discouraged by the community.

Two other types of case may be mentioned to illustrate our general principle.

Free love. A young man and woman married with the understanding that each should be permitted 'free love' with others if they wished. After a time another young man invited the wife to go off with him for a weekend. Encouraged by her husband, she did so, not very enthusiastically, but to live up to her principles! The result? – the husband who had encouraged her developed an anxiety neurosis and came to me for treatment, at the same time kicking himself for his inability to maintain his principles without working himself up into a state of anxiety about it. It was however his deep-rooted sense of guilt which was asserting itself: his 'free love' was merely a defiant rebelliousness not based on reason.

Religious people sometimes say that only by the Grace of God do they keep themselves chaste and their passions controlled. Well and good! But what about those who have not the aid of the Grace of God for the simple reason that they do not believe in God? For them there is another reason for their not giving way to their passions and that is that it is stupid.

Unlike the aforementioned Charlotte (p. 154) there are, still, girls who value their virginity, and are prepared to surrender it only to the man whom they select to be their partner in life, the father of their children, and the protector of their life and home, their companion through life. The female is selective, not prepared to unite with anybody. Even many females in animal life are selective and the lioness, like the female of the human species, will fight furiously against a male not of her choosing. This selective process on the part of the female is a provision of nature, by which the best of the species is chosen so as to produce the most vigorous race. This selectivity is an innate propensity, not lightly to be cast aside. To many girls therefore their virginity is their most priceless possession, the most valuable gift they have to bestow. For a girl to surrender her virginity to a man, only to find that having satisfied himself he decides he does not want to marry her, is a shock and a humiliation. She feels that she has made herself 'cheap', by which she means she has sold her virginity for a passing pleasure, instead of its being the symbol of permanent love and happiness. For, as Dr Mace has rightly said, there is a difference in the sexes, for whilst a man gives love in order to get sex, the girl gives sex in order to get love. To be refused that love after surrendering her sex is a humiliation and a disillusion. As one girl said, after spending the night with a sailor, 'I have never had so much "fun" with so little pleasure'.

In bringing forward these cases I am not pretending to lay down the law as to what our moral standards should be. That is not the job of a psychologist, whose concern is with the facts, and these I have tried to present.

It is said that moral decisions must ultimately be the responsibility of the individual, and that is correct. But in coming to a decision the individual has to take into consideration two important factors – first, the possible harmful consequences to himself and those immediately concerned, and in this he would be wise to take into consideration the long term view of the community with its wide experience as to what those consequences are likely to be; and secondly, he must take into consideration the welfare of the community as a whole whose privileges he enjoys, and to whom therefore he owes responsibilities. When it is claimed, however, as so often it is in the matter of extra-marital relations, that what two people do is their own concern and no business of anyone else, that is entirely false. 'No man liveth unto himself'; every person is not only individual but a member of the community. All that he does affects the community; on the other hand, the community is concerned with the welfare and happiness of each of its members.

When a youth on a summer holiday defies the local fisherman and sets sail in a threatening storm, or swims in dangerous currents, one may say; 'If he drowns himself, it is his own concern!' That is not so, for when he capsizes or gets carried away by the current, others have to go to his rescue at the risk of their lives and not infrequently at the loss of their lives. He should have listened to the advice of those of greater experience.

It is precisely the same with problems like those of sex relations. It is *not* merely a matter for the individual; it is the concern of the community as well.

But suppose the community itself adopts wrong aims and standards? Then it decays as so many nations have done in history, and must give place to others of sterner stuff.

CHAPTER XIX

The New Morality

THESE PRINCIPLES AS to the origin and basis of moral behaviour may be illustrated by the modern movement known as the 'New Morality', a sample of which is contained in a pamphlet by a group of Quakers under the title 'Towards a Quaker View of Sex'.

Most of the pamphlet is common sense and sincere, containing facts and opinions generally accepted by most intelligent people. In other aspects I found the pamphlet rather amusing, for the writers try so hard to be ambiguous with very little success. For it is clear that, in plain language, whilst disclaiming promiscuity (though they do not say why), they condone fornication and adultery *in certain cases.*

One of the writers for instance takes up the point that a *ménage à trois*, the one man/two women partnership, may work out very happily. Another takes the view that it may do a 'nervous youngster' a lot of good to fall in love with a happily married woman – presumably having sex relations with her. They also seem to regard homosexuality as natural and normal in some people.

I am myself of Quaker ancestry though not myself a Quaker (my great-grandmother, a Quakeress, was 'converted' by John Wesley himself, but remained a Quaker. Later she contracted a runaway marriage – which shows a catholicity of interest which I think I must have inherited!). But in this matter I must declare myself on the side of the angels, not of the Quakers.

It is a little difficult to know precisely what these writers are getting at – indeed, they confess they don't quite know themselves. The first thing that springs to the mind of a psychologist (they are suspicious people) looking impartially at these statements is a suspicion that in advocating these views they may be simply excusing their own earlier, or perhaps present, peccadilloes; or else that they would like to commit them but daren't. Then there is the subtle influence of rationalization which is such a trap to the unwary. It is so easy for anyone to say that he is actuated by sympathy for the poor unmarried girl (who may be neurotic anyway), when it is mainly for his self-gratification – and so to give motives for his conduct more plausible than the real motive. A normal healthy girl takes not being married in her stride; she has plenty of outside interests, and soon accommodates herself to unmarried bliss, which has many compensations. Many women do not marry owing to their having neurotic disorders; but it is an logical fallacy to assume that they became neurotic *because* they did not marry!

Ménage à trois. But to look at these statements: if they are taken to be mere statements of fact, what they state cannot be denied – for sometimes, though rarely, the *ménage à trois* may work out quite satisfactorily and no doubt some nervous youngsters would be thrilled to have affairs with happily married women in which they have all the fun and no responsibilities. But these opinions are obviously intended not merely as statements of fact, for in that case it would have been incumbent on the authors to have balanced them with the other side of the picture – those numerous cases in which they work out badly and do harm. That is completely ignored. For what concerns society is the welfare of the community as a whole, and that what may work out quite satisfactorily in exceptional cases would, if generally accepted, work out disastrously for members of the community as a whole. Society has to watch out that what is advanced as a permissible exception does not become the rule.

For this is quite certain, that human nature being what it is – and certainly it *is* – every married man who has the inclination to take another girl friend into his house as a second 'wife' would claim that his is the exceptional case. He would persuade his reluctant wife that it would be so kind to give the girl a home, that in fact it is the only Christian thing to do; and if he put forth high enough motives no doubt some wives would be won over, although it is difficult to see what she gets out of it, unless she is bored with her husband, or is taking a fancy to another man and is glad to have an excuse to be 'kind' to *him*! One or two rare cases where the *ménage à trois* works out satisfactorily do not off-set a hundred other cases where it works out badly and engenders jealousy and hatred. One has only to look at the divorce courts to see what bitterness and hatred can replace love in such cases – and the disastrous results on the children.

But there are also personal reasons. Years ago I was consulted by a woman who had lived with a Member of Parliament and his wife. The wife disliked sex relations and was glad to have the other woman to relieve her of this, and all was amicably arranged. After two years the third party left, for although she had a comfortable home, the love of a man she liked, and satisfaction for her sex desires, there was the fact that she was *not* his wife, and that on all public occasions it was the wife who accompanied him and received the honours, while she was put in the background. It was to regain her self-respect that she abandoned all these not inconsiderable pleasures and privileges. The right solution of course would have been for the wife to have treatment for her frigidity – or for their marriage to be lived on a higher plane of love, although that is probably too much to expect of ordinary human nature.

The acceptance of this 'new morality' opens up all kinds of possibility. If one man/two women, why not two men/one woman? This indeed was the case of my neighbours living in the next shack to me on a ranch near Calgary, where two men shared one 'wife'. That also seems to have worked out satisfactorily because of the shortage of women. Farther north, near Edmonton, so I was informed by a friend, there was one woman who 'served' all the men in a lumber camp, some dozens, and preferred this life to married bliss. Would the 'new morality' approve of this since it worked out satisfactorily, and the woman was being 'kind' to the sex-starved men? Most people would look on it with disfavour in spite of the exceptional circumstances since it is a perversion of the sexual instinct from its original purpose of reproduction and is also altogether devoid of love.

In any case why stop at two 'wives'? Why not several, as in the case of the clergyman who some years ago set up an *Agapemone*, an Abode of Love, with a number of women cloistered with him in unmarried bliss? There would nowadays be no difficulty in a man having several wives on grounds of finance for the wives could easily earn their living, and any children could, as in some African communities, be regarded as having a number of mothers. Indeed it might be quite a good financial proposition. As far as I know it worked out quite satisfactorily but I have not yet heard that it has been generally adopted by the Lambeth Conference.

There is a good deal to be said for polygamy, especially as a social service for the surplus women; but somehow it has not caught on. In fact the trend in evolution is in the reverse direction, towards monogamy. There are indeed cases where polygamy may be regarded as perfectly justifiable and works out very satisfactorily, as at one time amongst the Mormons. Settling in a newly undeveloping country there was need for all the children they could produce, to populate the region and develop their religion. Nor did it work out as badly as one would imagine. I have stayed, during a trek on horseback from Calgary to Montana, at a Mormon Settlement, and there, although polygamy was prohibited by United States law, the men had several 'cousins' living with them. They lived in peace and there were no jealousies amongst the women, who preferred to be one of several wives, and have a home and children, than remain spinsters. The original need for such polygamous marriages has now passed and Mormon families have settled down to monogamy and that not only because of the compulsion of the law. It is extraordinary to what human nature can accommodate itself as in the abolition of jealousy in such homes. The fine German frauleins chosen by Hitler to mate with the finest specimens of men to produce the Master race quite willingly gave up their babies after birth, so I was informed by a British officer who after the war had charge of such a camp. The girls accepted the conditions from the first and did not demur; though what the ultimate effect of the suppression of the maternal instinct was is not related. But if they later married and had children of their 'own', probably it worked out quite well. But no other country, as far as I know, has taken up this excellent idea!

So amongst the Moslems the constant wars in the name of Allah meant a depletion in the male population, and a great surplus of women. The need for more children made polygamy desirable and justifiable. As this need is passing (for in the world today, the danger is not under- but over-population), many Moslems have by choice one wife only and a country like Turkey has definitely pronounced for monogamy. Why they should have proclaimed this self-denying ordinance is a psychological problem which those who advocate any breach of the monogamous impulse would do well to study. Queen Soraya could still be Empress today if she had acquiesced in the King taking another wife even for the admirable object of getting an heir to the throne. But she preferred exile. Let it be noted, however, in both these cases – the Mormons and the Moslems – the 'exceptions' were for the good of the community, not for the convenience of the individual.

The reason for this trend towards monogamy is not only because it works out better; but it works out better because as I have explained there is a trend in evolutionary development towards monogamy since by that means the family is established, with the result that the offspring are better cared for, and are therefore better able to survive. Thus polygamy is becoming 'outmoded'.

Homosexuality. As for homosexuality, however sympathetic we may be with the homosexual who has a condition for which he is in no way responsible (p. 139), the fact remains that it *is* an abnormality, and cannot be regarded in the same light as heterosexuality. To treat it, as in a poem quoted with approval in this Quaker pamphlet, as equivalent to being condemned for having red hair is to misrepresent the facts. It is true that the homosexual is not responsible for this condition, but that does not mean that it is innate or constitutional like red hair: for when we analyse homosexuals we always find that this condition arises from specific and abnormal conditions in early childhood: homosexuality is acquired not innate, although constitutional factors do play a part.[1] Moreover many of these men come for treatment, realizing that there is something abnormal about them and that not just because of social disapproval. Thirdly because homosexuality is usually associated with other symptoms, especially depression (one of them told me he could always recognize other homosexuals by the sad look in their eyes).

The third instance of the 'new morality', as mentioned in the Quaker pamphlet, says, 'By the same token, it would surely help a nervous youngster to fall in love with a happily married woman' – presumably from the context, having sex relations with her. We are of course familiar with this same idea which was the theme of Marie Lloyd's famous song 'A little of what you fancies does you good!' If it does you good it is apparently permissible! Such affairs between a young man and a married woman, far from being 'new', were the common practice in this country during the Romantic period – and were 'outmoded' long ago.

It is also the line taken by some psychiatrists who, to overcome sex complexes, recommend a young man or young woman to 'take a lover' – advice which Freud went out of his way to denounce as bad psychotherapy. In some cases it may work; in others it may precipitate a greater sense of guilt and anxiety.

[1] See my *Psychology and Mental Health*, pp. 379 f.: and *British Medical Journal*, June 7th, 1958, p. 1323, 'The Cure of Homosexuality'.

If one is going to encourage the 'nervous youngsters' to fall in love with a happily married woman (First catch your woman, as Mrs Beeton might say, although I suspect there would be little difficulty if she were appealed to on high enough moral grounds!) I have a suspicion that there will be a great increase in the number of 'nervous young men' in the community, all ready to join the queue.

What I should like to know from the Quakers is on what principles one is to judge of exceptions. I suspect that what the advocates of this 'new morality' are sincerely aiming at in putting forth these exceptions is to counter the idea that forms of moral behaviour like honesty and chastity are 'right' or 'wrong' *in themselves* or as such, so that exceptions are permissible.

It is a little difficult to understand in any case what is meant by right and wrong '*in themselves*' – unless we take it to mean the absolute Will of God. It would take a philosopher to explain what is meant, and then we should probably be no farther.

But when ordinary people claim that some forms of behaviour like kindness or honesty are 'right' and others like cruelty are 'wrong' *in themselves*, they mean that they are contrary to the principles of conduct which have been adopted by oneself and others as a guide to communal living (see p. 142). By 'wrong' in themselves they mean that such forms of behaviour are contrary to the principles which they and the community have adopted such as kindness, honesty, truth and not pushing people off the pavement because you are in a hurry.

It does not mean that there are no exceptions. You would not hesitate to push someone aside on the pavement in order to save a child being run over. But you would apologize to him and explain that you had reasons for your exceptional behaviour. It has been established by sociologists for instance that people being 'kind' to beggars encourages vagrancy, and a surgeon often has to inflict cruel pain on a patient to make him well. I would not tell a man that he is going insane for that would make him worse; but neither would I tell him that he was not going insane if he were. But these exceptions do not deter us from accepting and living up to the principle; and if anyone claims exception to the general principle, they must have very good reasons for departing from these principles accepted by the community. (See also p. 150.)

If the advocates of the 'new morality' mean that there is a higher law than a strict moral code, and that the law of love supersedes such moral injunctions, one cannot but agree. There is of course nothing 'new' about this, for it is the basis of Christian teaching. Love is the fulfilment of the law. As we have said, the person who is actuated by love does not steal from his neighbour; he also does not seduce a girl to the detriment of her ultimate happiness although not perhaps to his immediate pleasure.

There are many high-minded people who adopt that basic principle of love and live up to it in their everyday lives. They have no need of moral rules, and indeed can defy them if they consider them detrimental to the good of the community. But the trouble in adopting the principle of love as the universal basis of true morality, true though it be, is that the word 'love' is capable of so many different meanings to different people. A man may claim that he is actuated by love for a girl when he seduces or even rapes her. The fact is that whilst some men and women of high culture may be capable of living up to the principle of love in all aspects of life, human nature is not yet ready to be trusted with it as the one law of life, because of its various interpretations – just as we cannot trust everybody to be activated by consideration of others in driving a car on the main roads. That may not be as we should like it, but it is an unfortunate fact. Meanwhile what they require are more definite rules – illustrative of the principle of love and consideration of others – by which to regulate their lives.

Morality is progressive.

But the fact that moral rules and principles are necessary does not preclude others of higher intelligence and with a deeper concern for the welfare of the community from living lives wholly dedicated to love of their fellows. By so doing they will gradually leaven the whole community with the same principle of love and consideration.

One of the main principles followed by such men and women is that they will do nothing, however harmless to themselves, which if generally adopted would lead to the hurt of others.

There were those, for instance, in a former generation, when drunkenness played such havoc in the community, who were teetotal, not because they thought it was 'wrong' to drink, nor that they thought there was any harm in taking a glass of wine at their meals, nor had they any fear of themselves becoming drunkards; they refrained for the sake of others who might not have the same self-control, or whose circumstances of life, the misery, the poverty were so severe that they were only too glad to get some moments of oblivion, only to increase their misery. They denied to themselves a harmless and even beneficent pleasure lest it might give encouragement or sanction to those others, to their harm.

In this connexion there is an intriguing story told of King David, who in the heat of battle thirsted. Three warriors at great peril of their lives dashed through the enemy's lines and brought water from the brook. But 'David would not drink thereof, but poured it out unto the Lord and said God forbid it me that I should do so; shall I drink of the blood of these men who have put their lives in jeopardy? for with the jeopardy of their lives they brought it'. A very sporting gesture! A less high-minded man would have said 'Really, you shouldn't have done it, old boy! But, as you have, it is a pity to waste it; so here's to your good health!' But, David's thought was for others not of himself. He did not even claim that, as King, his was an exceptional case.

Countless teenagers are in jeopardy of their lives and happiness because of this acceptance and condonation of pre-marital relations. They are in a sorry plight, left on their own for the most part without help or guidance and without principles to help them through life. There are many high-minded people who therefore refrain from doing anything, however harmless to themselves, or giving vent to opinions which would jeopardize the health and happiness of these youngsters. They are not being self-righteous; they are merely sincere.

What then should be regarded as the New Morality?

There is no doubt that morality is changing; it always is and always must. The New Morality, if there is such a thing, stands on different ground from the old. The Old Morality condemned the instincts as sinful and must be crushed. The New Morality regards the instincts and their emotions as biologically necessary, and useful, for the purposes of life. Moreover, they are capable of being re-directed to higher ends [as Wm. McDougal has demonstrated in his *Social Psychology*, and as Freud has recognized in his theory of sublimation (Chapter XXV)].

The New Morality therefore, if there can be said to be one, consists neither in the indulgence of our basic instincts for pure self-gratification, nor on the other hand, in their repression. The New Morality consists in the *acceptances* of our instincts, and the *re-direction* and re-orientation of the surplus of their emotions to the social and spiritual well-being of man, raising them to a higher potential.

This is a task worthy of our highest endeavours; it is the essence of progress in civilization; and it makes for peace and harmony in the individual and in the community alike, for the fulfilment of life.

That we sometimes fail in so high a task is not to the discredit either of ourselves or of our endeavour.

CHAPTER XX

Evil

THE NEW PSYCHOLOGICAL conception of the nature and value of the instinctive emotions is in contrast with any ethic of repression. Its teaching may be summarized thus:

There is no instinct in man but has been of value in the biological development of the race, and may be of value in the higher ethical development of civilized life.

It is true there are activities which appear in themselves evil – conceit, vanity, avarice, hypocrisy, or lust, the unbridled exhibition of the sex instinct; and definite names are given to these forms of perversion or excess. But it cannot be too strongly emphasized that these vices are not primary impulses, but are only the perversions of primary instincts, in themselves valuable. Vanity is the perversion of self-display, avarice the perversion of acquisition, lust the perversion or excess of sex. They can, by appropriate treatment, be cured and their impulses directed to normal and right ends.

Jealousy, for instance, is condemned as a vice; it is green-eyed, no poet sings its praise, no preacher defends its value, or urges its necessity. Yet, suppose we could abolish this so-called vice, so that all marital jealousy be done away, and the wife be unmoved at the infidelity of her husband, what would happen to the stability of our social life and the security of family ties?

Nature is wiser than her sons. When she seeks to establish the security of family life she places jealousy as the guardian of the monogamous impulse to preserve the sanctities of love.[1]

[1] Juries have instinctively recognized this, and in face of the written law of the land have maintained the validity of the 'unwritten law', even when jealousy has avenged itself by violence. In doing so, they have maintained the primal law of nature, without which the social fabric would crumble.

That jealousy is not the highest law is admitted, for it must be ultimately developed into the higher law of trust. That jealousy can be perverted is also acknowledged. Its primal purpose is to sustain sexual fidelity and the family tie; it may be perverted into an exhibition of petty jealousies that destroy rather than protect family life. But this should not blind our eyes to its essential value and virtue as the guardian of the monogamous impulse – an impulse which will permit of no trifling with the sanctity of love. When mutual trust has been established, natural jealousy passes, and becomes transformed, e.g., into jealousy for our cause.

As with jealousy, so with other primal instinctive tendencies.

Pride is often looked on with disdain; it is regarded as a vice, and as a sin. But pride may be of great value. Is not the artist justified in being proud of a good work of art and the business-man of some achievement? The pride we have in our work and the commendation we get from others is of value in that it encourages us to greater endeavour. We can get the best out of children not by pointing out the faults in their work, but by encouraging them with praise of good work.

Pride is only an evil when it is not associated with any such achievement. Indeed such pride or conceit probably arises from a feeling of inferiority. A young woman came to a priest and confessed that she was proud of her beauty. He replied, 'My daughter, that is not a sin, it is a mistake!'

To the psycho-physician there are no vices in their own right; there are only perverted virtues – if we give to 'virtue' its original meaning as something of 'value'.

We are not born evil; nor are we born in sin. Original sin – *Peccum originale* – means the sin of our origin, not that we all suffer because of Adam's sin! In other words it means hereditary traits. But even so these hereditary traits are not to be regarded as sinful. The hereditary capacities and potentialities with which we are all born have been developed in the course of evolution mainly for the survival of the species. It is true that in the progress of civilization some of these, particularly the aggressive and the sexual impulses, are overdone, for we have found more effective means of gaining our ends than fighting, and have devised better methods of caring for offspring than the earlier method of producing thousands in the hope that a few will survive. The result is that this surplus of these instincts causes trouble. It leaves civilized man with the task of transferring the surplus energies to social uses as in sublimation. It is a task which confronts every one of us, and some of us lamentably fail so that these instincts emerge in crime, vice and neurosis.

Good and evil depend not on the nature of our hereditary instincts, but on the way these are used, the end to which they are directed. Even anger may be rightly directed if it makes another desist from evil. I should like to hear some sermons on the value of jealousy, pride, anger and other so-called vices.

Evil, like dirt, is misplaced matter, or rather, misdirected function, valuable in itself, noxious if out of place. The instinctive impulse is misplaced if it persists beyond its phase; it is misplaced if it is directed to wrong ends; it is misplaced if attached to wrong objects.

(*a*) *Evil is misdirected impulse.* It is misdirected if it is attached to *wrong objects.* The attachment of the emotion of fear to an imagined illness, to darkness, or to an open space, is evil. Scorn is right if directed towards baseness, it is wrong if directed towards those who are simply of humble birth. The attachment of the instinct of acquisition to our neighbour's ass, the sexual attachment of a grown girl to her father, of a man for himself, are evils. All complexes are evil, for they are the attachments of our emotions to objects and repressed expressions of the past instead of their impulses being directed to the purposes of the present. They are, however, not sins, for they are unconscious and dissociated so that we have neither knowledge nor control over them. They require psychotherapeutic treatment to discover their origin, to bring them into consciousness, and so bring their impulses under the control of the will.

(*b*) *Evil is the discarded good of yesterday.* We have already seen that as our psychological development advances we pass from one phase to another by a process of re-birth.[1] Self-display and the desire to attract is the normal phase of the girl of 15 and 16; being the healthy expression of her instincts, it is for her good. But while the desire for admiration is good for a girl, it is evil if it dominates the psychology of a woman of 55, for whom it should be a discarded phase. The flapper of 50 is an 'evil' woman.

Pugnacity, as such, is an evil in the man of 40, though a valuable and necessary impulse in the boy of 12. As in the individual, so in the race, pugnacity has served its purpose, which was the development of the race morally as well as physically. It succeeded in developing courage which even today remains one of the greatest of virtues, a racial disposition accepted as noble. That pugnacity has outlived its use when it leads to the war of nations is equally accepted. In the individual, pugnacity should develop into confidence and quiet determination, which are much more effective than hitting out.

To the young married man and woman the sexual impulse is good; its physical expression develops and increases spiritual love, the absence of its physical expression produces a thin dilution of love falsely called spiritual. But the good of today will be the evil of tomorrow, if the sexual instincts are permitted to dominate the man of 40. This does not mean that these earlier impulses must die altogether. They are accepted by the self, they are modified by it, but cease to dominate the psychology.

Again, there was a time when slavery was a good thing, being a decided step in advance of the earlier custom of murdering off the victims captured in war. We have progressed, and the good of yesterday is now admitted an evil.

Indeed the conception of evil is contained in the very idea of progress, for if we do progress, that from which we have

[1] See Chap. XVI.

progressed must henceforth be evil. We cannot conceive of progress without conceiving the possibility of evil.

Evil then is not a 'thing', it exists as a misdirected function; it does not exist externally but only in the hearts of men. It is not objective except in so far as the actions of men are evil. Still less is evil a 'person' although it is very convenient to have the devil to blame for our misdeeds.

It is not surprising that this evil has been personalized as the devil, for to the patient suffering from obsessional compulsion it is experienced as an outward force opposed to the self, and compelling him to do silly and wrong things even against his will. The patient feels himself to be possessed or dominated by another personality which he cannot resist. But the modern name for the 'devil' is a complex, which being powerful but dissociated has all these compulsive qualities.

Nevertheless *evil is positive*: it is a positive force. It is the misdirection of forces in themselves valuable: it is the use of a valuable impulse in the wrong way, at the wrong time, in the wrong place and directed to wrong ends. It is that which constitutes an evil, and it is a very positive evil. The principle that all the primary impulses in our nature are to be regarded as of value and as 'good' is therefore not inconsistent with the idea of evil as a positive force in the world: but the force springs from the hearts of evil men.

To sum up: in essence, vices are only the perverted use of valuable instincts, and the cure of evil is not in eradicating but in diverting them to right uses. *To the psychotherapist there are no vices in their own right; there are only perverted impulses, which, when wrested from their morbid attachments, may be turned into positive virtues.*

How this may be done we must discuss later (Chap. XXV). Meanwhile we must take a closer, though brief, glance at the neuroses, the nature and causes.

CHAPTER XXI

What is a Neurosis?

EVERY NEUROSIS SPRINGS from an unresolved problem. An unresolved problem is unbearable; therefore we repress it; because we push it out of our minds it becomes dissociated; and because it is dissociated it is beyond the control of the will.

But it is still active, though dissociated, and when reactivated emerges into consciousness in the form of a symptom; but because it is unacceptable to the conscious self, which represses it, the symptom must take a substitute or symbolic form.

Most of these unresolved problems naturally arise in childhood, since the child's personality is immature and not fully organized to cope with them. Such problems relate mainly to matters of insecurity and fear: and if the child does not receive the necessary help and sense of security, it falls victim to fears and distresses of all kinds.

The basic cause of neurotic disorders is therefore the sense of insecurity, but since the child's security comes from the protective love of the mother, this insecurity is experienced by the child as deprivation of love.

The first need, then, of every child is protective love providing it with a sense of security and so of confidence to face life.

Denied that protective love – or *feeling* itself deprived of it – the child falls into various forms of neurotic reactions, the nature of which depends on its age and the circumstances of the deprivation. One child falls into a state of anxiety; another into depression and misery; another becomes angry, jealous and resentful; another falls into self-pity, whilst another resorts to auto-erotism as a solace for the lack of love. All these, which are the main neuroses, are reactions to the deprivation of love.

The need for protective love is also the main *repressing* force in the form of fear. For when the child resorts to these reactions such as jealousy or masturbation, it is rebuked and punished by the mother, so that, because of its need for its mother's love, it has to repress these forbidden tendencies, with the result that they are transformed into neurotic symptoms. Thus a child full of self-pity because of a lack of affection, and finding this a very poor substitute for the mother's love, represses the self-pity, which then emerges in the form of a hysterical pain, unconsciously designed to get the sympathy of the mother.

This conflict in the mind, one part repressing, the other reviving our problem, constitutes a problem itself which the child is often quite incapable of solving. It gives rise to distress and anxiety.

We find then that there are certain typical situations in early childhood which give rise to these unresolved problems.

First: birth itself. Birth is a severe traumatic event. From being warm and comfortable and secure in the mother's womb the child is suddenly subjected to pressure on the head, and to suffocation, sometimes prolonged; finally it is thrust out with great force into a cold and barren world, exposed, isolated and cut off from all contact with the mother.

These conditions are often found to be the predisposing causes of *claustrophobia* – the fear of close places like a cinema, tube train or church in which the patient feels the sense of suffocation and 'must get out'. These attacks of claustrophobia, when analysed back to their source, are often found to be an actual reproduction of the birth experience. It is also the origin of many cases of *agoraphobia*, which is defined as the fear of open space, but which is in fact fear of a loss of contact, sometimes called 'separation anxiety' – separation from one's base. In analysis, in tracing back the separation anxiety to its source, we frequently find that it is an exact reproduction of the separation after birth, especially if the new-born infant is not given proper care, but left by the midwife who is attending to the mother.

In reviving these experiences at birth by free association, the patient relives with 'hallucinatory vividness' the terror he felt at birth. He also comes to realize that this terror is precisely the same as he experiences now at the cinema, or when taking a journey: in fact he realizes that his symptoms are a factual reproduction of the original experience.

It must not be assumed that these early experiences alone are themselves sufficient to produce a neurosis: there are many children who have bad births who do not suffer. But they are an invariable and necessary factor in the production of a neurosis. Provided the child later has a sense of security from the love of the mother, it outlives the early fear; for it discovers that life is not so bad after all. But if the child is not reassured, then this early fear is apt to be revived, any later fears confirming the child's first impression. Or if later the person is subjected to great strain or to some severe problem in business or domestic life which he cannot solve, he may feel stifled and the original fear is likely to be revived, called up like an evil genius, so that he suddenly begins to suffer from claustro- or agoraphobia.

Another common situation creating an insoluble problem occurs when the child has developed strong self-willed tendencies, say, by being spoilt or allowed his own way, and then is subjected to punishment or to over-severe threats for being self-willed. In such a case there is a violent conflict between the child's self-will and the fear of consequences. It is the irresistible force of self-will against the immovable post of the fear of consequences. Neither will give way and the child is subjected to an insoluble problem. The problem is particularly severe in such complicated cases as this: the child feels deprived of love and therefore resorts to masturbation as a solace. This is discovered and the child severely threatened.

To give up the masturbation means the loss of the only joy and solace left in life: to continue means to risk the punishment and threats. What is the child to do in the face of that problem? He has to compromise: he allows himself the forbidden desire, but vows that he will be very, very good and obedient in everything else. The child who constantly has to say to his mother 'Am I being a good boy?' probably has something to hide. His question is motivated by anxiety that he may not be a good boy. He becomes over-conscientious, over-scrupulous and often very religious.

Or the child may resort to compulsive acts, like Lady Macbeth's handwashing, or making sure that the gas fire is turned off time and again. The purpose of these compulsive acts is propitiatory; they are designed to avert the inevitable consequences of our forbidden desires. It is a method of removing the guilt by symbolic acts (the gas for instance representing his emotions which are liable to explode at any moment), but of course it does no such thing, because as with Lady Macbeth the patient refuses to face the real source of the guilt. In any case the source of guilt is usually unknown, being some experience in early childhood.

A further situation commonly giving rise to symptoms is that of jealousy of a younger child. A girl of 3 who has up till now received all the attention and admiration of the mother is suddenly confronted with the situation in which the mother is giving all her love and attention to the baby boy. She naturally becomes jealous: for jealousy is a natural reaction of self-preservation, since the older child is thrown into a state of insecurity. She shows her anxiety by trying to push the baby off the mother's knee to get the love and security she needs; but all she gets in reply is a rebuke and a smack from her mother who says, 'Can't you see I am busy?' That is precisely what she does see, and what she objects to.

But she is faced with this intolerable problem: the more the mother rebuffs her the more angry, unloved and jealous she becomes; but the more angry she becomes the worse the consequences. That problem is insoluble as far as the child is concerned. Ultimately, since self-preservation is the first law of life, she has to be good and represses all her anger, self-pity and misery.

From that various results may follow. The repressed jealousy may later come out in compulsive form, so that she becomes insanely jealous if her husband even speaks to another woman, although she is ashamed of her jealousy which she realizes is irrational. That is a compulsive neurotic character trait, the repressed emotions emerging in their original form. On the other hand the child may find that, when she is ill, her mother shows a great deal of concern and gives her the attention she craves. She thereafter resorts to illness as a means of getting the lost sympathy. Later, if she is confronted with a similar situation – if, for instance, she thinks her husband is showing her less affection than before, or showing preference for his own daughter, the old jealousy is revived but in this case she automatically develops symptoms of illness, which *unconsciously* is designed to win back the attention of her husband, as it did with her mother in childhood. In most cases, of course, it does no such thing, for it only irritates him to have a sick wife, but the subconscious mind can be very pig-headed. So when in analysis she realizes what she is doing and why, she abandons that stupid method of trying to win back her husband's love and resorts to more sensible methods.

The same mechanism applies to the sex perversions like homosexuality or fetichism. If a child feels unloved, he may resort to masturbation as a solace; if no one loves him he at least can love himself; he can do without them!

If discovered, he is then threatened, with the result that his sexual activities have to be repressed out of fear. This means that they are arrested in development: so that when, later, in puberty and adolescence, sex emerges as the result of physiological development, it emerges in the form in which it was originally repressed. A fetichism for instance, that is to say the sexual instincts being attached to some inanimate object like a shoe or a corset, we find always to be a breast substitute. It arises when for instance a baby boy feeding at the breast is sexually aroused and gets an erection, which scandalizes the mother, who then deprives him of the breast. He is forbidden the breast pleasure, which is taboo, but resorts to a breast substitute. A corset is of course a very natural substitute. Shoes are a common fetichism because two shoes together look similar to the two breasts, and leather has the same body smell.

It will be observed that in all these cases there are aroused natural propensities which are then repressed. It is the repression which causes the damage and which makes these impulses appear in a substitute form as a neurotic symptom – although for some peculiar reason Freud says that the sex perversions are not due to repression but to mere persistence of infantile activities.

We cannot agree with Freud that the essential nuclear complex is the incestuous desire of a child for the opposite parent – the Œdipus complex. We find the basic cause to lie not primarily in sex, but in the feeling of insecurity experienced as the deprivation of love, as in all the instances given.

CHAPTER XXII

Therapeutics

METHODS OF HEALING

Can we change human nature? We can and we do. The methods used may be divided into those of

(*a*) The moralist
(*b*) The religious man
(*c*) The medical psychologist

(*a*) The moralist – using the term in a somewhat narrow sense – regards evil as a perversion of the will. For cure he relies upon the *exertion of the will*, and uses persuasion to encourage the delinquent to follow a higher standard of behaviour. 'Pull yourself together!' is the effective phrase. This is most valuable in many cases, for many cases of evil are due simply to low ideals. The man of bad temper, the anti-social youth who steals, or the girl who indulges in sex adventures can be persuaded that their line of life can only lead to unhappiness for themselves and for others.

It is effective, however, only in what I call 'simple character traits' in which the person had been brought up with poor ideals and lack of discipline. It is useless where these same disorders are due to repressed and dissociated complexes over which the person has no control. It is useless to tell the girl with morbid self-consciousness or the one with claustrophobia, or the one who has obsessional compulsions, to exercise her will; she replies, 'I only wish I could.'

(*b*) The religious method is that of *Conversion*. This applies particularly to those forms of conversion in which there is a complete churning up of all the emotions, including the complexes, with the result that the person has an entirely new orientation to life. William James in his *Varieties of Religious Experience* mentions cases of this kind and so does Begbie in his *Broken Earthenware*; and I am sure the Salvation Army could supply thousands of other cases. The strange thing about these conversions is that they not only rid the person of his faults and sins, but cure him of his neurotic disorders such as drug habits. Nor is it simply that the converted now have power to resist their impulses; but they lose all *desire*, say, for their homosexuality or drunkenness. That is why we say the emotional turmoil must reach down to the complexes. The fact that many of these 'converts' fall back does not discredit those whose whole lives have been changed.

But unfortunately we cannot command religious conversions; 'the wind bloweth where it listeth'. We are therefore compelled to resort to slower but surer scientific methods.

THE METHOD OF ANALYSIS

The aim of all modern methods of psychotherapy is to produce a healthy, whole, or complete man. This can only be done when those elements which are excluded from the organized self, the repressed complexes and suppressed instincts, are liberated and brought into harmony with the 'self'.

Our first endeavour must, therefore, be to discover those complexes; secondly, to wrest their instinctive emotions from the morbid attachments, and finally harness them to the will and use of man.

This method of psychotherapy secures two results: (*a*) It cures the symptoms of moral and nervous disorders, which depend for their existence on repressed complexes; and (*b*) it liberates powerful instinctive emotions for the building up of a full and perfect character.

The difference between the moralist's approach and the scientific approach is that the moralist approaches these disorders from the point of view of a *standard of behaviour*, of right and wrong, of a failure to reach that standard. The scientific approach is that of *causation*, to discover what are the causes of the disorders and by discovering their causes, to cure them. The moralist condemns hypocrisy; the scientist asks what is the cause of hypocrisy; why and how do people become hypocrites? Condemning the hypocrite does very little good; how can you cure him without discovering the cause?

Surely one of the greatest services that the clergy can render to humanity is by studying such behaviour disorders as hypocrisy, lying, jealousy, conceit, indolence, self-indulgence and defeatism, and deal with them scientifically by discovering and treating their causes. Such behaviour disorders are within the province of the minister and clergyman, but he will not get very far without the new approach – that of the scientist.

A repressed complex manifests itself in *conduct*, in *physical symptoms*, in *moral diseases*, or in *dreams*. By following any of these paths, therefore, we may track down the complex.

An illustration at hand exemplifies all of these. A lady protests that she and her husband are most devoted to each other, and to all outward appearances they seem to be so. Yet it was obvious to a psychologist that the opposite was the truth, from four casual incidents – first, she forgot to meet the train by which he was returning after a week's absence; secondly, she dreamt that some harm had come to him; thirdly, she had a habit of unconsciously moving her wedding ring on and off her finger as she talked; and, fourthly, she protested her devotion over-much. The first incident showed her indifference, the second and third her repressed wishes, the fourth her attempt to hide her true feelings. This diagnosis was confirmed, for it turned out that she was all the time in love with another man. Unconscious signs like these tell us more about the real character than conscious speech.

Intuition. What the psychologist does deliberately and consciously, most people do by intuition. *Intuition is the unconscious notice we take of things.* Intuitions spring for the most part from our *dispositions*, for these represent the accumulated experience of the years; they therefore serve as a reliable guide in action and thought. So we judge aright of people's character even in the absence of logical reasons. When we like or dislike people by intuition, it is because we have unconsciously noticed things about them which are pleasant or unpleasant to us, according to our previous associations. Intuition is not a 'sixth sense', but the unconscious deduction we make from all our senses. The most trifling things about people may thus justly make a profound impression upon us. The conclusions we draw may be of great value. The psychologist, like everyone else, makes use of intuition, but, besides this, takes conscious notice of these signs, and draws logical conclusions. Thus, in her dream, conduct, and symptom the lady was proclaiming to the world her infidelity more loudly than her speech protested her devotion.

ANALYSIS THROUGH CONDUCT

(1) Having already discussed the mechanisms of conduct, especially by *over-compensation* and *projection* (p. 36 f.), it will not be necessary to deal further with them.

A just estimate of character and a wise dealing with it depend on our interpreting the conduct of others, not at its face value, but according to what it tells you of their unconscious motives. The man who boasts of his wonderful achievements of daring invites you to recognize that he is morally a coward. His bravado before the world proclaims his lack of courage in facing his own passions and desires. The man who announced, 'My father is an important man in the business world, and in some ways I seem to have inherited his genius and brains', is trying to hide from you that he really has a feeling of terrible inferiority.

A very thorough analysis of any person's character may be deduced merely from the interpretation of such indications of character and the discovery of their underlying motives.

The analyst may appear to have his eye on the stage, but his attention is really absorbed with what is going on behind the scenes.

DREAM ANALYSIS

The most usual form of investigating the 'unconscious' is by means of dream analysis, for as speech is the language of the conscious, dreams are the language of the 'unconscious'. There must be a right interpretation of dreams; but the language of dreams is symbolic, and the trouble about the interpretation of anything symbolic is that it is so easy for everyone to give it an interpretation in accordance with his own pre-conceived theory. The result is that at the present time you may take a dream to half a dozen analysts and receive six different, and often contradictory, interpretations – to one the symbols are sexual, to another they are images of the primitive unconscious, to another they are compensatory, to one they are teleological, to another reminiscent, whilst to another they serve the function of preparing for life.

Dreams are the emergence into consciousness, during sleep, of our unresolved problems.

The function of dreams is that by repeating the problems of the day they tend towards a solution of these problems.

In this respect they are like symptoms, which also are an attempt to solve our problems, but they do so much more successfully than symptoms. For the symptom represents a complete failure to solve the problem and has to resort to compromise. Thus a telephone girl, hating her job, but having to stick at it, develops an 'occupational' deafness which solves her problem but at the expense of a symptom. It is a most unsatisfactory solution. A man who in his childhood days developed a fear of sex, had a fear that if he left home and went into the world he would be tempted to sex indulgences; so he developed an agoraphobia, a fear of leaving home and this solved his problem, since he found it impossible to leave home, but at the expense of a permanent phobia.

Dreams tackle the problem much more directly than symptoms and give a much clearer image both of the problem itself and its solution.

I have given a full account, with many illustrations, of the 'problem-solving' function of dreams, which I call the 'biological theory of dreams', in my book *Dreams and Nightmares* (Penguin); but as dreams deal very largely with the moral problems of our lives, a brief account of their nature and function is here called for.

When we cannot solve a problem of any kind we tend to push it aside – for we must get on with the job of life. But at night when the problems of the day are laid aside and the inhibiting forces of our minds are in abeyance, the repressed problem emerges once more, pressing for solution. Such are our dreams: they are problem-solving.

The material of dreams. Dreams do *not*, as Freud maintained in his book on Dreams, deal with sexual problems only, but with any and every sort of unresolved problem.

Some of these dreams are concerned with the ordinary everyday objective problems of our lives, with our business, our domestic life, how we can best deal with the children, or our anxiety about our examinations. Very commonly also they deal with our psychological and moral problems.

In many cases no solution can be offered and then we wake up. For just as we go to sleep to escape the cares and problems of the day, so we wake up to escape the unresolved problems of the night. Typical of such dreams are nightmares many of which reproduce terrifying problems of infantile life. A common one is the nightmare of passing down a long dark passage with great dread and anxiety, a dream which is traceable back to the anxiety of a long and difficult birth.

In many other cases, however, dreams, by repeating the problem over and over again, in many forms and by many symbols, do in fact offer a solution.

Sometimes very naturally, the solution may be a very

poor one, such as a mere wish fulfilment. The starving man may dream of a wonderful meal, but he wakes up hungry. We may 'solve' the problem of sex deprivation by imagining our sex feelings satisfied. That may ease our physical tension and allow us to sleep, but it is no real solution.

But consider a dream of this kind: a man who chafes under the irksome tyranny of his boss may dream of himself standing up to his boss, and finds that his boss respects him the more and does not bully him so much. Such a dream is not a mere wish fulfilment; it relates to something going on in himself: it is factual. The fact that in his dream he sees himself and *feels* himself being more courageous and assertive actually encourages him to *be* so during the day: he realizes that he has it in him: he has done so once, why not again. The dream tells him in effect: 'If you were not such a worm and did not take things lying down, as you do, you would find that people respected you the more!' So the dream by worrying over the problem points to a solution.

Take another simple dream like this: a man dreams that he and his daughter are seated at a restaurant table at which two other people, strangers, are seated. At the end of the meal the strangers find they have no money to pay for their meal, whereupon the man generously offers to pay for them. But when he comes to open his wallet he finds he had only a ten-shilling note, not enough to pay for himself and the strangers. His associations were that he had recently given considerable sums of money to his daughter, but the thought crossed his mind that he might be running himself short in his retirement – a thought which he immediately dismissed from his mind as 'unworthy' – saying he had given the money and that was that! But the problem must have been still worrying him at the back of his mind, so that when he was asleep, and his will in abeyance, this problem returned. The dream says in effect, 'Look here! it is all very well being generous but you haven't got enough money to be so lavish in your generosity.' The dream brings him down to earth, to take a common-sense view and compels him to face facts.

It is trying to point out to him that as it was quite unnecessary to pay for meals of perfect strangers, so it was quite unnecessary to stint himself for his daughter, who in fact has plenty.

The problem-solving function of dreams can be confirmed from many sources, and concern many other problems than that of sex. Many mathematical and scientific problems, such as the discovery of the Benzene ring in Chemistry, and the conservation of energy in Physics, both of which were discovered in such dream-like states. In ordinary life when we are confronted with a ticklish problem to which we can find no solution, we say 'Let's sleep on it!' and we find the problem solved for us. The function of dreams is thus precisely the same as that of intuition which is a subconscious method of drawing inferences, as distinct from reason, which is drawing inferences from conscious data.

Perseveration. The return of the problem in dreams is by virtue of a quality of the mind we call 'perseveration' – which is defined as 'the tendency of the mind to revert back to an unfinished train of thought'. This of course includes unresolved problems.

The simplest illustration of perseveration is in ordinary worry. If we have a problem in the mind which we cannot solve, we tend to push it aside – for the simple biological reason that we have to get on with our job in life and with other problems and difficulties. But everyone knows that every now and then, especially in moments of relaxation, the worry intrudes into consciousness again – as though to say 'Now you can attend to me!'

Thus we have two opposing forces in life in our mind – one which tends to repress what we cannot solve, and the other insisting on coming up for solution.

Both of these opposite devices have their biological value. We need to push aside problems we cannot solve because we must get on with the job of life. On the other hand it would never do for us always to be shelving our problems in this way: to be efficient we must be prepared to face up to our problems, for that is the way of progress. So the mind has the tendency to throw our problems back on us.

The conflict between repression and perseveration itself constitutes one of the main problems of life.

We conclude then that dreams have a far greater significance than mere wish-fulfilment in order to allow ourselves to sleep, which is Freud's view: they are of biological value. They tackle the problems and worries of life, including our moral problems and work towards a solution.

The difficulty about the interpretation of dreams is that so many of them are symbolic, and symbols are capable of almost any interpretation.

The only safeguard against the arbitrary interpretation of dreams is to rely upon the patient's own free association and to discover what the dream means *to him*. By such free association we find that dreams relate far more to *actual experiences* than is usually supposed; experiences which are found to contain unresolved problems. These experiences may relate to the actual object of our symptom, whether headache, phobia or paralysis; or they may be simply *instances*, representative of the deeper problems of the whole personality. That is why dreams are so valuable in discovering what is the problem which worries and besets the patient, and frequently offering a solution which, coming from the patient's own intuition, is likely to be more correct and of greater value than any solution we may have to offer.

DIRECT REDUCTIVE ANALYSIS

Every neurotic symptom emerges during life as the result of an unresolved problem. It seems reasonable to suppose that by tracing back this symptom to its historical origin, we shall there find its real cause. This applies also to disorders of conduct and character. The best means of understanding a character is to go back to its sources in childhood. The adult psychology is very complex, and it is exceedingly difficult to discover the exact motive or cause of any action, for so many factors are involved. But in childhood we see the character in its simplest forms, and having once secured the key we find the interpretation to all kinds of traits of character. It may be difficult to discover from the 'present psychology' what is the origin of an inability to work, the lack of will. Is it laziness, is it conceit, is it fear, is it an inability to face responsibility? We go to childhood and there find an abnormal craving for approbation associated with fear of a morally severe mother. So terrible were the consequences of the slightest wrongdoing that the child assumes the attitude 'Rather than risk doing wrong, I shall not do anything'. This attitude, which was the original cause of the lack of will to work, is also the cause of his present indisposition. He still has an abnormal craving for approval, he is still terrified of doing wrong. The *reductive analysis* into childhood gives us the key to his present psychology.

The method we employ to investigate the original cause, which, as I have indicated, is always forgotten, is that devised by Freud, the method of *free association* upon the symptom, the patient being in a quiescent, hypnoidal condition, or, in difficult cases, by hypnosis, automatic writing, or unconscious drawings.

As long as the mind *tries* to remember it will fail to do so, for the repugnant complexes elude search. But if the mind is quiescent and uncritical, and the idea of the-origin-of-the-symptom is suggested to the mind, there will come to the mind pictures of the earlier instances of the symptom until ultimately the earliest and original comes to mind.

When we have the incident, then we may proceed to discover the emotional conflict that accompanied the incident. The recovering of this conflict is often sufficient to cure the symptom.

It is then found that 'in the unconscious' there is a repressing force and a repressed force. The *repressing* force may be a primitive emotion, like fear in a case of sex assault, which represses the sex sensations; but more commonly it is the moral 'Self' or Super ego. The *repressed* force is usually of an entirely primitive kind and is variously conceived. We may regard it with Freud as ultimately sexual, or with Jung as the repressed primitive experiences of the race contained in the 'collective conscious'. For our own part we seem to detect two phases: the earlier and more primitive one belonging to the body and its sensations, the sensuous layer, which gives rise to the perversions; and a later phase expressed in the primary instincts, such as fear, sex, self-assertion, curiosity, which belongs not to the sensational but to the perceptual plane and which have largely sprung out of the earlier sensuous level. Disorders may arise from either of these levels; sometimes it is necessary to analyse down only to the instinctive layer, at other times the disease must be traced down to the deeper sensuous layer.

One case will illustrate these points. A barrister suffers from severe pain in the leg, and from moods of depression and bad temper, the one a functional nervous disease, the other a moral disease. The pain in the leg was suggested by an incident in boyhood, when on the way to school he witnessed a severe accident, in which a man's leg was smashed. Consequently, he did his work badly at school, yet the horror of the incident prevented him from explaining. This incident was not only associated in his mind with horror, but what affected him more particularly was that he, a clever and 'bright' boy, was blamed for inattention. The symptom was thus associated with a complex of humiliation. By this means we discover not only the historical origin, which in itself is unimportant, but the repressed emotion, in this case, *the over-sensitiveness to blame* which not only then, but now, unknown to himself, plays an important part in his psychology and in the determination of his character. The recovery of the original experience was sufficient to cure the pain symptom; but it did not cure the depression, nor, of course, did it cure the sensitiveness to blame, which was the fundamental disease. The analysis, therefore, had to proceed, and revealed the fact that for five years he was the only child, petted and admired by fond parents, who loved to show him off. His instinct of self-display was exaggerated; he was, in fact, 'perfect'. Then, in succession, came five other children, and this oldest boy was shelved, and retired to brood over his miseries in sullen rage, and became morbidly sensitive to blame. The endo-psychic conflict between self-importance and insignificance thus gave rise to all his symptoms, both nervous and moral. It originated his morbid depression and bad temper, and later, by association, it was the cause of the pain in the leg.

The next phase in the analysis is then to bring the psychological conflict up to date and demonstrate it in the present psychology. This is done by analysing not the original but the most recent occurrence of the symptom. In this case it was found that whenever the symptom recurred, it was always associated with some incident in which humiliation and an over-sensitiveness to blame played a part; for instance, when he lost a case owing to slackness, which he was unwilling to admit, and when he arrived a few minutes late for a consultation. This bringing up to date of the analysis is most important.

A third stage is the process of re-adjusting the personality to the recovered experiences and the resolving of the problem. The method here advocated differs radically not only from Freud's later method of analysis by dreams and the transference, but also from his original method by 'abreaction'. 'Abreaction', which is the liberation of the repressed emotion, is only the first stage of analysis. What is of more importance for a radical analysis is that we should discover the nature and origin of both the complexes which combine to produce the breakdown.[1]

[1] The case also demonstrates several processes we have already described (Chap. IV). (*a*) The formation of complexes, their repression, the endo-psychic conflict between them and their emergence as moral and nervous disorders. (*b*) The illustration also shows that, although the origins of the neuroses are forgotten, they nevertheless continue to affect our life and conduct, but that they may be recovered by the method of free association. (*c*) The case also illustrates how a symptom, the pain in the leg, may originate in later life, whereas the pre-disposing cause, the over-sensitiveness to blame, originated in childhood. The immediate cause of the symptom may be a love-affair, overstrain at work,

The method of analysis may be summarized thus: we trace the symptom to its historical origin; discover the emotional complex from which it springs; find that the emotional conflict is still present, the cause of the persisting symptom; and, finally, readjust the elements of the complex by bringing them under conscious control of the will.

This method of reductive analysis by means of the symptom has very obvious advantages over that of dream analysis.

(*a*) We are dealing with facts and not with arbitrary interpretation. It is true that in free association the patient often produces what are obviously imaginary fancies of early childhood, but these can be sifted from the visualizations which are later recognized as real occurrences, and which may often be confirmed. Even the phantasies are valuable as exhibiting the psychology of the patient, for they are themselves a product of the facts of mental experience.

(*b*) It is unnecessary to deal with the 'transference'[1] of the patient. Since the neuroses are due to a maladaptation of a patient to himself all we require to do is to show him to himself, which we do by the recovery of his past experience. We do not require his acceptance of anything *we* say: all we require is that he should co-operate in the method; he himself reproduces the experiences of childhood and sees the facts of his character for himself.

(*c*) Reductive analysis is, as we have seen, the most direct and rapid method of investigating the *present* character. We reductively analyse into the past only to discover the present psychology.

[1] Transference is here used in the Freudian sense of a displacement of affect to a person to whom it does not properly belong; for instance love or hate being transferred from the parents in childhood to the analyst.

the explosion of a shell, but the ultimate cause is an abnormality of one's attitude towards life, or, still more, one's attitude towards oneself, which are dispositions developed early in childhood. Thus, an analysis as far as the immediate cause may frequently produce a cure of that symptom, but the analysis is not really satisfactory which does not set right the whole attitude to life. The 'neuropathic disposition' can be cured as effectively as the neurotic symptom, though, of course, with considerably greater difficulty, and requiring a much longer treatment.

(*d*) The reductive method described enables us not merely to *recognize*, but to *realize*, the morbid origin of disease. We may recognize our weaknesses of character without realizing them. The difference between recognition and realization is that realization carries a certain emotional tone which is wanting in recognition. Realization and not merely recognition is necessary to cure. It is quite possible for a man to know and even recognize a fact without its benefiting him. A soldier may know from others exactly what happened to him when he was buried; but this knowledge has no effect upon his condition. We may recognize that we are proud and vain, but this recognition may have no effect until we realize what snobs we are. We may make a show of admitting a fault in order to disarm further criticism; or we may declare that we are selfish or sinners to lead others to think how righteous we must be; or, having admitted a fault, we hold ourselves free to continue it. We only fully realize our failings when, by recalling instance after instance, we react emotionally. Then we begin to realize that we are still egotistic, want attention, like to show off, are selfish, are virtuous only because it pays. Realization takes place when the recognition is accompanied by emotional reaction, and when this takes place we know that the emotional tone of the complex has been released. Such release is necessary to cure, and indeed is sufficient for cure.

But the simplest and most convincing method of realizing our present morbid traits is to analyse them to their origin. One may not be convinced by the uncertain interpretation of dream analysis and so fail to realize unpleasant traits in one's character. One cannot but be convinced when recognition and realization spring from a definite recollection.

So, in reductive analysis we take the soldier back to live again the horrifying experiences of being blown up, so as to liberate his repressed fear; we revive sexual experiences of childhood, buried because of their repugnant character; we let the patient see his conceit, his humiliations, his cruel traits, his cowardice, his selfishness, his perverted tastes.

But this raises many questions.

(*a*) What is the use of raking up the past? How will that cure? It will only make the patient worse!

(*b*) After all, it is said, repression is nature's method, we must repress. If we did not suppress our instincts – our pride, our sex, our fear, our pugnacity – they would get the better of us; we should become immoral; the soldier would become a coward; the pugnacious man unbearable; we should go to the dogs; our vanity would make us socially impossible.

(*c*) What are we to do with our instincts when we have brought them up? May we not cure our nervous and moral diseases at the expense of our morality?

CHAPTER XXIII

The Cure

WHAT GOOD WILL it do to rake up the past? To bring up repugnant and unpleasant memories cannot but do the patient harm. Best 'let sleeping dogs lie!' To compel the woman to remember the humiliating experiences of the past, to make the man live again through those experiences which, in the providence of nature, he has completely forgotten will surely make them worse.

It is admitted that this is what we should *expect*. But it is found in *experience* that the bringing-up of the complexes into consciousness actually relieves the patient and cures the morbid condition. 'It is extraordinary,' a patient has just said to me, 'how getting up all these horrible things makes you feel so much better!' We appeal to the facts of experience.

As regards the theoretical explanation of *how* the cure comes about, there are conflicting opinions.

One theory suggested is that repressed emotion, like pent-up steam, can cause damage as long as it is repressed. The recovering of the emotion to consciousness 'lets off the steam', which therefore becomes harmless. This is the essential though not the only feature in the theory of 'Abreaction'. To anyone who watches a patient pass through the process of getting up the emotional experience with hallucinatory vividness and then lose his symptom, such a theory is most plausible and convincing. But an experiment of the following kind seems to disprove it. A patient with a severe head-shake was hypnotized, and in hypnosis recovered the memory of his shell-shock experience, and the origin of his head-shake, which meant, 'No, no, the shells won't drop here.' He let off a great deal of emotional 'steam' during this process. But when he wakened from his hypnosis he did not remember what he had recalled, and *his symptom was not cured.* Later, he was again hypnotized, and told he would remember the experience on waking. He did so, and his symptom was cured with the recovery into consciousness of the experiences. This illustrates, first, that the recalling of such an experience does not cure by the mere letting-off of emotion, for this was more effectively done in the first hypnosis, but, secondly, that the recovery of the fear complex into consciousness does cure.

A truer explanation of the facts would then seem to be that *whenever material is brought up into consciousness and recognized and accepted by the self, it immediately comes under the control of the will.* But the question remains, How can analysis cure? Analysis does not cure any more than a surgeon cures a patient when he removes his appendix. It is not the surgeon who cures, but the healing forces of the body. All that the surgeon does is to remove that which was obstructing and poisoning the healthy flow of life in the body. So the analyst 'cures' by removing those repressing forces which obstruct the flow of mental energy, that the emotions may emerge again into a free and active life, under the control of the will.[1]

REPRESSION AS NATURE'S METHOD

It is further objected that, in unearthing the complexes, we are interfering with the process of nature which represses the complex for very good reasons – the preservation of the individual's peace of mind. That is partially true. Repression is a provision of nature, but it is to be observed that she only resorts to this method when she has failed in her main purpose, namely, adaptation to the new experience. When a bullet enters the hand, nature's first endeavour is to expel it,

[1] It is often urged against the psycho-physician that he claims to cure moral ills that God alone can cure. That is not the case. Analysis is only a *method* of cure; it is the means of grace, not the grace itself; and there is no reason why the religious, if so inclined, should not employ this as a means for bringing life to the morally sick.

and in this she frequently succeeds. Only when she cannot do this does she surround it with fibrous tissue, and thus renders it more or less harmless by disassociating it from the rest of the body. The surgeon then cuts down and removes the bullet, for as long as it is present it may 'light up' and become a focus of inflammation. But let it be observed that in extracting what nature has repressed, he is not acting contrary to nature, but in line with nature's *first* purpose, which was to remove the cause of irritation. So by the surgery of the mind, the psycho-physician seeks to remove those complexes which clog the channels of life and power. In every experience of life our minds seek first to adapt themselves to the new condition; only when we fail to readjust ourselves do we resort to repression. An illustration will demonstrate this principle and the methods of nature's cure.

A patient, suffering from speechlessness and severe headaches, happened to see in the streets a huge crane, and thought, 'Suppose this fell on me!' That night he dreamed of all his experiences of being buried in France – experiences he had forgotten, but now remembered on wakening. With the recovery of the memory his speech returned. *This was nature's own method of curing this patient.* One would have expected this to have suggested to the neurologist who had charge of him the right method of cure for his headaches, which continued. But whilst nature in his dreams was trying to make him *remember* his war experiences, the neurologist continued treating him with bromide and continued to tell him to *forget* about the war. He was later sent to a psychotherapist, who, following the hint suggested by nature as to the method of cure, used means to recover to his mind a previous incident which originated his headache. The recovery of this to consciousness cured the pain as effectively as the dream had cured his mutism. The methods of nature and of the psycho-physician are the same. The method of repression which nature first resorted to in this case did, indeed, deliver the patient from mental distress, but it left him dumb and in pain. It was a poor substitute for the radical method which the physician, following the hint later given by nature, used to cure him.

We may, therefore, take it that not only does this method lead to cure, but that it is in accordance with the principles nature herself employs. It should, however, be added that the bringing up of the complex must be complete. If a surgeon only half extracts a piece of shrapnel, it is much worse than if he had never done anything at all. So with complexes, and it is failure to realize this fact which has given rise to the opinion that it only makes one worse to remember these things, and has led people to speak of the 'dangers' of psychotherapy. Like all forms of medical practice it is dangerous, and may be harmful in the hands of amateurs. But in the method itself there is no danger. The most real danger in amateur analysis is that it may raise questions and arouse emotional forces which it cannot control. It is essential that, when an analysis is commenced, it be carried through to the end. If we simply probe into a shrapnel wound without extracting all the shrapnel, we make the patient worse: when it is completely extracted the pain ceases and the wound heals. So it is with the mind. A neurasthenic patient is always introspective – *nature makes him so*, to compel him to devote himself to the problem of the mind, and that is why he finds it so difficult to concentrate or to remember, so absorbed is his mind with its own problems. Only when that problem is *completely* discovered and solved does he cease to be introspective, and becomes healthy-minded and able to devote his attentions to things around.

REPRESSION AND SELF-CONTROL

It is urged that we must repress our instincts or else we cannot get rid of them and they would get out of our control. We reply that, on the contrary, *we cannot control our instincts as long as we repress them*; only by bringing them into consciousness and accepting them as part of ourselves can we control them. We do not seek to 'get rid of them'; we seek to use them.

The will has no direct control over any impulses of the mind, except those which are constituted as part of the self. It may repress those elements it has itself rejected as painful or repugnant, but that is not self-control. Indeed, these repressed forces constantly burst forth as impulses, obsessions, fears, and neuroses, which sweep before them the feebly protesting will. *Self-control is the conscious and voluntary direction of the instinctive emotions to the will and service of man.* This is the essential and important difference between repression and self-control. Repression excludes the complexes and instincts from the self, whereas self-control admits them as part of its self and thereby brings them under its sway. As long as they are excluded they are like bad boys thrust out from school who continue to torment us by throwing stones; our only hope of controlling them is to accept them back. Peace of mind can never be secured by rejecting passions which are unruly, but only by recognizing, accepting, and sublimating them.

We may now distinguish four processes – restraint, suppression, repression, and self-control.

In *restraint* we recognize and accept our instinctive desires as natural and right – for instance, the desire to possess the etchings of a friend, or the youth's sexual desires for the girl he loves – but we restrain ourselves from giving full expression to these in conduct. In *suppression* we recognize the impulses but do not accept them, regarding them as abhorrent, as many people do their sex feelings. It will be observed that what we *sup*press are the *recognized* complexes. *Repression* is an unconscious process in which the complexes are so repugnant that we refuse either to accept or even to recognize them, but they are apt to burst forth in abnormal ways. In *self-control* we not only recognize but accept our impulses, and give them expression in conduct by redirecting them to higher ends. It is true that we may frequently need to *restrain* our anger or sex instincts, but only temporarily, whilst we re-educate them in the process of self-control. Restraint is necessary to self-control. But repression makes self-control impossible by putting impulses beyond the control of the will.

PSYCHOLOGICAL EXPRESSION

The contrast between repression and self-control is of the greatest importance in dealing practically with moral problems. *It is only in so far as we admit our instincts that we can control them and sublimate them.* A lady told me that while nursing in a raid area in France she began to develop an 'anxiety neurosis'. Then she suddenly recognized that she was afraid, a fact she had previously refused to admit. Her anxiety neurosis immediately disappeared, and her fear, now recognized, was easily controlled. When she returned home after the war she developed neurasthenia, and again some accidental occurrences brought home to her the fact that she had strong sex feelings, which had previously been repressed. She accepted these as right, and immediately her neurasthenia, caused by the repression, disappeared. I asked her if accepting them made her feel like 'going to the dogs'. 'On the contrary,' she said, 'I had even more control over myself.'

Only by admitting all our thoughts, good and bad, into the mind can we control them and give sublimated expression to them. This is the principle of *psychological* acceptance, which means the acceptance and expression *in the mind* of all our desires and impulses.

We are asked: 'Do you mean that when evil desires present themselves to my mind I am not to shut them out, but to accept them?' That is precisely what we do mean.[1]

It may be replied that it is wrong to permit evil thoughts in the mind at all. The reply for the time being is that in the interests of a moral life it is temporarily better to accept the impulse of fear or sex as natural and right, and so control it,

[1] The injunction of Christ about 'looking on a woman to lust after her' is not hostile to this principle. Incidentally, the injunction particularly referred to the *married* woman (γυναικα), and was therefore made in the interests of the monogamous principle. But, more important, the context shows that it was concerned with *intention* to lust, which is very different from the desire. If the saying is to be taken literally as referring to all sex feelings towards women, the only men amongst us who have not committed adultery would be the sexual perverts like homosexuals and neurotics whose sex instincts are repressed!

than it is to be obsessed with it by continuing to repress it. The ultimate reply is that only by so doing can we use and sublimate them. When evil thoughts come we are told to drive them out of our mind and forget them. This is exactly what was advised to the shell-shocked soldier, to try to forget about the war! We ask, with what success? Experience proves that we cure the soldier best by taking him back and inducing him to accept the fact he was loath to admit, that he was afraid. The psychologically healthiest man in the trenches was the man who was not above admitting that he was afraid; he was also the most self-controlled. The acceptance of his fear whilst in the trenches does not make him run away: it enables him to control it and he remains healthy. It is found, too, that 'evil thoughts' obsess the mind far less if they are given psychological expression. The best way to get rid of a tune in the head is to sing it out, and of a repugnant desire, to accept it. The repressed impulse *needs* expression. It is only because we do not give it right expression that it comes out in morbid ways. There is something abnormal about a mind that cannot look naturally upon the impulses.

What, then, prevents us 'going to the dogs'? Simply the influences of the rest of the mind – the remaining sentiments and dispositions, into the circle of which the instincts are now brought; in other words, the control of the will.

What people usually mean when they say, 'But we *must* repress our instincts!' is that we must *restrain* them. That is quite true. If the bus conductor treads on my foot it is perfectly natural for me to be angry, and it is far better that I should admit that I *am* angry. But there is no necessity for me to express my anger in an outburst. I restrain my anger, natural though I recognize it to be, since I recognize that it would serve no good purpose if I did lose my temper.

If, on the other hand, I *repressed* my anger and pretended to myself I was perfectly amiable and that it is impossible that *I* should be angry, as likely as not my repressed ill-temper would come out towards my wife at home during the evening on some trifling pretext. In such circumstances, then, we need to restrain, but we do not need to repress the impulse. We may give them psychological expression without giving them expression in conduct – and it gives us relief when we do.

The principle of psychological expression is therefore of the utmost importance in ethics. In the interests of moral life and health of mind our repugnant complexes and 'animal passions' must be accepted before they can be controlled. This does not mean that it is necessary to give outward expression to them in their crude form.

To give them crude expression in conduct is to do violence to our ideals: to give them psychological expression, that is to say, to accept them and control them but not suppress them, means that we can modify them in accordance with our ideals.

If I am a man of strong sex passions, I recognize that such desires, as desires, are natural and right, but that it is inexpedient to give them crude expression in conduct since this would not conduce to self-realization and happiness. It is only by accepting and controlling them that I can sublimate them into the higher forms of love.

The principle of psychological acceptance is therefore as important in morality as in the treatment of nervous ills. It provides us with two essentials: (*a*) it enables us to control our impulses which we cannot control as long as we repress them; (*b*) it puts at our disposal instinctive forces of great power for the building up of character.

CHAPTER XXIV

Re-association

EVERY MORBID COMPLEX consists of a group of emotions centred round an object or idea. In analysis we bring this complex into consciousness and so under the control of the will. By this means we are able to break up the complex. We then take the object or idea forming the nucleus and associate it with healthy emotions – Re-association; and finally take the emotions liberated from the complex and redirect them to new ends – Sublimation.

The thought of a base action may be associated with shame, the recollection of an 'insult' with anger, the sexual instinct may be attached to a fetishistic object.

In treatment, these thoughts and events are wrested from these emotions, and are associated with new emotional attitudes such as humility, a sense of humour, or indifference respectively; whilst the emotions of fear, shame, anger, and sex are redirected to new ends.

To take a specific example from psychopathology.

An airman has a crash and fractures his skull. He continues to suffer from severe headache and some anxiety. Under hypnosis, he is taken through all his experiences again until he comes to the crash, when he nearly jumps off the bed. This incident is at present associated with terror. Keeping the incident before his mind we associate it with the idea that the whole thing is over, and there is nothing to worry about. The next day he is again put through the experience, under hypnosis, but when he comes to the crash he quietly says, 'Tut! there goes two thousand quid. But, never mind, I'm getting my own back!' The event has been successfully re-associated with confident emotions.

As with nervous, so with moral conditions. When an object arouses emotions in a way which is unacceptable to us, we call it a temptation. But such objects may be robbed of these emotions by being associated with new emotions. People who before aroused our anger by their baseness may now arouse our pity; an insult may be so re-associated that we see the humorous side of it; to the fetish which aroused our sexual passions we become indifferent; the difficult task stimulates our determination instead of our despair; the worthless wastrel moves our chivalry instead of our scorn; when we realize that our 'righteous indignation' is mere intolerance born of moral conceit, we become helpful instead of censorious towards the weak. Thus, the process of re-association is in its way just as important as that of sublimation.

Treatment by suggestion depends upon this process of re-association. By suggestion we associate the morbid object with a new emotion. If standing up to make a speech makes us nervous, by suggestion we link it on to the feeling of confidence: we associate in our minds the speech-making and confidence. We visualize ourselves beforehand speaking calmly and easily. When the occasion arrives, we find that the association is reproduced, the one recalling the other by association, and we find ourselves speaking with extraordinary ease.

Suggestion is of great value in the treatment of minor ailments. A morphino-maniac could not pass a chemist's shop without the desire to go in and buy chlorodyne. By suggestion he was made vividly to picture himself *passing* certain shops where he gets the dope, the idea of a chemist's shop being thus associated with the thought of passing it. The suggestion was so effective that he complained later, 'I found the greatest difficulty in going into a chemist's shop to get a toothbrush!' Treatment by suggestion may thus effectively dismiss the symptom. It does not, however, cure the underlying disease, though it inhibits the symptom of the morphino-maniac, for his real disease is his moral inability to face the responsibilities of life. As long as the complex remains it may 'light up' again.

This objection holds good of all those forms of 'faith healing' by the laying on of hands, unction, and prayer. We have already protested against the treatment of organic diseases by these means. But even in the treatment of functional disorders they fail of their purpose if they cure the symptom without securing a radical change in the moral outlook of the patient. We may cure by unction, or the laying on of hands, the nervous backache due to repressed self-pity without curing the self-pity. Indeed, our main criticism of these forms of treatment is not that they cure physical disorders by spiritual means, but that they too frequently treat these diseases, which are essentially moral, by non-moral means.

The practice of auto-suggestion is of value in overcoming minor traits of nervousness from which so many suffer, but which are too trifling to submit to a prolonged psychological analysis. I need emphasize only one or two points which have not received sufficient notice elsewhere: (*a*) Suggestions should always be positive. To suggest before making a speech, 'I shall not be nervous', is to associate the idea of speaking with the idea of nervousness, in which case the last state is worse than the first. The sub-conscious deals in broad ideas, and is indifferent to negatives. Suggest rather to yourself, 'I shall be calm and confident', and picture yourself so. So, instead of suggesting, 'I shall not be disagreeable with the club bore', we suggest, 'I shall be pleasant'. The effect may be remarkable. (*b*) The suggestion should precede the occasion. In time of peace prepare for war; to wait until the occasion comes is to court defeat. If we wait till we sit in the dentist's chair before suggesting courage, the stimulus to fear will be too much for us. If in anticipation of temptation we link the coming event with the right emotions of courage, determination, calmness, and confidence, we find the moment of temptation pass as by a miracle.

Suggestion is the first method of psychotherapy, and valuable as it is in minor ailments, or for alleviating serious ones, yet it often fails to cure because of morbid *auto*-suggestions which obsess the patient's mind. Conscious auto-suggestions are of undoubted value. But we must remember that auto-suggestions may also arise from repressed complexes. There is, therefore, a conflict between the new and voluntary auto-suggestions and those from the complexes, whose impulses are often so strong that they overpower the new auto-suggestions, however strongly emphasized these may be.

If a woman suffers from a pain in the back due to repressed self-pity, she may say to herself that she is free from pain, and this conscious suggestion may produce an immediate effect. But it does not get rid of the repressed self-pity which continues to throw up its auto-suggestions, and since it is strong and of old standing, it commonly wins in the end, so that cure is not permanent.

The only radical method of treatment is to discover and eradicate the complex, split it up, and re-associate it, so that its voice is for ever silenced.

CHAPTER XXV

Sublimation

Sublimation is the process by which instinctive emotions are diverted from their original ends and redirected to purposes satisfying to the individual and of value to the community. In treatment, when we have brought up the complex and re-associated the nucleus with a new emotion, we proceed to sublimate the emotions now liberated from the complex.

(A) *Surplus Emotional Energy.* Every instinct is primarily directed towards a definite and specific end of biological value to the animal. So the acquisitive instinct is directed towards the accumulation of the raw materials of life, food, shelter, and weapons. In the course of biological evolution means are devised by which these ends are more easily effected, and thus an economy of energy is secured. This means that the full strength of the original instinct was not required.

The need for the young animal to fight is diminished by the care it receives as the result of the maternal instinct, and therefore there is a superfluity of the pugnacious instinct which issues in play. Again, we have observed that the full strength of the sexual instinct was originally required to reproduce large quantities of the species, but that this is made less necessary by the emergence of the maternal instinct and the care of the young. The result is that as life becomes more specialized and civilized, and more economical means are adapted to ends, there is a large amount of primitive energy which is 'going loose', which man does not need for the ordinary purposes of life, and which he has at his disposal for sublimation. This energy, by being re-directed, gives rise to all those activities of culture, of art, and of learning, which adorn civilized life.

(B) *The Right to Sublimate.* It is sometimes objected that we have no right to sublimate our instincts to ends other than those for which they were naturally intended.

If, as we have held, the instincts are good, why should we seek to sublimate them to something 'higher'? We appear to say: 'The instincts are good, but let us try to get away from them.' Let us be clear as to what is our aim in sublimation, and why we should sublimate. Our purpose in sublimation is to produce a condition of harmony and happiness. We have the following justification for sublimating:

(*a*) Sublimation is a natural process, to be observed not only in the play of the young, but also in the natural development of music and the arts, which we find even in lower phases of evolution, e.g. among birds and savages.

(*b*) Furthermore, we have to face the fact that instincts are, in fact, redirected to other than their natural ends in morbid conditions. The end of the sexual instinct is reproduction, and its emotion is aroused by an attractive person of the opposite sex. But the sex instinct, instead of being aroused and attached to such a person, may be attached to an object like a girl's shoe, and produce a fetishism; or to one of our own sex, homosexuality; or to ourselves, auto-erotism. These objects may completely monopolize the instincts so that they and they only arouse sex feelings. In neuroses instincts are attached to morbid objects; in sublimation to healthy ones.

Any kind of activity may serve as a sublimation. Pent-up instinctive energy will be eased by any form of outlet; for instance, a man may find relief from his sexual troubles by going to the wars. But for a satisfactory sublimation we should discover in what specific form the energy is repressed, that is to say, what mode of instinctive expression, whether maternal, sexual, or pugnacious, so that the mode of sublimation may be appropriate and specific.

(C) *The Directions of Instincts.* An instinct, say that of acquisition, may take three directions: it may be directed to its *natural* end, the accumulation of the necessities of life; or to a *perverted* end, say the accumulation of old clothes or papers; or a *sublimated* end, the collecting of art treasures giving pleasure and profit to oneself and others.

In the study of each instinct we shall observe (1) the original direction; (2) the perversion; (3) the sublimation.

We shall deal briefly, not with all the instincts, but with the most important, viz. fear, curiosity, sex, self-display, self-assertion, submission, and the maternal instinct.

FEAR

There is no more common nor more valuable instinct than fear: without it we should constantly step into danger and be killed. The function of fear is to provide the body with mobility and muscular tone, and the mind with alertness to meet danger. The protection of civilized life leaves us with little to fear, and, therefore, with an enormous surplus capacity for fear. So the superfluous fear becomes attached to all kinds of indifferent objects and we fear ourselves and develop 'phobias', the *perversion* of fear, in which fear is attached to morbid objects. This commonly takes the form of pantophobia, the fear of everything, which is characteristic of adults who are still children in their relation to life, having been arrested in their emotional development. Or the fear may be projected to some one external object giving rise to all those phobias like agoraphobia (the fear of open spaces), claustrophobia (the fear of closed spaces), fear of marriage, fear of being alone, of being in a crowd, of pillar-boxes, of tunnels, and a thousand other fears for which the Greek language is impotent to provide names. It is not without reason that some schools of New Thought make fear, or fear-thought, the chief foe of man's happiness. We should distinguish fear, anxiety, and phobia. *Natural fears* are fears directed to objects really dangerous to life: *anxieties* are fears without an object, and are usually due to fear of a threatening impulse within. They are *unrecognized* fears of ourselves. *Phobias* are fears attached to objects not in themselves dangerous. They are *projected* fears of ourselves. This is true of all phobias – they are all fears of ourselves, fears of some impulse in ourselves, fears of 'unconscious desires'. The greatest fear of civilized man is himself. The difference between a normal fear and an abnormal fear (or phobia) can easily be recognized. The normal fear leads to biological efficiency, whereas the abnormal fear leads to inefficiency. So the chemist has a normal and sublimated fear of making a mistake in his drugs and poisoning some one; he therefore takes precautions. But he may develop a phobia that he has poisoned somebody, which may in fact be due to a repressed and unrecognized sadism or impulse to inflict cruelty on others which obsesses his mind day and night. Far from making him efficient, it makes him lose his head.

The *sublimation* of fear is found in that alertness of mind which is able to perceive emergencies and prepare to meet them in any sphere of work, business, or profession. It is the opposite of the carelessness of the man who is unconcerned in danger. To fear is not to be afraid. I had rather trust myself in dangerous waters to a seaman who had some fear than one who had none. So would I avoid the surgeon who has not the least fear of making a mistake on the operating table. Fearlessness is wedded to recklessness. Confidence, as distinct from recklessness, is given to him who realizes the danger, but realizes, too, his power to meet it.

SEX

It is difficult to define the sex instinct.[1] Its end is normally that of reproduction of the species, but to confine the term merely to the reproductive act is to exclude activities like kissing, or perversions like exhibitionism, homosexuality, and self-abuse, which are obviously sexual. In the curiosity of the prying gossip there may be little consciousness of sex feeling, and yet it would be difficult to deny to such curiosity the

[1] See 'The Conception of Sexuality', a symposium by the present author and others, in *The British Journal of Medical Psychology*, 1925.

character of sex. Freud has pointed out this difficulty but has gone to the other extreme, and seems to identify the sexual with sensuous gratification,[1] which involves him in considerable confusion. He admits, for instance, the existence of a nutritive instinct (expressed in sucking) as distinct from the sexual instinct, and yet he calls the gratification in sucking 'sexual'. This shows the futility of defining sex in terms of its affective or feeling tone, instead of defining it in terms of its biological end. Between the too limited and the too vague definitions we must seek one more in conformity with the use of the term in ordinary language. We define as sexual *that group of impulses whose natural end is reproduction.* Such impulses as exposing oneself are not reproductive, but they naturally lead up to reproduction, and are therefore sexual: so with kissing, so with stimulating the sex organs. On the other hand, sucking with its pleasure is entirely nutritive, passing motions and its pleasure, purely excretive; and therefore while they are sensuous they are not sexual, as they do not in any sense lead to reproduction. Indeed, their influence upon ordinary sex feelings seems to us in the direction of 'drawing off' the gratification from the latter, when they are too persistently indulged. Other impulses like curiosity and self-assertiveness are sometimes sexual and sometimes not, their morbid attachment to sexual objects being given specific names such as 'observationism' and 'sadism'.

Again, perversions like homosexuality, self-abuse, and exhibitionism do not as perversions lead to reproduction, but, on the contrary, often oust normal sex desires. Why then call them sexual?

We call them sexual because their impulses – stimulation of the sex organs, self-display, and the rest – *naturally* lead up to reproduction: it is only because they are turned away from these ends and are attached to unnatural objects that we call them perversions. We may, therefore, justifiably speak of them as *sexual* perversions in the terms of our definition.

[1] *Three Contributions to the Sexual Theory*, p. 44.

This definition appears then to fulfil all the demands of the word sex as used in everyday language without involving us in the confusion into which Freud has led us.

Whatever views we may hold, and in our opinion the time has not come for dogmatic statement, the sex instinct is undoubtedly charged with extraordinary power and primitive emotions. This instinct, and fear, are perhaps the most primitive. Sex is also the most repressed; fear is the main repressing agency. We are not surprised, therefore, to find that sexuality plays a predominant part in the formation of a vast number of the neuroses and phobias.

The sex instinct may be viewed in relation to its *object*, or as an *impulse*. As it develops it passes through certain phases, being attached to various objects at different times of life. In childhood our love is attached to ourselves, as auto-erotism, and frequently persists as such. The habit of self-abuse or masturbation, which may be regarded as 'having sexual intercourse with oneself', is characteristic of those who are in love with themselves; it is for this reason psychologically and morally morbid. Normal homosexuality, the exclusive love of one's own sex, is a normal characteristic of puberty (13 and 14 years of age), when, however, it should be directed not so much to individuals as to the gang of other boys. Hetero-sexuality, the love of the opposite sex, and polyerotism, the love of several such, are characteristic of later adolescence. Monogamy is characteristic of adult life. Any of the earlier phases may persist to such an extent that they exclude the normal sexuality of adult life, and so give rise to perversions.

To sublimate sex emotion we must observe all the phases of its development. For instance, the auto-erotic stage characteristic of childhood may persist in the normal and healthy desire to make ourselves pleasurable to others and liked by them; homosexuality is characteristic of early puberty and may be normally sublimated in loyal co-operation with those of our own sex; the polyerotic tendencies of later adolescence in chivalry to those of the opposite sex; the monogamous tendencies in loyalty to and love for an ideal.

Further, viewing sexuality from the point of view, not of its object, but of its impulses, we observe that many impulses go to the making of the sex instinct – self-display and the craving for admiration; self-assertion, characteristic of the masterful male; coyness and submissiveness, at one time characteristic of the female; the creative impulse primarily for the creation of the child; and closely allied to the sex instinct, the maternal instinct for the care of the offspring.

The sublimation of the sex instincts means, therefore, the redirection of each of these impulses to sublimated ends. But since individuals vary very considerably in the development of these different impulses, we must, to effect an adequate sublimation, discover which of these impulses is strongest in any particular individual and then secure the redirection of this impulse, so that it may be given its fullest development. In one the craving for admiration is strongest when it may be sublimated in a desire to secure admiration for good work; in another the creative impulse may be sublimated in all forms of creative work, and many women, whilst still recognizing and desiring natural expression for the sex instinct, have found happiness in creative work of other kinds, whether in art, writing, or handicraft.

But the sex instinct is so many-sided, and its impulses manifest themselves in so many forms, that the forms of sublimation must correspond to these, several of which will be dealt with in the following paragraphs dealing with some of these impulses.

THE INSTINCT OF SELF-DISPLAY

In nature self-display seems to be essentially sexual: the plumage of the bird attracts the male; the display of manly strength impresses the female. As in beauty of form and strength of motion, so in the beauty of song: the first song, like the croak of a frog, was a love song, and the majority of songs still retain their original theme of love.

Self-display as an instinct normally blossoms into full

flower about the age of 15 and 16, and forces the attractions of love. At this age the girl displays her loveliness, the boy his prowess. But the tendency to display is found even in children. In its earliest phase the instinct of self-display takes the form of a desire to expose themselves and run about naked. This is not merely a desire for primitive liberty, for it is usually accompanied by the desire to be seen, and most often seen by one of the opposite sex. This is a perfectly natural phase in the child, but if it is unduly repressed it may become a 'perversion', to which the name 'exhibitionism' is given. The perverted 'exhibitionist' may have no normal sexual desires, but merely wish to expose himself. In women it is exemplified in the 'dressy' type, who seem to be oozing sexuality from every pore, by every article of dress, and in every perfume. It is a strange anomaly that such women, who appear to be so highly sexed, are frequently devoid of any localized sexual feeling whatever. Indeed, outwardly attractive as they may be in appearance, they make very disappointing partners in marriage, because of their sexual frigidity, and their marriages are frequently failures ending in the divorce court. The reason for the lack of localized sexuality is that their sexuality has been arrested in an early 'diffuse' phase, and has never developed into adult localized sexuality.

Normally, the child passes from the display of its body to that of its clothes, its cleverness, its prowess – 'See how clever I am! Watch me do this!'

The sublimation of the instinct of display takes place when beauty is admired and sought for, not as a symbol of sexual love, but for itself. Such is considered by most to be the origin of Art and Music, in which beauty is loved for its own sake. Indeed, we use synonymous terms when we speak of beautiful things as though they were sexually attractive, and call them 'lovely'. So successfully have the sexual associations of the instinct been sublimated in a love of the beautiful that in the symphony or the colour scheme its origin would not so much as be suspected. So close is the connexion, however, between this instinct and the sex instinct that its complete sublimation in art relieves the tension of the sex instinct, and many women have found happiness in a life devoted to music and the arts. Such an outlet is satisfying to the individual and is *sometimes* of value to the community.

Æsthetic taste is thus one of the most beautiful forms and sublimations of the sexual impulse. If the artist is himself normal, then his expression of art will concern itself with those qualities of form and colour which have always been associated with feelings of love. If, on the other hand, he is perverted or neurotic, his work will depict the symbols of his morbid state. Some artists are sadists, and depict cruelty and bloodshed, the guillotine, and burning of martyrs. Others are masochistic, depicting sordid, coarse and depraved women, drunken men. Every artist perforce must paint what is the beautiful to him. We can have no objection to such an artist expressing himself, for he cannot do otherwise.

But self-display may be manifested in other directions satisfying to oneself and of value to others. The child who has strong instincts of self-display may become a poet in which his imagination is displayed, a lecturer who displays his thoughts, a preacher who displays his beliefs, an actor who visibly interprets the thoughts and emotions of others. When such actors and preachers are analysed, it is frequently found that in childhood they were 'exhibitionists' with a strong tendency to self-display. There is no need for such men to be ashamed of this tendency; they may use and develop it to right ends, and should find their delight in giving expression to such forms of self-display.

SELF-ASSERTION AND SUBMISSION

The self-assertive instinct establishes the dominance of the individual, and since the advancement of the race depends upon the emergence from the crowd of individuals of outstanding and commanding personality, this instinct is of paramount importance. But, like all the instincts, it may be perverted to base uses, or it may dominate the mind too exclusively.

The ideal expressed in the phrase, 'The will to power', is an exaggeration of the self-assertive instinct. Such an exaggerated ambition or 'power' psychology is usually to compensate for a feeling of inferiority. Indeed, Adler traces all nervous breakdown to the attempt to compensate for physical inferiority. The Kaiser's ambitions of power were probably a counterblast to the paralysis of his arm. Roosevelt and Sandow were both delicate children, and Napoleon was laughed at by his fellow-students. Many of our most reckless airmen and soldiers in the war were 'mothers' boys', who were trying to prove to themselves and others, often with great success, that they were not weaklings.

It is because the 'will to power' is an over-compensation for a feeling of inferiority that it sometimes fails so miserably. It commonly produces a nervous breakdown with the sense of failure and lack of confidence. Besides which, it impoverishes our character in that it represses the qualities of love and tenderness. There are two great principles in life, the principle of power and the principle of love, both of which must find expression in a healthy life. They are the two wings by which man soars to his ideal. The 'superman' despises the 'sentimental', the 'unmanly'; he is the man's man, the strong, silent hero, the man of iron – firm, hard, unyielding, scorning all that he calls 'effeminate'. But in saving his power he loses it; for he tries to fly to the sun on the one wing of power, fearing to surrender any of his libido to love lest he should lose power. But the one wing of power soon tires, and he falls exhausted. He must learn to surrender some of his ambition, to yield himself to the principle of love, that so, by spreading both wings, the wing of power and the wing of love, he may mount easily to the heavens. Only by losing his power does he find it: by surrendering his ambition he secures it. The 'will to power' is the direct road to impotence. Power can only become omnipotent by being wedded to love.

The self-assertion instinct manifests itself in primitive life in two main activities – the subduing of the foe and the over-powering of the female by the male; that is to say, one of its activities is sexual and the other not. This gives rise to two forms of perversion – one taking the form of sheer cruelty and brutality, and the other to the perversion known as sadism, the pleasure of overmastering and even inflicting pain upon the sexually loved person. Famous instances of the former are found in tyrants like Nero, and of sadism in the Marquis of Sade, Jack the Ripper, and Landru. History repeats itself in examples of 'Bluebeards', who murder their many spouses. The wife-beater is an example of less romantic type: so is the schoolmaster who loves the cane; others still less romantic bite their nails, the loved person in this case being themselves. Others take a pleasure in saying biting and cruel things to their friends.

The term sadism should not be used therefore of all manifestations of cruelty, but only those which are directly or indirectly sexual in nature or, to put it otherwise, all cruelty should not be regarded as sexual, as is done by some psychologists. The impulse itself is self-assertive, though the object to which it is directed is sexual.

These two forms of abnormality – brutality and sadism – must be separated and distinguished. The sadist is merely a brute in the ordinary sense of the term, for his sadism is due to *repressed* brutality. Indeed, he is frequently, like Landru, the gentlest and most courteous of men in ordinary life; and it is the mildest of girls who wear their nails long like talons.

Sublimated, the instinct of mastery and self-assertion makes the firm statesmen, army generals, great employers, and foremen, leaders of men who rule their fellows by force of character. Nor do they shrink from inflicting pain if this is necessary to bring about a reform for the greater good of men.

The *Submissive* instinct is as truly instinctive as any other, and demands recognition in a life of perfect self-realization. We must know how to be abased. The instinct was originally developed in obedience to the herd instinct, for without submission to the pack, or tribe, social life would be impossible. The reason why the instinct is stronger in women than in men is probably due to the primitive custom of 'marriage by capture' amongst animals and men, in which the pursuit and capture of the female served the biological purpose of ensuring that only the strongest and bravest of the males should propagate the race. This custom finds its echo down the ages in the cry which still escapes the lips of the amorous damsel of the Old Kent Road – 'Chase me, Charlie!'

The instinct of submission is perversion in 'masochism', the pleasure in being overmastered, even to the infliction of pain. This is very common, especially amongst women, although they may not recognize it. It gives them the reputation of being able to endure pain more than men. The strongest argument against caning in schools is that it often arouses the sexual instincts of the boy who is thrashed. Masochism is seen in early childhood in the child who deliberately bangs its head against a wall. The pleasure most of us find in increasing the pain of a loose tooth by pressing the tongue against it gratifies both our sadistic and our masochistic tendencies, for at one and the same time we both inflict and suffer pain.

The sadistic tendency is shown in the schoolboy who spends a Saturday afternoon bullying his sister – it is usually the favourite sister – and the masochistic tendency in the sister who is bullied. Her pleasure in the proceeding is proved by the fact that though she protests against the brutal treatment, as soon as he shows signs of desisting she immediately provokes him to make him continue. The wife-beater is a sadist, but the wife who is beaten is commonly a masochist, admiring and loving him the more for his brutal treatment of her.[1]

Nothing is more aggravating to some women than a husband who is always mild and never loses his temper, in spite of her provocation. Only those women who have

[1] One ventures to suggest that the Eugenic Society might arrange marriages between sadistic husbands and masochistic wives, so that they may find their pleasures at home in mutual love by castigation!

experienced living with such a husband know its utter misery and the longing for a husband who can lose his temper once in a while.

Submission is sublimated in the man or woman who is indifferent to the pain they suffer in espousing a great cause; it is the stuff out of which martyrs are made. If such suffering is assumed merely for its own sake and to no useful purpose, it is an example of the perversion of masochism: if, in spite of the actual pain, one suffers gladly for some great cause, it is a true sublimation.

CURIOSITY

We have already described the function of this instinct. It is not primarily sexual, like that of self-display, but is directed towards examining every strange and possibly dangerous object, with a view to self-preservation. In early life, however, it frequently gets attached to sexual objects, and takes the form of 'observationism', or the tendency of sexual curiosity, which, if it is repressed, may persist as a definite perversion, so monopolizing the sex instinct that all desire for the normal expression of this instinct may be obliterated. There are other manifestations of morbid sex curiosity. Prudery is ill-disguised sex curiosity, and the prude, like other sexual perverts, is frequently lacking in normal sexual desires. Nothing is more calculated to stimulate morbid sex curiosity than the suppression of its normal psychological satisfaction. This is very commonly done by parents, who will answer the questions of their children on all other subjects except that of birth and sex, a procedure which makes this subject excessively fascinating to them. We are fascinated by what is hidden. Clothes may serve the purpose of stimulating curiosity in sex. Complete nudity, physical and mental, is excessively boring; suggestiveness, on the other hand, stimulates the appetite, in the lowest as well as the highest forms of literature and art.

The sublimation of the instinct of curiosity gives rise to all forms of scientific research. Instead of being curious only as to whether an object is dangerous or not, the scientist is curious about the heavenly bodies, about the formation of the earth, the constitution of matter, the nature of mental processes, and these give rise to the sciences of astronomy, geology, physics, and psychology. Without curiosity there would be no incentive to research, whereas if the instinct is consciously and voluntarily restrained and controlled it may be re-directed to these sublimated ends. Thus, the age of conscious restraint in the nineteenth century was the age of greatest scientific discovery.

THE MATERNAL INSTINCT

The functions of this instinct have already been discussed. It is naturally directed to the care of the young. It is perverted in the woman who spends her time in caring for a cat or fondling a toy dog. Its sublimation is obviously found in nursing or in the teaching and training of the young. A special form of its sublimation is found in women who have reared families, and whose instincts are no longer required for the care of their family. Nature, it is said, has no use for women after forty-five. But such women may trick nature and avoid disappointment by finding happiness in redirecting the instincts to the larger interests of the community – becoming the mothers of the people.

SOME PROBLEMS OF SUBLIMATION

In connexion with such sublimations as we have illustrated, such questions as the following arise:

'Is it possible to sublimate in every case?' 'What of people who have taken up work such as we have indicated and are yet unhappy?' After all, one has known governesses who are unhappy in caring for children, although they are doing good work, and girls at the School of Music who break down with neurosis.

It is true that there are many people who are living virtuous and useful lives, apparently sublimated, who yet find no satisfaction in life, and are certainly not the envy of others. Some further observations of sublimation are therefore necessary.

(*a*) *We cannot sublimate unless we have material to sublimate.* It is worthless to try to sublimate the sexual instinct by creative work whilst the sexual instinct is repressed in some complex, or regarded with disgust or suspicion. The emotion must first be released before it can be employed. The woman of 35 who has 'never had a sexual feeling in her life' cannot easily find happiness in the supposed sublimation of instincts which are unexpressed. Her work becomes wearisome for lack of emotional energy. The instinct must be liberated; she must recognize and accept these feelings, and then, perhaps for the first time in her life, she becomes happy and works well. There is no more common mistake amongst moral people of our day than the attempt to sublimate without the material of sublimation, and they pay for their mistake by constant breakdown. The instincts refuse to be regarded as poor relations of which a haughty self is half-ashamed: they are the partners which give power to the enterprise of our ideals.

This point needs emphasis, for one of the greatest difficulties faced by a psychotherapist is 'over-sublimation'. A large part of our race is over-civilized, and the psychologist is urging the return to nature, human nature in its primitive strength, for the means of culture and the acquisition of power. There are high-browed souls, refined, sensitive, intellectual, idealistic, whose characters are nevertheless thin. The blue veins of our aristocracy of taste and idealism are seen beneath the thin veil of their flesh, but their arteries do not pulsate with the rich blood of life. It is a paradox that these people of an over-sublimate refinement have to be brought to accept the primitive in their own souls, to know that out of the animal may spring the spiritual, to recognize that the human is fashioned not only out of the breath of God, but out of the dust of the earth.

As a physician, I would rather deal with a healthy, primitive soul, innocent of any sublimation, than deal with one possessing a perverted idealism, which is the most common type of those visiting the psychotherapist.

The latter class, hedged about with prejudice, needs to recognize their primitive savage selves before they can be built up again into a healthy sublimation. In practice, therefore, repressed instincts must first be psychologically liberated. Before we sublimate, we must have material to sublimate.

(*b*) *Every sublimation must be satisfying to the individual.* Many are engaged in sublimated activities who are yet unhappy.

The teacher and the art student may be unhappy and break down: the business-man may take no pleasure in accumulating money. These are not sublimations, however valuable they may be to others, for every sublimation must be satisfying to the individual. The lack of 'joy' is a sign that the sublimation has not been properly brought about. The reason for this may be the attempt, previously described, to sublimate instincts which are still attached to repressed complexes. These must first be freed.

But it may also be because every individual must discover the right form of sublimation, and failure is commonly due to the fact that the right form of sublimation has not been discovered.

It is useless for the woman with strong creative instincts to devote herself to playing the violin; or for a woman with strong instincts of self-display to become a children's nurse. It is quite a different type of girl that one meets at the Academy of Music from those of the School of Handicrafts. The man with sadistic tendencies may make an excellent surgeon, but a poor physician. The man with repressed criminal tendencies may make an excellent lawyer, but would probably make a poor banker. It is most important that the 'bent' of each individual should be discovered, as it may be by analysis, if not otherwise. What we call the 'bent' is not inherited, but is based on the development of the instinct as the result of the early environment of its home. If a child's early conditions call forth his acquisitive instincts or his pugnacity, it is these which represent his bent, and these which should be used. The old principle which urged us to repress any instinct which we found strongly developed in us, and develop the weak ones, is directly opposed to the principle of modern psychotherapy. Our business is to use and develop the talent we have, not to try to cultivate those of others. If, as a result of childhood experiences, our observationism was developed, we should follow our bent, and become scientists; if our exhibitionism, then we should become actors, lecturers, or artists, recognizing the while the instinct to which we are giving expression. That is why every adolescent boy or girl needs to be given a say in what shall be their career, and not be forced into a career chosen by their parents, which may be incompatible with the youth's own bent.

(*c*) *Every sublimation must be of value to the community.*

No form of sublimation can be ultimately satisfying to the individual unless it commends itself to the community, for the individual cannot be happy except as a member of a community, and giving expression to those social instincts which, however lately developed in evolution, are so firmly rooted to man's nature that, as James points out, there is no torture more awful than solitary confinement, no punishment so severe as social ostracism.

There are many activities which appear to be satisfying to the individual but, in so far as they are selfish and contribute nothing to the life of the community, they cannot be ultimately satisfying to a being in whom the social instincts are as strong as they are in man. A woman may gratify her maternal instinct by keeping a toy terrier, but as this is of no particular value to the community it is not sublimation. Letting the hair grow long, whether in professional footballers, musicians or labour leaders, may be of great satisfaction to the self-display of the individual, but is of no great value to the community. It is most gratifying to the masterful impulses of a boy to slash off the tops of plants with his newly-acquired walking-stick, but it is not sublimation. The activities of tyrants are of this order. Many raconteurs one hears find great pleasure in their art, but give satisfaction to no one but themselves. The superæsthetic young man and the bossy young woman are other instances of such psychological types, gratifying their own appetite at the expense of others. Those cannot be ultimately happy, for their instincts and their activities have no end but their own gratification.

(*d*) Further, it may be asked: 'Is sublimation as good and satisfying as the natural uses of the instinct?'

No! In ordinary cases sublimation of such instincts as the sexual and the maternal is not as satisfying as the natural use of the instinct in reproduction and care of children. This is particularly obvious when we remember that even when we use the instinct in the natural way there is still a large excess of emotion which may be sublimated. Married people may employ the sexual instincts naturally, and at the same time sublimate, and there is no proof that they are behind others in artistic, creative, and social work. Nevertheless, sublimation, though it is 'second best', saves us from neurosis and gives us happiness, and may be of immense value to the race.

Moreover, it is conceivable that for some people, and in some work, complete sublimation may be preferable. A woman with a maternal instinct completely repressed in childhood by her masterfulness would make a poor mother, even when this is liberated in later life by analysis. Her own happiness and the good of the community are perhaps better served by devoting her masterful instincts, say, to running a business instead of running a husband.

(*e*) *Sublimation does not destroy the instinct.* Many women are reluctant to plunge into a form of sublimation and divert their instincts, as they still hope for marriage and the normal expression of their instincts. To sublimate appears to them to burn their bridges and cut themselves off from marriage or, at least, to be a concession to the idea that they will not get married. Such an idea is quite unjustified. The sex instincts are far too strong to be so easily sublimated and, whatever their sublimation may be, their normal instinct will rapidly be restored to their primitive functions. A woman does not make any the less a good wife for having been in business, nor does work as a nurse make her the less tender as a mother.

CHAPTER XXVI

Motives: Selfish and Altruistic

IT IS NOT without reason that one of the main charges brought against the new psychology is that it reduces everything to low motives. It is nevertheless a false charge.

A lady whose life was devoted to 'rescue' work amongst fallen girls believed herself to be actuated only by what she would call the highest motives, the well-being of her fellow-creatures. On analysis she recognized that she was originally attracted to this work by sexual curiosity. The barrister, whose case will later be mentioned (p. 235), considered that he was actuated in his profession by a desire to help the oppressed; on analysis his original motive was found to be self-importance. Another is devoted to good works and has a reputation for unselfishness. She discovers on analysis that she originally took to being 'unselfish' because this was the best means for securing praise and admiration, for which she had an exaggerated craving. She must needs be the centre of interest, and this was secured when people said, 'How unselfish!' The craving for admiration was the motive for her unselfishness.

These motives were not imputed by the physician, but were discovered by the patients themselves in investigating their past by free association.

But we are reducing everything to low motives. What of altruism? Are we all so selfish?

We admit that we reduce our conduct to its *original* motives; we deny that they are low. Before we can understand our motives of conduct, we must understand what we mean by 'motive'. The confusion in which we find ourselves is due to the fact that we use 'motive' in two senses – the *primary or initial motive* and the *end motive.* When, for instance, we say that 'the motive for the crime was theft', we mean that this was the 'end in view' which moved the prisoner to commit the crime. But it would be equally true to say that the motive of the crime was avarice, or the instinct of acquisition, in which case we use 'motive' to mean the instinctive motive or *force* which impelled him to perform the theft. The money was the *end* motive, the greed the *primary* motive, or motive force which urged him to the crime. These two are, of course, related. It was the end, viz. the thought of the jewels, which actually aroused his instincts of acquisition, and it was these instincts which in turn made him desire the jewels and impelled him to steal them. Every instinct which forces us to action is aroused by, and directed towards, a certain end.

So, using the term motive as the 'end motive', we may say that a man's motive was the good of his fellows, to serve his country, to do his duty. We may with equal truth say that his motive is his self-display, his gregarious instinct, or his craving for approbation. In the first case, we are stating the end motive; in the second, the primary motive. This distinction was clearly recognized by the child who was being reproved by her mother for biting her brother's nose: 'It must have been the devil that put such an idea into your mind,' said the mother. 'No,' replied the child, 'the devil made me angry, but biting his nose was entirely my own idea.' Behind every action we perform lies an instinctive impulse which finds gratification in its expression. When that impulse is accepted by the self, and directed towards an end satisfying to the self, it becomes a *motive.* We recognize both elements in the definition. '*The motive is a desire directed towards an end approved by the self.*'

In every action both these factors play a part.

Some people over-emphasize the end motive, others the primary or instinctive motive.

(*a*) *We must recognize the instinctive emotion as the motive of our actions*. In ordinary life we are apt to recognize only the end motive because in the nature of the case our conscious attention is directed towards the end. It is true, we do seek the good of our fellows, but what gives driving force to that end? There are those who insist that their motives are 'purely altruistic', and that they are actuated by nothing but the 'highest motives' and a sense of duty towards others. Such people deceive themselves if they fail to realize that their action gives them personal gratification, and the satisfaction of some desire. They fail to recognize the instinctive motive force which urges them to act, and failing to recognize it they pride themselves on the 'purity of their motives'.

The instinctive emotion which urges us is usually unrecognized and constitutes the unconscious. This is the 'unconscious motive' so much emphasized by the modern psycho-physician.

People who fondly imagine that they are actuated by nothing but a sense of duty are often surprised to discover that the real motive of their conduct is the gratification of some latent desire. The politician, of course, desires only to serve his country, the clergyman to preach the truth, the ascetic to practise self-denial, the doctor seeks only the health of his patients, the researcher the interests of science, the slum-worker to uplift the masses, and the saint seeks holiness. These are the conscious motives. When analysed, it may be found that the original motives which led them to these lines of action were – in the politician, self-importance; the clergyman, self-display; the ascetic, a shrinking from the responsibilities of life; the saint, self-righteousness; the slum-worker, a social snobbishness which urges him to seek the society of people amongst whom he will be 'somebody'. These are their *unconscious* motives, which *originally* determined their line of conduct.

But why not? Why should they not continue gratifying these instincts by employing them to these worthy ends. A patient cleverly remarked that all the first part of treatment consisted in asking the question, 'Why?' (to discover the unconscious motive), and that the second part of the treatment consisted in asking, 'Why not?'

When a man discovers on analysis that the original motive of what he took to be altruism was a desire for approbation or the feeling of self-importance or self-display, his phantasy is often humiliated. When the rescue-worker discovered that while her conscious motive was to help her fallen fellow-creatures, her unconscious motive was to satisfy sex curiosity, she remarked, 'Then I must give up my work. I see I was actuated by low motives.' But if one has an instinct strongly developed, why not accept it and use it? One will do the work better but will be free of self-righteousness.

If a girl, owing to childhood experiences, has developed a strong sex curiosity, why not recognize and use it? How better can she use it than by finding an outlet for these desires in rescue work? By recognizing these desires in herself, she will sympathize more deeply with those she is seeking to help, and therefore help them the more effectively. We do not condemn a girl for satisfying her maternal instincts in nursing, nor should we consider it a disgrace that she should give satisfaction to her sex instincts in work of this kind, *provided always that she recognizes the fact and that her interest is consciously directed towards her work and the welfare of those for whom she works; to the end motive and not to the mere gratification of her desires.*

If a man originally became a preacher to gratify his instinct of display, why should he abandon his calling on the discovery of this? If he has a strong instinct of display, how better can he use it than by illuminating great truths and moral principles? And if he can use his instinct of display in such a service, why not recognize and enjoy its use? The recognition of such motives brings happiness and increases power.[1] The instincts are not 'low'; *instincts are ennobled by*

[1] It is an extraordinary fact that, although I have analysed a large number of clergymen in whom the instincts of self-display or self-importance, and sometimes self-righteousness, have played so large a part, in no case has any one of them ultimately felt it necessary to abandon his calling, but they have returned with fuller, stronger life to use and enjoy this instinct in the service of

their uses. As St. Paul said, *first* the natural and *then* the spiritual.

(*b*) *We must recognize the end motive of our actions*, for it is equally false to go to the other extreme and over-emphasize the primary or instinctive motive. Whilst we must recognize the instinctive motives which give power to our activities and joy in our work, it is equally necessary to recognize the end motive towards which the instinctive emotion moves. Advocates of the new psychology have an unfortunate habit of saying of our motives: 'It is *only* self-display, it is *only* sexual curiosity, or *only* a desire for approbation.' They fail to recognize that these emotions would have lain inactive were they not stimulated towards some particular end.

(i) *In the stimulation of any instinct the end is the determining factor.*

It is not true to say that the motive of the rescue-worker was *only* sexual curiosity. The desire to help others was at least as important in judging the quality of her act, for without it her sex curiosity would not have followed this course, but might have developed into 'observationism' or some other form of sexual perversion. It was the end motive which determined her conduct.

Again, it may be true to say that it was the paternal instinct which moved Wilberforce to work for the emancipation of the slaves, but it was not 'only' this which constituted his motive, for he might much more easily have gratified this instinct by keeping guinea-pigs. These creatures did not, as far as we know, move him to pity, whereas his pity *was* aroused by the thought of the slaves. The primary motive of his conduct was the paternal instinct, the end motive was the liberation of the slaves, and it was the latter which was the determining factor.

A man may kill another either to secure his property or to protect a girl from rape. A man whose instincts would be

---

their work. It is the preacher or lecturer without self-display who is hopelessly dull. It requires more than a little of this instinct to make some theological truths attractive. There are some who pour scorn on those who speak 'for effect', yet what other object has a public speaker in view? Oratory is effective talking.

moved by the first might not be influenced by the second, whereas a man who might commit the second crime would be horrified by the first. The arousal of the pugnacious instinct and anger depend in these cases on the end motive. *In judging our motives everything depends on the kind of end which arouses our instincts.*

It is of the greatest importance that both factors be recognized, for no action is complete in which both these factors are not fully represented. The force of an act depends on the instinctive emotion, the quality of the act depends on the end: the one gives power, the other direction. We can be saved from self-righteousness only by recognizing the instinctive desires which lie behind every action: we can be saved from moral chaos only by recognizing the right end towards which all our instincts should be directed.

(ii) The end not only determines whether we act or not; *the end determines the* QUALITY *of the act, whether it is selfish or altruistic.*

If it is right that we should find joy in expressing our instincts, where does altruism come in? Are all our actions selfish? What do we mean by selfishness and altruism?

Altruism means that we find our joy in doing things for others.

The barrister, we say, should recognize his self-importance and find joy in its expression. Is this selfish or altruistic? That depends on the end motive towards which the instinct is directed.

As long as he uses his rhetorical powers in the defence of his client he is acting altruistically, whatever joy he derives from it; indeed, the more joy he derives the better he does his work. But suppose an opportunity to arise for a witty remark or brilliant repartee which would bring him applause *but which would prejudice his client's case*; to indulge in this self-gratification would be an act of selfishness. In both cases he finds pleasure, but in the first his pleasure is expressed for another's good, and therefore is altruistic, whereas in the latter case it is directed towards himself, and, being so, it is selfish. That is to say, *so long as the pleasurable impulse is directed towards the service of others, it is altruistic; as soon as the gratification of the instinct becomes itself* THE END MOTIVE AS WELL AS THE MOTIVE FORCE *it becomes selfish.*

This point must be emphasized. For an action to be unselfish and altruistic it is not sufficient that it be for the good of others; it must be *consciously directed* towards the service of others. Altruism must thus be distinguished from the principle of 'enlightened self-interest' which many have accepted as the guiding principle of their life. They say: 'I shall best serve my own interest by being moral or kind.' It implies that as soon as being kind ceases to contribute to our self-interest we are free to abandon it. Or take that horrible remark, 'To be generous (or to be honest, or courteous) *pays dividends*'; it is true that being kind does bring happiness. But enlightened self-interest, in directing its attention towards itself, defeats its own purpose; for as soon as we begin to make our own pleasure the end motive, and do things for others only so as to get pleasure for ourselves, the pleasure vanishes as fleetingly as when we seek to enjoy music by attending to our feelings of joy. An altruistic act must be directed towards the happiness of others: only by so doing can we find our own happiness.

Many activities which appear to be selfish, in that they are extremely pleasurable, must be looked upon as altruistic. So the rescue-worker's recognition of the joy she experiences in satisfying her sex curiosity does not make her work the less altruistic; it merely makes it more effective. If as a result of childhood experiences I have an abnormal craving for admiration, let me gratify it in activities serviceable to others. The pleasure is mine, the good is theirs and mine. If I have a feeling of self-importance, let me use it in excelling in my profession, or in building up my business. To take pleasure in being a successful accountant or plumber, in so far as it is directed towards the good of others, is altruistic.

On the other hand, many activities thought to be altruistic are, in fact, utterly selfish.

For instance, it is right that we should be ready to suffer

for our cause, and to find joy in suffering. But if we deliberately put ourselves into positions in which we receive insults for the pleasure of self-pity or posing as martyrs, even giving our bodies to be burned would be a selfish act, an indulgence of self-gratification worthless to others. There are some instincts like the maternal and the herd instinct, which appear to be essentially altruistic, yet even these may be selfish if wrongly directed. I have in mind a case in which a man when recovering from a serious illness was nursed by his sister, who positively kept him an invalid by over-care, in order to indulge her maternal instincts. Many mothers to gratify their mother instincts so devote themselves to their children that these never grow up but remain hopelessly arrested in development.

Pity may be a form of self-indulgence; benevolence may be a form of vanity; forgiveness may be due to a weakness of character which cannot bear to have enemies, or it may be granted in scornful disdain; whereas pugnacity, self-assertion, sex, and fear, by their direction to noble ends, may give expression to the highest forms of altruism.

Altruism does not mean that we do for others what is irksome to ourselves: altruism is finding joy in doing things for others. The determination of whether our activity is selfish or altruistic does not depend on whether or not it is pleasurable in its expression, but upon the end towards which it is directed. If what we do is consciously directed towards the happiness of others, it is altruistic; if the instinct is directed purely towards self-gratification it is selfish.

Altruism is, therefore, accepted as a higher moral law than egoism, and is encouraged by the herd, in that it serves social ends as well as giving joy to the individual.

CHAPTER XXVII

Know Thyself, Accept Thyself, Be Thyself

THERE ARE THREE principles of psychological and moral health – Know thyself; accept thyself; be thyself.

KNOW THYSELF

The purpose of all 'self-examination' is to know oneself, yet the injunction of the Greek sage has never till recently even approached realization. Most people think they know themselves; in the course of analysis they usually discover that what they think of themselves is rather what they want to be thought than what they really are. When we remember that what we want to be thought is obviously what we are not, it is not surprising that our characters are often the opposite of what we think them. This has been amply illustrated in the earlier pages of this book.

To see ourselves as we really are is an event of profound importance. It is sometimes brought about by the presentation of a new ideal with which we compare ourselves, as in religion. It can also be brought about by analysis. The purpose of all analysis is to discover the whole person, and to reveal a man to himself. This is always a surprise; it is often a shock.

ACCEPT THYSELF

One of the most difficult things in life is, having known oneself, to accept oneself. There is the whole world of difference between *admitting* and *accepting* oneself. When one 'admits' anything it is usually an indication that he does not 'accept' it. We 'admit' that we lost our temper, that we were vain or avaricious, that our minds were obsessed with 'evil thoughts', but in the very act of admission we dissociate ourselves from them. To 'accept' them we make them part of ourselves. We must accept ourselves *as* pugnacious, vain, and sensuous. If we are to win the instinctive emotions to our side, we must be prepared to make unto ourselves friends of this Mammon of unrighteousness. The man who feels himself to be effeminate and tries to hide it by a manly pose, needs not merely to admit his effeminacy, which he is loath to do, but to accept it and give more play to it. He will find that the feminine in him, including, for instance, the quality of sympathetic intuition, is his real strength. The vain man, instead of repressing his vanity, will accept it and win the applause of men for noble deeds. The man constantly obsessed with passionate thoughts must not merely accept them as his, he must discover more outlets for his emotional life, which craves for expression.

It is often objected that if we accept ourselves as we really are it would destroy all moral endeavour. We reply, on the contrary, that there can be no moral progress until we do accept ourselves. The refusal to accept ourselves is not righteousness but self-righteousness.

The real difficulty we have in accepting ourselves as we really are is that it pricks the inflated phantasy we have of ourselves. Reductive analysis abolishes our phantasies of ourselves and makes us accept the fact that we are for the most part extraordinarily ordinary – which, when it is once accepted, is not only a great relief, but a great impetus to moral progress.

BE THYSELF

It is a right impulse that makes us concerned with what others think of us; but to identify ourselves with what others think of us is to adopt a pose, and to try to be someone other than ourselves is to lose our character.

We all have many selves, one of the most important of which is the self we present to our fellows, the self *we appear to be*.

This is our *persona*, the mask or character we assume, and which we want others to recognize. This self or character is often entirely inconsistent with, and even antagonistic to, our 'dominant' psychology, or what we term our 'real self'. Persona and Psyche may not be on speaking terms. The one emphasizes outward conduct, the other the soul. We all know that we often *behave* very differently from what we *feel*. The rough rider may be a hopeless sentimentalist, with a mother complex. The natural and deep-rooted craving to act and pretend to be other than we are makes us love to clothe ourselves in the attire of others and fancy ourselves to be them.

Napoleon prided himself more on being a musician than on his victories; the Kaiser fancied himself a sculptor; the profiteer assumes the persona of landed proprietor; the hairdresser a 'tonsorial artist'; the owner of a shop becomes 'proprietor of an emporium'; a college 'don' likes to think himself a 'man of the world'; the burglar likes to be thought a genial good sort. Such pleasurable romances need not be destroyed as long as we recognize them to be romantic, but when we identify ourselves with such as phantasies we do violence to our real selves.

Language, it has been said, was invented to hide thought; so conduct seems often designed to conceal our true character. The persona is the mask we assume before our fellows. The garb of the official is the most common of these masks, turning many a weakling into a man of importance. The clergyman's voice, the doctor's bedside manner, the lawyer's air of wisdom, the shop-girl's elegant accent are all signs of weakness designed to cover up the poverty of the real self.

But as soon as a man ceases to be himself and assumes the persona he loses power. Whenever we try to be someone else than ourselves we do dishonour to our own nature. One of the greatest acts of daring a man can perform is to be himself: it is humbling, but ennobling, whereas pretence is humiliating and degrading. Better call oneself scavenger than 'a representative of the cleansing department'; better let the tears come at a sentimental play than blow your nose; better admit a liking for being in a crowd than pretend one goes to 'study the people'.

The world curiously enough respects people who are honest and daring enough to be themselves, but shows no inclination to follow them. Yet there is no greater relief in life than that of accepting ourselves. James somewhere quotes the lady who said that the happiest day of her life was when she ceased trying to be beautiful. The strain after the impossible is so taxing that thousands break down over it. So few of us are content to be ourselves, yet by seeking to be another we end by failing to be either. *No man can ever be other than himself*, and the attempt to be what we can never be is a hopeless misadventure, resulting in the loss of individuality.

The discovery of our real selves and the acceptance of the motives which govern our actions put at our disposal resources out of which we may build a character truly our own, an individuality fashioned by ourselves out of the material of life presented to us.

Yet to be content to be ourselves is not to be satisfied with ourselves. For we cannot 'be ourselves' in the completest sense until we are perfectly fulfilled. We are not merely the self we are; we are the self that we can be.

Self-realization carries a twofold meaning. It means that we recognize and realize what we are; it also means the realization or attainment of the full and complete self which it is our purpose, like that of every organism, to achieve by the pursuit of a great ideal.

KNOW THYSELF: ACCEPT THYSELF: BE THYSELF

Index